LONDON GIG VENUES

CARL ALLEN

AMBERLEY

ACKNOWLEDGEMENTS

Thanks to friend and gig companions David Whybrow, Mark Russell, Steve Swain, Rita Vail, Rupert Jones, Ashley Spindler, Chris Harden, Rosie Dinnen, Brad Heffer, Sally Harrington, Boz Boorer, Libby Kirby-Taylor, Richard and Amber Wilsher, Nigel Meffin, the venue staff who have allowed me into the venues to photograph inside them and the bands/artists who have led me inside many wonderful buildings – especially Morrissey, The Go-Betweens and Robert Forster.

Special thanks to my very understanding wife Hilary Collins and our children Ciara, Toby and Harlyn.

twitter.com/musicvenueman
facebook.com/musicvenueman

First published 2016

Amberley Publishing
The Hill, Stroud
Gloucestershire, GL5 4EP

www.amberley-books.com

Copyright © Carl Allen, 2016

Photographs © Carl Allen, 2016.

The right of Carl Allen to be identified as the Author of this work has been asserted in accordance with the Copyrights, Designs and Patents Act 1988.

ISBN 978 1 4456 5819 3 (print)
ISBN 978 1 4456 5820 9 (ebook)

British Library Cataloguing in Publication Data.
A catalogue record for this book is available from the British Library.

Typesetting by Amberley Publishing.
Printed in the UK.

CONTENTS

Introduction   9
London's Music Scene   11

The A–Z Guide   19

Central London   23
  Aeolian Hall   23
  Africa Centre   23
  Ain't Nothin' But … Blues Bar   24
  The Albany   24
  The Apple Tree   24
  Arts Theatre   24
  The Astoria   24
  Bag O'Nails   26
  The Barbican Centre   27
  Beat City/Tiles   27
  Betsey Trotwood   28
  Blitz   28
  Bloomsbury Ballroom   29
  Bloomsbury Theatre   29
  The Borderline   29
  Bunjies/Folk Cellar   30
  Cadogan Hall   31
  Central St Martin's College (School of Art)   32
  Central St Martin's College (School of Art)   32
  Conway Hall   32
  Cousins/Les Cousins   32
  Cromwellian Club   32
  Dominion Theatre   33
  Drummonds   34
  The Flamingo Club/The Temple   35
  The Fly   35
  Heaven/G-A-Y/Global Village   36
  Hippodrome/Talk of The Town   36
  HMV (East Oxford Street)   36
  HMV West Oxford Street)   36
  Horsehoe Hotel   37
  Hyde Park   37

ICA	38
Imperial College	38
Kings College/KCLSU	39
Kings Place	39
LA2/Mean Fiddler	39
Live! On The Park at Pizza On The Park	40
London School of Economics (LSE)	40
Lyceum Theatre	40
Madame JoJo's	41
Marquee 1958–1964	42
Marquee 1964–1988	42
Marquee 1988–1996	42
Marquee 2002–2003 (see Islington Academy)	42
Marquee 2004–2007	42
Marquee 2007–2008	43
Metro Club	43
Middle Earth/Electric Golden	44
Notre Dame Hall/Ad Lib Club/Cavern in The Town	45
100 Club/London Jazz Club/Hymphrey Lyttelton Club	45
The Palladium	46
Paris Theatre	46
Pigalle Club	46
Pizza Express	47
Portlands/The Pits/Green Man	47
Rock Garden	48
The Roebuck/Adams Arms	48
Ronnie Scotts	48
Rough Trade (Covent Garden)	49
The Roundhouse (Wardour St)/Blues and Barrelhouse Club	49
The Roxy (Covent Garden)	49
Royal Albert Hall	50
Royalty Ballroom	51
Saville Theatre	52
Scotch of St James	53
Scots Hoose/Spice of Life	53
Slaughtered Lamb	53
The Social	53
Soho Revue Bar	53
Somerset House	54
The Speakeasy/Bootleggers/Cameo	54
St James' Church	55
St Lukes	55
St Pancras Old Church	55
Studio 51/Ken Colyers Jazz Club	55
2i's	56
12 Bar Club	57
229 Club	58
Tiles	58
Turnmills	58
University of London Union (ULU)	59
Victoria Apollo Theatre	59
Virgin Megastore (Oxford Street)/Zavvi	60
Vortex (Wardour St)	60

The Wag Club/Whisky-A-Go-Go/Flamingo 60
Water Rats/Monto Water Rats/Pindar of Wakefield 61

North London 63
Alexandra Palace 63
Archway Tavern 63
Barfly/The Monarch 64
Birthdays 65
Bluesville 65
Boogaloo Bar 65
The Boston Arms/The Dome 66
The Brecknock 66
Buffalo Bar 66
Bull and Gate 67
Cecil Sharpe House 68
Clissold Arms 69
Coliseum (Harlesden) 69
Dingwalls/Lock 17 70
Drummonds 71
Dublin Castle 71
Electric Ballroom/The Buffalo 71
The Enterprise 72
The Falcon 73
Fiddlers Elbow 74
Finsbury Park 74
Fishmongers Arms/Village of The Damned 74
The Forum/Town and Country Club 75
The Garage/Upstairs at The Garage/T&C2 76
Golden Lion Camden 76
Granada (Harrow) 76
The Green Note 77
Hippodrome (Golders Green) 77
Hope and Anchor 78
Islington Assembly Hall 78
Islington Carling Academy/The Marquee (2002–03) 79
Jazz Café 80
Kalamazoo Club 80
Kilburn National Ballroom 81
Kings Place 81
Koko/Camden Palace/Music Machine 82
The Lexington 83
The Luminaire 84
The Macbeth 84
Majestic Ballroom 84
Mean Fiddler/Old Fiddler (Harlesden) 85
The Moonlight Club/Klooks Kleek 85
Moth Club 85
Nambucca 86
Northwood Hills 86
Portlands/The Pits/Green Man 87
Powerhaus (1996–2004)/Sir George Robey 87
Powerhaus/The Barn/Pied Bull 87
Proud Galleries 88

Purple Turtle 88
The Rainbow/The Finsbury Park Astoria 89
The Roundhouse (Camden) 90
Royalty Ballroom 90
Scala 91
Screen on The Green 91
Shaw Theatre 92
Silver Bullet 92
Sobell Sports Centre/Michael Sobell Sports Centre 92
The State Theatre/Gaumont State Theatre 93
St Pancras Old Church 93
Surya 94
12 Bar Club (Holloway Road) 94
Tinkers Folk Club 94
Torrington Arms 94
The Underworld 95
Union Chapel 95
The Verge/Bullet Bar/The Flowerpot/Heros 96
Vortex (Dalston) 96
Wembley Arena/SSE Arena/Wembley Empire Pool 96
Wembley Arena Pavilions 97
Wembley Stadium 98
The White Horse (Hampstead) 99

East London 101
Barking Broadway 101
Blackheath 101
Bridgehouse 2 101
Cabot Hall 102
Cargo 102
Cart and Horses 103
Catch 104
Docklands (London) Arena 104
Granada (Walthamstow) 105
Hackney Empire 105
Hoxton Bar and Kitchen 106
Hoxton Hall 106
Island (Ilford) 106
The Legion 107
93 Feet East 107
Ocean/Hackney Attic 108
The Old Blue Last 108
On The Rocks 108
Oslo 109
The Pleasure Unit 109
Red Lion (Leytonstone)/Chez Club 109
Rex (Stratford) 110
Rhythm Factory 110
Rough Trade East 110
The Roundhouse (Dagenham/Upney)/Village Roundhouse 110
Sebright Arms 111
The Shacklewell Arms 112
The Spitz 112

The Standard Music Venue 112
St Lukes 113
333 Club/333 Mother/London Apprentice 113
The Troxy 113
Turnmills 114
The Upper Cut 114
Village Underground 115
Walthamstow Assembly Rooms 115
What's Cooking Club 115
Wilton's Music Hall 115
XOYO 115

South London 117
The Albany Empire 117
Amersham Arms (New Cross) 117
Blackheath Halls 118
Borough Hall (Greenwich) 119
Brixton Academy/Brixton O2 Academy/Fair Deal/Sundown 119
Brooklyn Bowl 120
Cartoon (Croydon) 121
The Castle 122
Coronet (Elephant and Castle) 122
Coronet (Woolwich) 123
Crawdaddy/Station Hotel 124
The Cricketers 124
Crossfield Estate (Deptford) 125
Dirty South/Rose of Lee 125
El Partido 126
Fairfield Hall 126
Fellowship Inn/Railway Tavern 126
Fighting Cocks 127
The Fridge/Ace Cinema/Electric Brixton 127
The Glenlyn 128
Goldsmiths College 129
Granada (Dartford) 129
Granada (Kingston-upon-Thames) 129
Granada (Tooting) 130
Granada (Woolwich) 130
The Grand 131
Greyhound Hotel (Croydon) 131
The Half Moon (Herne Hill) 131
The Half Moon (Putney) 132
House of Vans 132
Indigo Club (also see O2) 132
Lewisham Theatre/Broadway Theatre 133
Mistral Club. 133
The Mick Jagger Centre 133
The Miller 133
Ministry of Sound 133
The O2/Indigo/Matter 134
Orchid Ballroom 135
Plan B 135
Pontiac Club 135

Purcell Room (Royal Festival Hall)   136
Queen Elizabeth Hall (Royal Festival Hall)   136
Ram Jam/The Fridge   137
Rivoli Ballroom   137
Royal Festival Hall   137
The Star Hotel (Croydon)   138
Stockwell Swan   139
Tunnel Club   139
The Venue (New Cross)   140
The White Horse (Brixton)/Brixton Jamm   141
The Witchdoctor/Savoy Rooms/Mr Smiths   141
The Windmill   141

West London   143
Bush Hall/The Carlton Club   143
Ealing Rhythm and Blues Club   145
Earls Court   145
Elgin Pub   146
Farx Club/Northcote Arms Hotel   147
Feathers Hotel   148
Goldhawk Club   148
Granada (Greenford)   149
The Greyhound   149
Hammersmith Odeon/Labatts Apollo/Carling Apollo
Hammersmith Gaumont/Eventim   150
Hammersmith Folk Club/Centre   150
Hammersmith Palais/Palais de Danse   150
Kensington Park Hotel/KPH   151
Lyric Hammersmith   151
Maida Vale Studios   152
Nashville Rooms   152
Notting Hill Arts Club   153
Porchester Hall   153
Red Cow   154
Riverside Studios   154
606 Club   155
Shepherds Bush Empire   155
Southall Community Centre.   156
Starlite Ballroom   156
Subterania/Acklam Hall/Bay 63/Neighbourhood/Mode   156
Tabernackle   157
The Target   158
The Toby Jug   158
The Troubadour   158
Three Tuns/Beckenham Arts Lab   158
Under The Bridge   159
Wallington Town Hall   159
West One Four/The Orange   159
Zigzag Club   160

INTRODUCTION

London dominates the UK and Europe music scenes, and its only competition for worldwide dominance is New York. While one city can register a trademark calling itself the 'Live Music capital of the World', it does not mean it is actually true (sorry Austin). If you are an English music fan the city will eventually call to you, pulling you like a magnet to its record shops and its venues. If you are some kind of music-loving hermit living in the Scottish Highlands then the music you are listening to is probably recorded in the capital's recording studios or inspired by its streets; certainly the group or artist would have played the London gig circuit to romance the London-based record company who released the album.

My own personal introduction to the capital's music venues started in 1986 when I was seventeen and lived in Colchester. I had just started going to gigs in the town at the students union in the University of Essex and at Colchester Arts Centre, but all my favourite groups had outgrown these puny venues and London seemed to be the place they were all playing. My first foray to a gig there was cautious: I paid £20 to go on an organised 50-mile coach trip to see my very favourite group, The Smiths, at the Brixton Academy.

So the Brixton Academy was my first introduction to live music in London. As venues go, it's not a bad place to start. The Academy's interior was wondrous: statues in alcoves, a giant stage; the roof of the venue appearing to be open to the heavens with the Galaxy painted on the ceiling, plus there were famous people hanging out in the crowd. It put the students union to shame, and it also made me wonder what the Academy was or used to be.

Needless to say I was soon going to more gigs in London and making my own travelling arrangements, and I soon found my way to the Town and Country Club, the Astoria and others.

Now nearly thirty years later I'm still undertaking the journey into London to gigs, and I have even spread my wings to other cities in the UK and have even seen my favourite groups in venues in Holland, Germany, Ireland, Spain and Australia. Through these musical wonderings it has been obvious that there is no city like London when it comes to live music, and so this book will be your guide to these venues. The book is set out in two parts: the first will give you, the reader, the background to the music scene in London. The second is the A-Z guide to the venues detailing the building's history, the groups who have played there, as well as the venue details.

This book is designed for a number of different users: long-time London gig-goers who may have wondered about a venues history, the out-of-London occasional gig-goer, musicians, and visitors to London who might be trying to find The Forum. Whoever you are, we have one thing in common: the love and the lure of live music – so enjoy!

LONDON'S MUSIC SCENE

When the London music scene is good, it's the best in the world. But when it's bad it's awful.

Chrissie Hynde (The Pretenders)

Walk around London and you'll soon discover that music pulses through the streets like blood through veins. From the fly-posting of gigs and new releases on telecom boxes through to the official advertising on boards and buses, the city lets you know what it has to offer. If you keep your eyes open you might even see a blue plaque to celebrate where Jimi Hendrix used to live. The list of songs that you could hum while passing through is endless (but you could start with 'Waterloo Sunset' by the Kinks or 'London Calling' by The Clash). From the start of 'pop' music in the 1950s through to the present day, London has inspired songwriters and artists to immortalise it in song. Eagle-eye music fans may realise that they are walking past the front cover of 'What's the Story Morning Glory' by Oasis in Denmark Street or they may be making a deliberate pilgrimage to walk across the Abbey Road zebra crossing. Whatever it is, it is further proof of the influence of the capital on pop music.

London's claim to be the world capital for music is reinforced by the sheer number of record companies who operate out of the city, from the giant multinationals in their skyscrapers to the indie labels run out of back bedrooms. The record companies call London home because the city has the talent that keeps them in business. But what came first, the talent or the business? Whatever act of nature it was, any UK-based group or artist who wants to live the rock 'n' roll dream has to move to the capital to give themselves the chance to achieve it. Once success has knocked and you are signed, the city has you for keeps. The Beatles may forever be associated with Liverpool or even Hamburg, but once they were signed they all lived in London. What makes it so hard to leave? That's simple – the city has the musician's support system. The employer (record company) is there, the management is there, and don't forget the publisher, the promoter, the recording/rehearsal studios, the venues, financial adviser, the journalists, the drug dealers, AA meetings, and the city has the best worldwide transport connections; London is conveniently close to Heathrow.

The capital throbs to a thousand different beats. The centuries-long history of immigration to the UK, and London in particular, has resulted in different cultures performing their traditional music and also adapting it to the new climate. The well-established Notting Hill Carnival is a Jamaican/West African street carnival that twists through council estates and exclusive streets alike, with its mega-mix of steel drums, reggae, toasting and dub. Brick Lane in East London is the epicentre of what is known as Bangra Town, where Asian music drifts with the scents of the curry houses. The song says it: 'Let me take you by the hand and show you through the streets of London'. Londoners are a diverse bunch and that is reflected in the music they make.

Equally diverse are the buildings that make up London's live music scene. Some have a long history of interesting previous uses and are really quite beautiful to look at, while others have been purpose-built and maybe lack some character (Docklands London Arena). There are a few venues in the capital that have been operating for well over forty years in the same location (100 Club), some names have existed for thirty-plus years at different locations across the city (The Marquee and The Mean Fiddler), while some buildings have long been a music venue – it's just the name that changes (Koko was previously The Camden Palace and The Music Machine before that). At the other end there are venues that have only been on the scene for a relatively short period of time and have yet to earn their place in the history. Into this mix are the ephemeral venues – those locations where a gig turns up totally out of the blue and are usually just one-offs. There are also venues that had one or two noteworthy gigs, but then nothing else.

Nearly any London theatre, pub, club or sports ground has or could host a gig, as the examples in this book illustrate, but it would be a thankless task to list every theatre in London on the off-chance that some group may decide to play there a few years from now. What the guide does is feature the theatres that have had a history of staging gigs, or some interesting one-off gigs. Into those categories fall The Dominion, The State, The Lyceum and The Shaw Theatres as well as others. It is worth noting that record companies will stage album launches in some quite frankly bizarre venues in which the group/artist may perform a showcase gig to an invited crowd. Once again, these venues would be too numerous and obscure to merit a comprehensive inclusion in the guide.

Record shops (how old fashioned is this author for still calling them that?) also host the odd live event, usually a group or artist on the promotional trail playing a short set followed by a signing session. The Oxford Street Virgin Megastore probably had the most regular events happening. Visitors to its basement stage included Dave Matthews, Natalie Imbruglia, The Hives (2001), Idlewild, Reef (2002) and Rufus Wainwright (2004). Other stores with a history of live sessions include the Oxford Street HMV, Tower Records (later Virgin) in Piccadilly and Rough Trade (Covent Garden, Talbot Road and East stores).

London offers a complete range of size of venues that can be broken down into the following five classifications:

1. 'Pubs'. London is scattered with a network of pubs, some of which have dedicated music rooms that have hosted performers who have gone on to be world famous, while others have gone on to work in music shops. Capacity can be anything from 50 to 200 people and includes venues such as The Dublin Castle.
2. 'Clubs'. These are the smallest venues with a capacity up to around 1,000. Into this definition would be very small venues like The Borderline, 12 Bar Club, Barfly, The Garage etc. These are the venues where acts with a cult following or who are on the rise play.
3. 'Theatres'. A venue doesn't need to have the word theatre in its title to be classed as a theatre, merely the capacity of up to 5,000. Include in this definition the Hammersmith Odeon and the Brixton Academy.
4. 'Arenas'. A capacity of around 12,000 means that these are the venues chosen by worldwide acts. Expect to see Madonna at venues like Earls Court, The O2 and Wembley Arena.
5. 'Stadiums'. The largest venues available apart from festivals, with capacities of 50/60/70,000. Home to superstars like The Rolling Stones, Bon Jovi, Michael Jackson etc. London offers Wembley Stadium, Twickenham or various sports grounds.

London also offers many other live music events such as The Camden Crawl, where practically any building with a roof can become a music venue for a night, and Carling 24 – non-stop live music across the capital's venue for twenty-four hours (in 2006 the Kaiser Chiefs, Ian Brown, Goldie Lookin' Chain, The Ordinary Boys and Razorlight all got in on the act). A new event in 2006 was 'The Electric Proms' with venues in Camden hosting gigs by The Who, The Guillemots, The BBC Concert Orchestra and Damon Albarn and Paul Simonon.

Since 2005 London has hosted the 'Don't Look Back' series of concerts where an artist/ group perform one of their classic albums. In 2005 The Stooges performed 'Fun House' at the Hammersmith Odeon (30 August), Belle and Sebastian played 'If You Are Feeling Sinister' at

The Barbican (25 September), Mudhoney played 'Super fuzz Big Muff' at Koko (16 September) and The Dirty Three played 'Ocean Songs' (5 October). 2006 saw Green on Red play 'Gas, Food, Lodging' at Koko (18 July), Teenage Fanclub performed 'Bandwagonerque' at The Forum and Ennio Morricone performed some of his classic soundtracks at the Hammersmith Apollo (19 July).

All of these events add to the already rich palette enjoyed by London gig-goers, but with so many artists playing the capital, which ones stay in people's minds? A pole undertaken by London's bible *Time Out* in 2005 to find the best ever London gig concluded the following list:

1. The Clash at The Rainbow, May 1977.
2. Brain Wilson at the Royal Festival Hall, February 2004.
3. Stevie Wonder at The Rainbow, February 1974.
4. The Rolling Stones at The Crawdaddy, April 1963.
5. Duke Ellington at The Palladium, June 1933.
6. N*E*R*D at Brixton Academy, November 2003.
7. Bob Marley at The Lyceum, July 1975.
8. The Smiths at Jubilee Gardens (GLC 'Jobs for A Change' festival), June 1984.
9. The White Stripes at Dingwalls, July 2001.
10. The Beatles at The Pigalle, April 1963.

Although the *Time Out* top ten is open for scrutiny, only 600 people could have seen the Stones at the Crawdaddy and anyone who saw Duke Ellington would have been at least eighty years old when the list was made – the list does illustrate the quality and diversity of acts and venues in the capital. The top ten also includes gigs at five venues that are no longer, so maybe demonstrating the kind regard the venues were/are thought of in the music fans' minds. It is worth noting that the top ten includes only three gigs since 2000 and five from the 1960s and '70s, which hints at the age range of those voting. It is worth underlining that practically all of the gigs are from theatre-sized venues or smaller, which would support the argument that 'atmosphere' is missing from large stadium gigs.

This book can only ever be a snap shot in time; the live music scene will continue to adapt and change as the music business evolves. With Sandi Thom conducting a virtual world tour over the internet from her Tooting bedroom in 2006, and attracting hundreds of thousands watching her, there may not even be a need for venues anymore. To go out to see a band in a dark, sweaty venue may be looked back upon as a rather strange, quaint past-time.

The Business of Music Venues (or Who Owns What)

The Mean Fiddler Group was probably the best-known venue operator in London and was started in 1982 by Irish promoter Vince Power. Based in Harlesden, north-west London, The Mean Fiddler venue (later The Old Fiddler) was the only venue the company owned. As the Mean Fiddler became more established and successful the company expanded and acquired further venues such as The Forum, Astoria, Jazz Café, Garage and Subterania. The Mean Fiddler Group also became involved in The Fleadh in Finsbury Park and festivals such as The Reading/Leeds Festival and Glastonbury. By 2003 the group had expanded into other ventures such as bars (Power's Bar and Bartok) and a radio station – Mean Country. Maybe as a result of straying away from its core business, the Mean Fiddler Group, with a turnover of around £25 million, reported a pre-tax loss of £8.3 million for 2002. As a result of this the group sold its bars for £2.3 million and radio station for £1.5 million, and stated that it would concentrate on the live venues, festivals and tour promoting (BBC News,0 1.07.2003). In November 2003 the Mean Fiddler Group bought the Borderline venue with Power stating that the Mean Fiddler Group were 'now able to progress artists through the various stages within the portfolio at every level of their careers, bringing them to the Borderline through the Mean Fiddler and eventually the

Astoria. This unique position ensures that (the) Mean Fiddler is, indeed, "the source of live music"'. (Mean Fiddler, 2003).

The Mean Fiddler Group was sold in 2005 to US-based Clear Channel Entertainment and Irish company Gaiety Investments (which owns promoters MCD Productions who run the Olympia in Dublin). The group was valued at £37.9 million and founder Vince Power received £13 million for his 35 per cent holding in the Mean Fiddler Group. Power said that he sold his interest in The Mean Fiddler Group because it was time to 'cash in his roulette chips, have a look around and then go back to the roulette table' (*The Independent*, 2005). Vince later set up Vince Power Music promotion (VPMP), which opened The Pigalle Club in Piccadilly in 2006.

Clear Channel had proven to be controversial in America where the company is involved in commercial radio, billboard advertising and live entertainment. In 2004 Clear Channel grossed $2.7 billion from its live entertainment division alone. This almost-stranglehold on radio and music venues has led to raised voices and questions being asked. Don Henley (The Eagles) claimed in the American Senate in 2003 that bands/performers were being pressured into playing Clear Channel music venues for fear of Clear Channel radio stations not playing their songs. Obviously, Clear Channel denied the claim and highlighted that Clear Channel were responsible for a third of Britney Spears' airplay in America, although she did not have Clear Channel as her tour promoter.

Live Nation was a subsidiary of Clear Channel until it was sold off from the parent company in 2005. Live Nation merged with Ticketmaster (a primary ticket outlet) in 2010 and the company became Live Nation Entertainment.

The McKenzie Group was formed in January 1998 for the management buyout of the Brixton Academy and the Shepherds Bush Empire from Break for the Border Group PLC. Shareholders in the new group included three UK music promoters: SJM Concerts Ltd, Metropolis Music Ltd and MCD Management Ltd. Since 2000 the group have opened further 'Academy'-branded venues in Birmingham, Bristol, Liverpool and Glasgow. In January 2003 the group entered into a three-year sponsorship deal with brewers Carling, which resulted in some of the venues being rebranded as 'Carling Academy's'. The group added further to its venue portfolio with the purchase in 2003 of the failed Marquee venue in the N1 Shopping Centre in Islington. The McKenzie Group is now known as The Academy Music Group (AMG) and has run the promotion off-shoot, Academy Events, since 2001.

Anschutz Entertainment Group (AEG) is an American-based company that operates the O2, Wembley Arena and co-owns the Hammersmith Apollo with Eventim – a ticketing agency.

Mama and Company was founded in 2005 and runs Hoxton Bar and Kitchen, The Forum, The Borderline, Jazz Café, Barfly and organises the Lovebox festival. In 2007 they bought the Hammersmith Apollo and Mean Fiddler Holdings. In 2008 it also acquired Heaven. The HMV Group bought a 50 per cent stake in Mama in 2009, making it 100 per cent in 2010 in a deal worth £46 million. In 2012 the Hammersmith Apollo was sold to AEG and Eventim for £32 million, while the remainder of the company was sold to the management for £7.3 million.

Sally Greene, an impresario who owns the Old Vic and Criterion Theatres, bought Ronnie Scott's for £3 million in 2004 and has spent a further £1 million refurbishing the venue. Although the venue will not make the size of profit of Greene's theatre productions, the venue does offer Greene something else: aside from lure of the jazz music itself, Greene was determined to have the venue because during its forty-six-year life it had performances every night (apart from the occasional public holiday), which is proof of a successful venue. No matter the size, a venue like this will always be an attractive business to a bigger fish. In an interview in *The Sunday Times* (2006) with Robert Sandall, Greene let slip another reason for buying the venue: she used to go to Ronnie Scott's when she was a child with her father. This would appear to be a jazz fan buying a jazz club for the love of the venue and what it represents, rather than being a cold business decision – no bad thing in the current overtly corporate atmosphere.

Metropolis Music is a Manchester-based company that was set up in 1985 to promote concerts. Metropolis Music promotes approximately 500 UK concerts each year and also became involved in operating venues under its joint takeover of The McKenzie Group (now The Academy Music Group, which of course has branched out into promotion with the setting up of Academy Events).

DHP Family is a Midlands-based company that owns Rock City, Bodega and The Rescue Rooms in Nottingham and Thekla in Bristol. In London its only holding is Oslo in Hackney. DHP stands for Daybrook House Promotions.

Red Tape, Planning etc.

For a music venue to operate it must have several things in place, namely planning permission and a licence, as well as keeping the local environmental protection/health officers happy. All of these roles are the responsibility of the local council.

Planning policies of the London boroughs take their lead from the London Plan, which is produced by the mayor. It is these policies that any planning application for a new live music venue will be considered against. Planning considerations for a new venue would include the impact on the night-time economy, cultural provision, access to public transport, amenity impact to neighbours and provision of jobs etc. While neighbours may not like the potential for noise if they live on, say, a busy road like Camden High Street, that is the choice they have made. There is a higher expectation of tranquility living on more residentially dominated streets than mixed-use areas.

In recognition of the importance of, and threat to, live music venues in London, the mayor published 'London's Grassroots Music Venues Rescue Plan' in October 2015. The recommendations of the report were interesting although some were somewhat idealistic. On the positive side it said that music venues should have their own specific policies in the London Plan. On the dreamier side, it was suggested that Article 4 Direction areas include pubs, so that they could not change their use without planning permission; also suggested was that developers could set-up 'music zones' for grassroots venues and for business rate relief for venues. All good stuff but I'm sure that independent, family-run businesses would feel aggrieved at the special treatment that music venues would receive. Possibly more beneficial is the Independent Venue Week, where small venues are celebrated and get some big names supporting the cause.

Planning permission – if granted – will condition days and hours of operation, signage, sound insulation and maximum noise levels. A licence will also cover hours and days of opening (but may not be the same as the planning permission and will not override the hours on the planning permission), how the venue is managed and set capacity levels. Environmental Protection will only be involved if there are noise complaints from residents, in which case the officer will monitor the sound and take action if there is a breach. For outdoor festivals it would be common practice for the council's Environmental Protection Officers to monitor the noise in residential streets, usually with the organiser's own Environmental Health professional. If the readings show a breach the organiser's team inside the festival will be notified and they would have to make a decision whether or not to turn the volume down or risk a fine. The organisers should also have their own Environmental Health team monitoring noise levels inside the festival so patrons are not exposed to damaging levels of sound. They would also check that connections to water supplies are safe as well.

Many of London's music venues are also listed buildings. Buildings become listed if they are deemed important due to their age, their design, building method, special architectural interest in a national context or association with an event or person. There are three levels of listing:

Grade I. The highest level of listing for the most important buildings. Only 4 per cent of all listed buildings fall into this category. They need to have an exceptional amount of original features still intact. Grade II*. An exceptional building but not quite good enough to make the highest grade. Grade II. By far the most common grade. Usually a good, sound building but possibly with too much damage/repair/alterations.

The implications of a music venue being a listed building are massive. The operator of the venue will need to apply for Listed Building Consent for any changes they may want to make to the building. While applying for consent is free, there is still cost involved in having plans drawn up and paying for specialists to undertake the work. A listed building will usually be over 100 years old and will have higher maintenance costs, let alone difficulties for sound-proofing and establishing fire exits.

The reuse of buildings gives London's music venues a real variety and character. Practically all the music venues in the capital have a history to them, whether they are theatres, cinemas, dance halls, libraries or rail sheds. A music venue will not need a licence for amplified music between 8 a.m. and 11 p.m. for a capacity of less than 500. If a licence is needed matters for consideration would be sound levels, how the venue is managed (including door staff), the size of the building, safety after 11 p.m. and if there are any under age issues. The licensing department will work with the poilice on these matters.

Born to Fail

Since I started researching these venues way back in 2004 many have been lost – the most heart-wrenching being The Astoria – but the winter of 2014 seemed particularly harsh on venues with Earls Court, 12 Bar Club, Madame JoJo's and The Buffalo Bar all either closing or announcing closure. While Madame JoJo's appeared to have some licensing issues that forced closure, the majority of venues close due to the pressure of redevelopment. This is an understandable pressure as most venues only open in the evening and not even every night. When they are open for business they may not even be half full and so the operators can easily fall into financial difficulty. If there is a landlord (there always is) then they can get higher and more guaranteed rent letting to an office or shop, or simply selling the land for housing. A lot of venues take up a fair bit of room in prime locations and property value in London continues to soar. One only has to look at Soho to see how that area is changing, with traditional occupiers being forced out – goodbye Denmark Street and music shops! Business Rates, electricity bills and beer suppliers all need to be paid as well, let alone staffing costs. It is no wonder that small, independent venues are run on love and overdrafts and not profit!

But it's not all doom and gloom. By 2014 venues had sprung up all over Dalston and Shoreditch. These were also emerging cultural hubs attracting artists, technologies and other creative businesses due to the comparatively low rents for the then unfashionable areas. Some of these venues are also open during the day as cafes or restaurants.

The Rules of Gigs

1. You will stand next to a farter and they will stink! Packed in like sardines you'll be unable to escape the foul bowels of a stranger and you will not know who the villain is. However, neither will anyone else and they will think it is YOU; even your wife will give you a damning stare! (Note: this will also apply to body odour.)
2. Just before the group come on stage there will be a drunken moron making a nuisance of themself on the other side of the room, and they will be magically transported right in front of or beside you. Please God let them move on or security eject them.
3. Can you smell someone smoking? You bloody well can. Which idiot has lit up in complete defiance of the smoking ban? You may love 'Anarchy in the UK' but smoking indoors is where the line is crossed. Times this by ten if you can smell a joint.
4. Running late. Come on, the curfew is 11 p.m. and it's 10 p.m. already with no sign of the headline act. It will happen once, but you will miss your last train home. Taxi or sleep in the station?
5. Is that really …? Yes, you will spot a minor celebrity or cult star in the crowd with you. Can't wait to tell your friends...
6. No matter how tall you are there will be a time when someone taller stands directly in front of you spoiling your view.

The Professional View of London

We may be the punters who pay to see a gig in London, but what do those involved professionally in live music think of London and its venues?

Boz Boorer has been Morrissey's guitarist, musical director and co-songwriter since 1991. Before that Boz was a member of rockabilly band The Polecats, who played all over London. Boz is ideally situated to comment on the sheer variety of venues in London having played many of them over the last thirty-plus years.

Q: Which London venues did you play early in your career with The Polecats and how important were they to your success?
Boz: The place I dreamt of playing was the Royalty Ballroom in Southgate – our rockabilly Mecca. We played there eventually in 1979. After that we played most of the great places – The Marquee was great, a place called The Venue in Victoria was particularly good for us. We got to play The Lyceum with Crazy Cavan; another early show was the Music Machine in Camden supporting Matchbox. There were also the regular rooms at the back of pubs that were very popular at the time. I remember The Fox in Turnpike Lane, upstairs at The Manor House pub and Fulham Place Greyhound supporting Little Bob Story.

Q: What was the first London venue that you played that made you think 'I've made it!' because you were on its stage and why?
Boz: Not sure. I liked the fact we played The Lyceum but we had just returned from a European jaunt and the gig was a bit underwhelming.

Q: What was it like playing the O2 in December 2014?
Boz: Great venue, lovely sound – very enjoyable night.

Q: How does playing The O2 or Earls Court compare to smaller London venues such as The Troxy or Brixton Academy?
Boz: They're all different; the smaller gigs have a close, intimate atmosphere. The Troxy had a bad sound; Brixton is much better.

Q: Do you ever have any moments when the musical heritage of a venue makes you think 'wow, I can't believe I'm on the same stage' as where one of your heroes played?
Boz: I remember playing The Roundhouse in Camden – a place I used to frequent in 1977/1978. Whilst on stage I looked up into the middle of the ceiling dome thinking of all the history it has seen and all the music that has been played in that place.

Q: Have you noticed any major changes to London's live music scene/venues over the years?
Boz: I don't mind the phones – it's a great way for history to be recorded. It's a shame there's less pub venues as I think they're the starting block for most bands, or they were.

Q: What for you as a performing musician makes a good venue?
Boz: There's a few factors – the sound system, acoustics of the venue, crowd participation, set list and last but by all means not least, the bands playing.

Q: What is your favourite London music venue that you have played and why?
Boz: The Brixton Academy has been good consistently because of all the reasons above. The Hope and Anchor was a very small but energetic venue, so was the old Fridge in Brixton in the early 1980s.

Q: What is your favourite London venue to go to as a punter?
Boz: Has to be a sold-out venue where you can get to the bar for a drink, like the 100 Club.

Q: What London venue has the best backstage area and what makes it good?
Boz: I can remember the new Wembley Arena being a bit chaotic backstage. The Electric Ballroom being non-existent, as was the Dublin Castle! But the best? The dressing rooms at Alexandra Palace were quite big and the after-show was OK. Hammersmith Odeon is a bit pokey – lots of stairs. The Roundhouse now has a nice backstage and the Festival Hall was very civilised too.

Q: You have played many of London's venues. Are there any left that you really want to play?
Boz: I haven't played the Electric Ballroom for about thrity years and it would be nice to return for old times' sake. I have never played the Barbican; sounded well when I was there for the Memphis Music Spectacular.

Q: How do London's venues compare to other capital cities across the world?
Boz: I think quite well as there are still a lot of venues to play so there is still a lot of choice.

Q: Are London audiences any different to play compare to other cities?
Boz: Of course every city has a different audience. In London they're at a big show – there's a lot of people who will travel in for it. But in the early days I thought it was a bit spoiled as everyone came through London and played.

Q: How important do you think London is musically these days?
Boz: I believe it's still pivotal in the growth of new bands and a great place to see everyone play. They all come to London – well almost.

THE A-Z GUIDE

What is London?

As far as this guide is concerned London is the current London boroughs, including Central and Greater London. In fact it is almost everything inside the M25 ring road that skirts the capital. Some parts of Essex such as Ilford are now classed as London due to local government reorganisations, which makes it part of the London borough of Redbridge.

The Guide

Every important or interesting venue has an entry. The buildings of London change so much that these photographs are just a snapshot in time. Just as the buildings are adapted for their musical use, they are equally accommodating to other users.

What this book is not is a record of every pub, university or college that has put some dodgy local group on occasionally or has a karaoke night once a week. With such a long history of live music, and the sheer size of London, some venues may have been overlooked. If you feel that there is a venue that should be included in future editions of this book, or can fill in some blanks, then please email me at carl@bigwavepr.co.uk.

Central London

Central London's only contender for the sheer number of music venues is Camden. While Camden can call Britpop its own, Central London can lay claim to having important venues – if not pivotal – to the jazz, folk, skiffle, rock 'n' roll and punk scenes. All the early teenage rebellions in London were fuelled by the coffee houses of Soho, such as The 2i's. However, a different liquid inspired the Punks at The Roxy or St Martin's School of Art.

North London

The epicentre of youth culture from the 1970s onwards, in Camden music actually throbs onto the streets. This North London Borough was practically the birthplace of Britpop. The most important Britpop venue was Camden's The Falcon, where Blur, Lush, Suede and a host of other guitar-welding, hook-infected groups played.

The Camden/Kentish Town area of North London was also the birthplace of Madness. The Nutty Boys played venues all over North London including The Hope and Anchor and Dublin Castle (where they also shot the video for 'My Girl').

North London was also home to The Kinks, with the Davies brothers living opposite The Clissold Arms where they played their first gig and returned to play in the late 1990s. The band posed outside The Archway Tavern for the front cover of their album 'Muswell Hillbillies' and had their Konk studio in North London too. The Studio has hosted Blur, The Stone Roses, and The Arctic Monkeys.

East London

East London is most associated with The New Wave of British Heavy Metal (NWOBHM), if only because Iron Maiden lived in Leyton and played in such pubs as The Cart and Horses, The Bridgehouse and The Ruskin Arms almost every night during the mid-1970s.

Members of The Libertines also had a strong affiliation with the East End, shooting videos in Bethnal Green, living at 112a Teesdale Street, Bethnal Green, and playing in its pubs and clubs such as The Rhythm Factory, The Pleasure Unit and The George.

South London

South of the river in any city is always a bit more gritty and urban, so it is no surprise that Brixton's venues have attracted similar artists, and that the area is at the cutting edge of Grime and Hip Hop. However, South London has also been home to Squeeze and Dire Straits, with both groups playing gigs in the area and members even living in the same housing estate.

West London

West London was important in the 1960s for being the home of The Who. This goes someway to explain why they played everywhere from Acton to Greenford, Ealing and to Putney. The Who even rehearsed in the building now called Bush Hall in Shepherds Bush. West London is also an important area in the history of Punk as members of both The Clash and The Sex Pistols lived here.

Who Were ...

A small handful of men dominates the design of many buildings that have been used for live music. Ladies and gentlemen, I give you brief profiles of George Coles, Frank Matcham, E. A. Stone and Beard & Bennett:

George Coles

George Coles was a London-based architect born in 1884 in Leyton (East London). In 1912 he became partners with Percy Adams to form Adam & Coles and had an office in Craven Street, WC2. He specialised in Art Deco cinemas (mostly for the Odeon chain) in the 1920s and 1930s, designing roughly ninety cinemas in the UK. He lived in Bucks Head, Sussex, and died in 1963.
London Designs: Coronet (Woolwich), Granada (Kingston), The Rex (redesigned Matcham's exterior), State Theatre (Kilburn), The Trocadero (Elephant & Castle) and The Troxy (Stepney).

Frank Matcham

Frank Matcham was born 1854 and died 1920. He was possibly the most important (and well known) theatre designer, responsible for theatres all over Britain.
London designs: The Hippodrome (Charing Cross Road), The Rex, Shepherds Bush Empire.

E. A. Stone

E. A. Stone designed the Astoria (Charing Road Road), The Rainbow (Finsbury Park) and Brixton Academy, as well as several 'Astoria' cinemas in London and beyond.

Beard & Bennett

John Stanley Coombe Beard (1890–1970) and Walter Francis Bennett (1904–74) designed The Forum (Kentish Town).

Cameras Used

Practica Super TL1000 35mm SLR (film)
Fujifilm Finepix S602 Zoom
Fujifilm Finepix F500 EXR
Canon 70D DSLR
Canon Powershot SX700 HS.
Samsung Galaxy 5

CENTRAL LONDON

Aeolian Hall

Address: 135–137 New Bond Street, London, W1S 2TQ
Tube: Oxford Circus (Central Line)

Built in 1876 as an opera house, the BBC took over the building as a studio in 1943. The Beatles recorded 'Taste of Honey' here and the hall was used for live sessions in the Jimmy Young and Terry Wogan radio shows. The Kinks played and were interviewed here in 1965. Now called Belstaff House and used as a retail unit for Belstaff Clothing.

Africa Centre
Address: 38 Kings Centre, Covent Garden, London, WC2
Tube: Covent Garden (Piccadilly Line)
Capacity: 200

The Africa Centre had a dual life: during the daylight hours the eighteenth- century building acted as an information centre on African arts, politics and culture. In the evening it transformed into a club which hosted the occasional live African group along with other types of music. Matt Johnston made his debut at the venue in 1979 while Carter The Unstoppable Sex Machine (October 1988), Ian McCulloch (of Echo and The Bunnymen) and Suede (April 1992) also played the venue. The Africa Centre moved out of the building in 2013.

Ain't Nothin' But ... Blues Bar

Address: 20 Kingly Street, Soho, London, W1B 5PZ
Tube: Oxford Circus (Central, Bakerloo and Victoria Lines)
Opened in October 1993 and puts on blues music seven days a week. Usually free entry before 8.30 p.m. There is a blues jam every Sunday between 3 and 7 p.m.

The Albany

Address: 240 Great Portland Street, London, W1W 5QU
Tube: Great Portland Street (Circle, Hammersmith & City and Metropolitan Lines)

Too Pure's Sausage Machine Club had a brief spell here (having previously been at the White Horse and the Moonlight Club) with Yo Lo Tengo and Courtney Love both performing. The Albany continues to host live music as well as comedy and cinema, but you may struggle to find an act's name you'd recognise.

The Apple Tree

Address: 45 Mount Pleasant, Clerkenwell, London, WC1X 0AE
Tube: Farringdon (Circle, Hammersmith & City and Metropolitan Lines)

After moving from The Golden Lion and the Fiddlers Elbow, the 'Come Down and Meet The Folks' club moved to this pub in Clerkenwell. Here on the last Sunday of the month gigs are put on as part of the club. In 2006 Hank Wangford and Vic Goddard and The Subway Sect performed here.

Arts Theatre

Address: 6/7 Great Newport Street, London, WC2H 7JB
Tube: Leicester Square (Northern and Piccadilly Lines)
Capacity: 342

This theatre was built in 1927 and had a long tradition of being the first stage for productions by Joe Orton, among others. In May 2001 the Arts Theatre was the venue for the Pet Shop Boys musical 'Closer To Heaven', which ran until October 2001 and starred Frances Barber. The theatre closed in June 2005 after lease problems, but was reopened and refurbished by April 2006. Lloyd Cole appeared twice in October 2006 and twice again in January 2007. Badly Drawn Boy played in September 2006, while former Throwing Muses frontwoman Kristen Hersh played in January 2007. Edwyn Collins played two nights at the venue in November 2007 with a backing band that included Roddy Frame (from Aztec Camera). The theatre continues to stage plays and comedians.

At the street level there is a bar area and some stairs at the rear lead down into the theatre's main stalls. Once inside the actual theatre there are framed pictures of actors on the walls and showbiz mirror light bulbs decorate the upper seating area. Also downstairs are the toilets and another bar/dining area.

The Astoria (see Pl.2)

Address: 157 Charing Cross Road, Soho, London, WC2 8EN
Tube: Tottenham Court Road (Central and Northern Lines).
Capacity: 2,000
Live releases: Radiohead '27.5.94 the London Astoria Live' video, Sugarcubes 'Live Zabor' video (June 1988), Ocean Colour Scene 'Filmed From The Front Row' DVD, Marc Almond 'A Lover Spurned' DVD.

The most centrally located of all London's venues, The Astoria was a few steps away from Tottenham Court Road tube station on Charing Cross Road. During daylight hours the box office sold tickets for all Mean Fiddler events and had boards on the street listing all the events, and cash customers could enjoy the novelty of gig tickets with no booking fee.

The building itself was originally built in 1893 as a Crosse and Blackwell pickle warehouse. In 1927 the warehouse was reconfigured into a cinema, with the redesign in the Halien Renaissance style by Edward A. Stone and built by Griggs & Sons (the team that also designed and built other Astoria cinemas in London). Being located on the edge of Soho, the next establishment was a strip club and then a music hall. The next change in direction was as a theatre and Shakin Stevens trod the boards in the 'Elvis' theatre production. The Astoria became a music venue in 1985 and has hosted gigs by Nirvana (November 1991, £7), David Bowie, U2, Eminem, Morrissey (December 1992, £12.50), Franz Ferdinand, The White Stripes and Oasis, to name just a few. The quality of these acts quickly led to the venue becoming a main stay of the London gig circuit. The venue attracted a wide range of performers from big named UK and US indie and metal groups to former Spice Girls and flavour of the month pop acts who were launching their new single at the venues popular GAY Pink Pounder nights (which started after the gigs had finished at 10.30 p.m). The GAY club nights had showcase performances from Kylie Minogue and others.

In 1994 Richey Edwards played what would turn out to be his last gig with the Manic Street Preachers at the Astoria before disappearing. Suede played a farewell gig here on 13 December 2003. U2 played on 7 February 2001 as part of their promotional tour for 'All That You Leave Behind' album. Tickets were only available to competition winners. Coldplay played in January 2000 as part of the NME Tour of Britain, which also included Shack.

The venue became part of the Mean Fiddler Group in May 2000. In 2004 the venue almost closed as it came close to losing its licence, however the threat was not implemented. In December 2004 there was a serious riot in the venue when Babyshambles failed to turn up; the crowd was told at 2 a.m. that there would be no show. Almost 200 fans invaded the stage to destroy the bands gear and to basically trash the venue. Needless to say the security acted in a way that rose to the challenge.

2005 saw the Foo Fighters play a warm-up gig for their appearances at the Reading and Leeds Festivals on the 24 August – £17.50 would have brought you a ticket for it. Robbie Williams launched his album 'Intensive Care' at the Astoria with a gig on 1 October 2005.

The main floor space was the ground floor, which was standing only. Upstairs was a (usually crowded) back bar named after Keith Moon, while at the front was a seated VIP only area with very unglamorous bingo-hall-style tables with seats and a general admittance area behind. The Astoria was demolished (along with Metro and The Mean Fiddler/LA2) in 2009 to be replaced by a new Tottenham Court Road Crossrail station.

Bagley's Warehouse. Prince played an aftershow gig at this Kings Cross club on 8 September 1993, taking to the stage at 5 a.m., after his gig at Wembley Arena. Became Canvas in 2003. The building has since been demolished.

Bedford College. It was here in 1970 that John Martyn, Nick Drake and The Spencer Davies Group played on the same bill. The college was in the South Villa in Regents Park.

Berkeley Square. Mika riding high with his number one single 'Grace Kelly' played in a big top in this square on 5 February 2007.

Blaises. Located in the basement of the Imperial Hotel at 121 Queens Gate, SW7 (Tube: South Kensington). Jimi Hendrix (1966), Yes (1968) and Pink Floyd played here. Has since been demolished.

Bloomsbury Bowling Lanes. Address: Tavistock Hotel, Bedford Way, London WC1H 9EU. Tube: Russell Square (Piccadilly Line). Located in the basement of the hotel, the Bowling Lanes staged gigs by up and coming bands on the London scene in 2005.

Blue Heaven Club. A 1950s Skiffle club set up by Cy Laurie in Ham Yard.

Bootleggers (see Speakeasy).

Bumpers. This club at 7–14 Coventry Street, W1, had Slade (1971), Status Quo (1971), The Sweet (1972) and Hawkwind (1972).

Bag O'Nails

Address: 9 Kingly Street, London, W1 5PH
Tube: Oxford Circus (Bakerloo, Central and Victoria Lines)
Capacity: 100

A basement jazz club that started in the 1930s and also hosted The Downbeat Club. Duke Ellington played in 1946 and was watched by Django Reinhardt. In 1967 Paul McCartney met future wife Linda for the first time while watching Georgie Fame play. It is also rumoured that John and Christine McVie also meet here.

The Jimi Hendrix Experience played a showcase gig for the London press here on 25 November 1966 while being watched by The Beatles, The Rolling Stones and The Who. Jimi's manager Chas Chandler sold some of his own guitars from his time in The Animals to finance the showcase. The risk paid off and The Jimi Hendrix Experience returned to the venue in January 1967 to play two shows.

The Libertines played early gigs here in 2003. The building later became a private club called Miranda's, but had reverted back to The Bag O' Nails in 2013. The venue was one of the legendary London venues that Prince stated a desire to play when he played a short series of small gigs in the capital in early 2014. However, he never turned up, preferring Camden's Electric Ballroom instead.

The Barbican Centre

Address: The Barbican Centre, Silk Street, London, EC2Y 8DS
Tube: Barbican (Circle, Hammersmith & City and Metropolitan Lines)
Capacity: 2, 026 (seated)
Live release: Calexico 'World Drifts In' DVD, Go Betweens 'Live in London' CD.

Building work started on the Barbican complex in 1971, and was designed by the architects Chamberlin, Powell and Bon at a cost of £161 million. The Barbican Centre opened on 3 March 1982 and is operated by the Corporation of London, forming part of the Barbican complex. The centre was built as the city's gift to the nation and was opened by Queen Elizabeth II who called it 'one of the wonders of the modern world'. The Barbican Centre is at the heart of the 35-acre residential Barbican Estate, and is a Grade II-Listed building. The main Barbican Hall had an acoustic refurbishment in 2001. The impressive stage usually hosts classical and world music, but the occasional 'rock' act slips in. Recent performers have included Billy Bragg, the Go Betweens, Ani Defranco, Kristin Hersch and Rufus Wainwright.

The venue is seated, with level stalls at the front of the stage that start to tier to the back. There are raised levels which usually have cheaper seat prices. Tickets are available from the venue's box office or from its website. The Barbican has curated the Beyond Nashville and Way Beyond Nashville festivals that spread across the capital's venues, usually late in the year.

Beat City/Tiles

Address: 79 Oxford Street, London.
Tube: Oxford Circus (Central Line)

The Spencer Davis Group played their first London gig at this basement club and The Rolling Stones played in July 1964. Them, featuring Van Morrison, played their first London gig here in July 1964. Later, in 1966, it became Tiles where Pink Floyd appeared in 1967 (see Tiles).

Betsey Trotwood

Address: 56 Farringdon Road, London, EC1R 3BL
Tube: Farringdon (Circle, Hammersmith & City and Metropolitan Lines
Capacity: 60

The venue was run by Plum Promotions who were involved with many other venues around the capital at the start of the millennium, and they operated from above the pub. At street level the pub is a fairly run of the mill London boozer; however downstairs in the cellar is a rather intimate venue with a small stage barely raised above the floorboards. To the left of the stage are a couple of alcoves which are sunken even further into the ground and offer a cozy atmosphere. A close-circuit TV screen is included so you don't miss any of the action up on stage. The alcove adjacent to the stage is the band area. A small bar with the mixing desk behind it is located at the entrance of the cellar the opposite end from the stage.

Artists who have played the venue since it opened in 2002 include early gigs by Keane (as a four-piece), The Subways, The Magic Numbers and KT Tunstall. Former James frontman Tim Booth launched his solo album here and former Suede guitarist Bernard Butler has played the Betsy. The pub takes its name from a character in Charles Dickens's *David Copperfield* and still hosts live music.

Blitz

Address: 4 Great Queen Street, Covent Garden, London, WC2B 5DJ
Tube: Holburn (Central and Piccadilly Lines)
Capacity: 350

The New Romantic club, which had Steve Strange (later of Visage) on the door, (for style control) and Boy George in the cloakroom (for coats!) started to attract attention in February 1979 when Strange started running his 'Bowie Nights' on Tuesday nights at this wine bar. The New Romantic customers soon became dubbed 'The Blitz Kids'. Spandau Ballet made their debut performance here in December 1979 and *Top of the Pops* dancers Hot Gossip performed even racier routines here than they did on TV. Members of Thin Lizzy, Japan, Ultravox and the Banshees used to hang out here as well as movie stars like Jack Nicholson. David Bowie filmed his video for the single 'Fashion' on the Blitz stage.

For a while the building was home to Browns nightclub, but is now a gentlemen's club called 'The Red Rooms'.

Bloomsbury Ballroom
Address: Victoria House, 37–63 Southampton Row, London, WC1B 4DA
Tube: Holborn (Central Line)
Capacity: 800

This 1920s Art Deco building contains the ballroom in its basement. Part of the former Mean Fiddler's main man Vince Power's new enterprise – Vince Power Music Group – the ballroom opened as a music venue in 2006. Amy Winehouse appeared in September 2006 and was quickly followed by Badly Drawn Boy, Kate Nash, Ed Harcourt, Edwyn Collins and Black Rebel Motorcycle Club.

The ballroom is also used for other functions such as corporate events, cocktail parties and even weddings, and these seem to have taken the place of live bands. The venue appears to have fallen off the gigging radar although occasional gigs have slipped in (Band of Skulls in 2013 and Hard-Fi in 2014).

Bloomsbury Theatre
Address: 15 Gordon Street, London, WC1H 0AH
Tube: Goodge Street (Northern Line)
Capacity: 535
Live release: Tindersticks 'The Bloomsbury Theatre' CD

Opened in 1968 as 'The Central Collegiate Building Auditorium', the building later became known as 'The Collegiate Theatre'. The venue became The Bloomsbury in 1982, reflecting the area of London where the building is located.

The Bloomsbury Theatre is part of the University College London and is in the heart of Central London's student zone. The venue is completely seated and also hosts plays and comedians as well as gigs. Artists who have played the Bloomsbury include Fairport Convention, Focus, Sandy Denny, Ray Davies (The Kinks), Ian McCulloch (Echo and The Bunnymen), Wreckless Eric and The Tindersticks. The Divine Comedy played for three nights in June 2004. Paul Simon performed a secret show here on 25 May 2006 that was later broadcast on Radio 2. Adam Ant took the stage here – his first performance for 10 years in September 2007, which included acoustic songs and readings from his autobiography.

The Borderline
Address: Orange Yard, off Manette Street, Soho, London, W1D 4JB
Tube: Tottenham Court Road (Central & Northern Lines)
Capacity: 275

This small venue tucked away near where the Astoria once stood has hosted some of the most intimate gigs by the world's biggest groups since opening its doors in 1985. The building itself dates from 1976. REM famously played here on 14 and 15 March 1991 (tickets £6!) under the pseudonym Bingo Hand Job, when they were joined on stage by Billy Bragg and Robyn Hitchcock. The group had previously played the venue on 28 May 1989 as Nigel and The Crosses (also with Bragg and Hitchcock). Other famous artists that have taken the Borderline's small stage include Crowded House, Pearl Jam, Bryan Adams, Blur, Sheryl Crow, PJ Harvey, The Verve, Lenny Kravitz and Pulp. These days it is the favoured venue by Americana artists (both UK & US) as well as singer-songwriter types and by UK groups in the sunset of their careers.

Upon entering the venue you go down some stairs which have the artist listings of every year it has been open painted onto the walls. These lead you down into the floor area of the venue. A cloak room is situated on the right next to the small stage. The main floor standing area is slightly sunken, while seating and bar areas are raised. Seats with tables are located left of the entrance at the rear of the venue, in the same area as the toilets. The bar is on the far side from the entrance and has a guitar hanging on the bar wall. The venues décor has a feel of the old Wild West to it and you could almost believe you were in some underground hacienda with its faded and stained paint on the walls. All of these features only aid to the charm of the venue and help make it probably the best small venue in London to see an act.

The backstage artist area is left of the stage and down a security pass only corridor. The artist backstage area is tiny, almost a wardrobe, and you have to wonder how all of REM fitted in there.

The venue was originally operated by the Break For The Border Group but was sold to the Mean Fiddler Group in 2004 and then to MAMA in 2007.

The Borderline continues to land special shows. Hollywood actress Minnie Driver launched her singing career here in 2004. The then unknown Tori Amos supported Dave Sharpe (ex The Alarm) here on 7 August 1991; a ticket would have cost you a fiver. Whatever happened to Dave Sharpe?

Debbie Harry played eight nights at the Borderline in October 1989 on her 'Def, Dumb and Blonde' tour. Suede played a gig here in October 1991, and Oasis shot their video for 'Cigarettes and Alcohol' at The Borderline.

Bunjies/Folk Cellar
Address: 27 Litchfield Street, London, WC2H 9NJ
Tube: Leicester Square (Piccadilly and Northern Lines)

Opened in 1954 as a coffee house that hosted folk gigs, Bunjies was also known as the Folk Cellar. David Bowie, Paul Simon and Rod Stewart all played here in the Swinging 60s. Bob Dylan played here in 1962. While the 1960s were definitely the period when the venue gained

its status as a venue, there was one last hurrah in March 1994 when Jeff Buckley performed in the cellar. The gig saw Jeff handing out white roses to those present and then over-running the curfew, so both singer and crowd relocated to the nearby 12 Bar Club where the gig continued. The building became a North African restaurant called Souk.

Café de Paris. 3–4 Coventry Street, London, W1D 6BL. Opened in 1924 and bombed in the Second World War, killing over thirty people including performers. Frank Sinatra, Marlene Dietrich and Noel Coward performed on the stage. Tube: Piccadilly Circus.
Café Freedom. Placebo played this Wardour Street café in November 1995.
Camden Centre. Located on Euston Road, WC1H 9JE, Terry Callier, De La Soul and Secret Affair played in 2009. Part of Camden Town Hall.
Cameo. See Speakeasy.
Camouflage. 84–86 Wardour Street, London, W1F 0TA, with a 450 capacity. A former restaurant called 'Spiga' until converted into a venue in 2006 by the Vince Power Music Group. However, nothing much really came of it.
Cavern Club. No, not the one in Liverpool, but at 5 Leicester Place. Also known as The Cavern in The Town and was located under The Ad Lib Club. The Small Faces played their first gig here in June 1965 and also went on to have residency. Also see Notre Dame Hall.
Club Eleven. Located at 41 Great Windmill Street, this was a jazz club was open between 1948 and 1950. Ronnie Scott and Johnny Dankworth were the band leaders of two of the house bands. Later moved to 50 Carnaby Street before closing soon afterwards. Also see The Scene Club.
Cross Kings. A venue in Kings Cross that closed in 2010.
The Condor Club. A 1950s rock 'n' roll venue in Archer Street, W1, where Marty Wilde was discovered. Known as a 'Beat Club' and a gambling den.
Covent Garden. Buskers are usually everywhere in this former market, Bon Jovi and Paul McCartney being the most famous and least needing of the buskers hat.
Covent Garden Spot. Address: 29 Maiden Lane, Covent Garden, London, WC2E 7JS. Tube: Covent Garden (Line).

Cadogan Hall
Address: 5 Sloane Terrace, London, SW1X 9DQ
Tube: Sloane Square (Circle and District Lines)
Capacity: 900 (seated)

Built in 1907 as the First Church of Christ Science, the church closed in 1996 due a decline in the congregation. The building was disused until 2000 when the Cadogan Estate took over the building. Since then it has been used mainly as a classical venue, although rock 'n' roll has been known to slip in unnoticed. The Magnetic Fields, Joe Jackson and Petula Clark appeared in 2008, and Patti Smith played in 2014.

Central St Martin's College (School of Art)
Address: Southampton Row, London, WC1
Tube: Holborn (Central Line)

Apart from having numerous musicians passing through its doors as students, the Southampton Row building also hosted the second gig by the Sex Pistols in November 1975. Generation X played their first gig here in 1976. The Paddingtons played in November 2005. The college had moved out by 2014 and the building was being prepared for redevelopment.

Central St Martin's College (School of Art)
Address: 107 - 109 Charing Cross Road, London, WC2H 0DT
Tube: Tottenham Court Road (Central and Northern Lines)

The Sex Pistols played their first ever gig here on 6 September 1975, at this part of the St Martin's campus. The gig lasted just 20 minutes as the promoter pulled the plug. A blue plaque marking the gig was inside the building. The building dates from 1939 and has witnessed many famous musicians, actors and designers graduate from its courses. The college gets a famous namecheck in Pulp's 'Common People' – Jarvis Cocker being a graduate of the school. No longer part of the college, it has been redeveloped (photo is shown when still an art college) into flats known as The Saint Martin's Lofts, where a two-bedroom apartment would cost you £2 million (2015).

Conway Hall
Address: 25 Red Lion Square, London, WC1R 4RL
Tube: Holborn (Central and Piccadilly Lines)
Capacity: 500

Since 2003 this humanist hall has hosted the 'Homefires' folk festival which has featured Willy Mason, Magic Numbers, Beth Orton, Badly Drawn Boy and James Yorkson. Previously the hall had staged occasional gigs including several by Hawkwind in December 1969 and April 1971 and Cure in 1979. Way back in 1957 Lonnie Donegan played the Hall.

Cousins/Les Cousins
Address: 49 Greek Street, London, W1D 4EG
Tube: Tottenham Court Road (Central and Northern Lines)

A 1960s folk club where Paul Simon, Bert Jansch, Nick Drake, Van Morrison and Al Stewart played. Also known as Les Cousins, the venue closed in 1979. It became a bar called Sak (around 2004) and is now a club called 'Club 49'.

Cromwellian Club
Address: 3 Cromwell Road, London, SW7
Tube: South Kensington (Circle, Piccadilly and District Lines).

Here over three floors Stevie Wonder and Reg Dwight (Elton John) played. Known for its jam sessions when the likes of Eric Burden, Georgie Fame, Eric Clapton and Hendrix use to get together and let the music talk. The basement is currently a bar, bistro and nightclub. It is located opposite the Natural History Museum.

Daybreak Club. Located at 44 Gerrard Street, W1, which also housed George Melly's West End Jazz Club in the 1950s. Also see Happening 44.

Denmark Street. Here in the street where every shop sells musical instruments, the 'Tin Pan Alley Festival' was held on 16 July 2006. Groups who played this free street festival included British Sea Power and Vincent Vincent and the Villians.

Diorama Theatre. Located at 15–16 Triton Street, Regents Place, London, NW1 3BF (Tube: Warren Street), the Manic Street Preachers played here in 1991. Has a tiny capacity of eighty.

Dover Street Arts Club. A private members club located at 40 Dover Street, Mayfair, W1S 4NP, that was founded in 1863 and moved to the current address in 1896. Most notable for soul legend Dionne Warwick performing in June 2014, where she stopped the gig to berate a crowd member for filming the gig on their iPhone before confiscating the phone. Her diva moment included the comment 'don't you know how much it would cost to film me?' However, she must have had a moment of self-awareness as she gave the phone back and invited the person to sing along with her.

Drury Lane Theatre. New Wave group Magazine supported by Simple Minds played this theatre in May 1979. Catherine Street, WC2B 5JF.

Duke of York's Theatre. Maria McKee played twice in October 1989, supported by the Black Velvet Band. Located at St Martin's Lane, WC2B 4BG.

Dominion Theatre

Address: Tottenham Court Road, London, W1T 7AQ
Tube: Tottenham Court Road (Central & Northern Line)
Capacity: 2,007

The theatre was designed by William and TR Millburn and opened on 3 October 1929. The theatre originally staged musicals, but soon showed films, opera, dance and variety shows. Big names from a bygone era such as Judy Garland, Maurice Chevalier and Shirley MacLaine have played the venue. Cliff Richard made his West End stage debut in *Time* here in 1985.

Although the Dominion Theatre was the home to the Queen musical *We Will Rock You* with the fake bronze statue of Freddie Mercury dominating the Building for twelve long years – one time the theatre really did rock people. Elvis Costello (supported by Richard Hell's The Voidoids) played seven consecutive nights here in December 1978, while in March 1983 Van Morrison played four nights in a row to launch his Beautiful Vision album, which went some way to count towards the eleven times he played the theatre during the 1980s. In the mid-1980s indie groups such as The Go Betweens and The Triffids graced the stage and invited the seated crowd to stand up. John Hiatt, Julia Fordham and Deacon Blue played in October 1988. In 2006 The Sugababes resurrected live music at the Dominion after the theatre had a long break with gigs when the 'babes launched their 'Overloaded' singles collection on 29 October.

We Will Rock You opened at the Dominion in May 2002 and closed in May 2014, after an estimated audience of 16 million had seen the show. Hopefully this will give bands the chance to return to its stage after being dominated by Queen for so long.

The Dominion Theatre is a Grade II Listed Building.

Drummonds

Address: 73–77 Euston Road, Kings Cross, London, NW1 2QS
Tube: Kings Cross (Circle, Hammersmith & City, Metropolitan, Northern and Victoria Lines)

Opposite St Pancras station, Drummonds would put on indie bands in the late 1980s. Television Personalities (October 1988), Motorcycle Boy (May 1988) The Jazz Butcher, Jesus Jones and Benny Profane (October 88) all played here. It is now part of the O'Neills chain of Irish pubs with traditional Irish sessions on offer.

> <u>Electric Golden.</u> See Middle Earth.
>
> <u>El Paradiso.</u> The Sex Pistols played a short residency in this Soho strip club starting on 4 April 1976.
>
> <u>Embassy Rooms/Empire Rooms.</u> Address: 161 Tottenham Court Road, W1. Tube: Warren Street (Northern and Victoria Lines). A venue used by Kilburn Polytechnic for gigs, the Empire Rooms had Black Sabbath and Van Der Graaf Generator play in the early 1970s. James played a low-key gig here (Embassy Rooms) in October 1999 to promote the album 'Millionaires'. The building is now home to Spearmint Rhino – a lap-dancing club.
>
> <u>Fabric.</u> Located at 77a Charterhouse Street, Farringdon, EC1, Bloc Party played a charity gig at this club in March 2006.
>
> <u>Fopp.</u> Address: 220–224 Tottenham Court Road, London.
> Tube: Goodge Street (Northern Line). A record shop that attracted some in-store gigs by the likes of Larrakin Love in 2006. The gigs usually took place in the coffee shop area in the rear basement of the store and purchasing the artist's latest product from the store was usually the requirement for entry. There was also a Fopp store at 287 Camden High Street, Camden (just before the lock) that also had some in-store gigs. The Fopp chain closed in June 2007, although a few stores have been revived since then. However, in-store gigs seem not to have been resuscitated.

The Flamingo Club/The Temple
Address: 33–37 Wardour Street, London, W1D 6PU
Tube: Tottenham Court Road (Central and Northern Lines)
Capacity: 400
Live release: Georgie Fame and The Blue Flames 'Rhythm & Blues From The Flamingo' LP

A jazz club started in the 1950s and had several addresses including the basement of 10–11 Great Newport Street in 1950, the basement of the Mapleton Hotel on the corner of Coventry and Whitcomb Streets in 1952, Brewer Street, a café in Leicester Square and the Pigalle Restaurant at 190 Piccadilly.

In 1957 the Flamingo found a longer-lasting home when it moved to Wardour Street. Georgie Fame and The Blue Flames, Dick Morrissey Quartet, Ella Fitzgerald, Billie Holiday, Dizzy Gillespie, Otis Reading and Ronnie Scott all played in the 1960s. The audience would consist of members of The Beatles, The Rolling Stones and The Who. Later in the 1960s, up and coming acts such as Them, Deep Purple, Status Quo, Led Zeppelin and Yes would play the venue.

The Flamingo was run by Jeff Kruger and was known for its all-night R&B sessions. The club later became The Temple before closing in 1970. The Wag Club would later be upstairs from the Flamingo. Now an O'Neills pub with traditional Irish sessions (also see entry for The Wag Club).

The Fly
Address: 34–36 New Oxford Street, London, WC1A 1AP
Tube: Russell Square (Piccadilly Line)

This venue was part of the Barfly empire which had venues elsewhere in London and all over the UK (as well as a free music magazine). The Fly attracted unsigned bands. The bar area was popular with indie and rock kids alike in the daytime hours while the bands played in the basement. The venue closed – like many other venues in the Barfly chain – and the building is now a Prezzo restaurant.

Gibson Guitar Studio. This studio at Global House in the West End saw Snow Patrol play an intimate gig to some radio competition winners on 4 September 2006, which was later broadcast on radio. Paul Weller and the Kaiser Chiefs have also played here, which is part of the Academy of Contemporary Music.

The Goings-on-Club. Pink Floyd played this club in Archer Street in January 1966.

Grosvenor House Hotel. The Park Lane location for the Mercury Music Prize where most of the nominees performed during the ceremony. The Beatles played a charity show in the hotel's ballroom in December 1963.

Hanover Grand. Address: 6 Hanover St, London, W1R 9HH. Tube: Oxford Circus (Bakerloo, Central and Victoria Lines). Capacity: 900. Suede played here on 27 January 1996, Dodgy (May 1996), David Bowie (1997), and Morcheeba, Lewis Taylor and Embrace appeared in 2000, with Idlewild playing in July 2002. Originally it was a Masonic hall.

Happening 44. Located at 44 Gerrard Street (also home to the Blue Heaven Club and Daybreak Club) in 1967, this was the venue for several early gigs by Fairport Convention and Soft Machine. The club was run by Jack Braceland. The 2i's was also housed here for a while.

Hard Rock Café. Opened in 1971 at 150 Old Park Lane, W1 1QZ, this music memorabilia-encrusted café has also hosted the occasional gig by the likes of Primal Scream (September 2013) and The Kaiser Chiefs (May 2014). Tube: Hyde Park Corner (Piccadilly Line).

Horse and Groom. This pub at 128 Great Portland Street, W1W 6PS, dates from 1826 and had the first London gig for the Manic Street Preachers in 1989 – and they played it twice that year.

Heaven/G-A-Y/Global Village

Address: The Archers, off Villers Street & Craven Street, London, WC2N 6NG
Tube: Charing Cross (Bakerloo and Northern Lines)

Formerly a club called The Global Village that had opened in 1973 and located in a small shopping parade in the railway archers under the approach to Charing Cross station. Heaven replaced Global Village in 1980 when Richard Branson took the building over as part of his expanding Virgin empire (Virgin also ran The Venue in Victoria). This notorious gay club hosts occasional gigs. New Order made their London debut here in 1981, Southern Death Cult (later The Cult), Spandau Ballet, Eurythmics, Erasure, Suede and The Orb have all played Heaven. The Pet Shop Boys shot some live footage for their video for 'Home and Dry' on Heaven's stage in 2002. The Fall's Mark E Smith's offshoot group Von Sudenfed played Heaven on 18 October 2007.

Heaven is (unsurprisingly) home to the G-A-Y club nights. Originally started as a club night at the Astoria on Charing Cross Road, these club nights always attract pop sensations for a very small, usually short, intimate gig. Nicole Scherzinger played a 25-minute set in July 2014.

Heaven can be accessed by either Villers Street or Craven Street.

Hippodrome/Talk of The Town

Address: Charing Cross Road/Leicester Square, London, WC2H 7JH
Tube: Leicester Square (Northern and Piccadilly Lines)
Capacity: 1,340

Opened in 1900 as a theatre and designed by Frank Matcham. As unlikely as it seems – if like this author you are of an age when you can only associate the Hippodrome with its tacky 1980s owner Peter Stringfellow –the Hippodrome was the venue for what could be considered to be the first ever gig in London when The Original Dixieland Jazz Band played on 7 April 1919. In 1950 the interior was ripped out and redesigned and became known as The Talk of The Town. Notable performers include Diana Ross, Judy Garland, Frank Sinatra and Tom Jones. The name reverted back to The Hippodrome in the 1980s when it became a nightclub. This Grade II-listed Building is currently a casino.

HMV (East Oxford Street)

Address: 150 Oxford Street, London W1D 1ND
Tube: Oxford Circus (Central Line)
Capacity: 400

Opened in 1996, the 60,000-square foot floor space made the building the biggest music shop in the world. Not strictly a music venue, the HMV Oxford Street store earned its place in this book because of the impressive amount of in-store performances which were often combined with signings. A-Ha played a short set on 30 January 2006, and Richard Ashcroft held an in-store signing on 23 January 2006. Others who have appeared here include Prince, Kiss, Sheryl Crow and Bros. In 1995 Michael Jackson had a private shopping session in the shop.

Store events were sometimes advertised in the *NME*, usually as part of an advert for the groups/artists new release. More informative however were the posters at the store entrance, advertising future events. For in-store gigs HMV usually issued special wrist bands that admitted the wearer to the gig. The wristbands were usually given away free on a first come first served basis on the day of the gig when that artist's new product is purchased. Gigs usually started at 6 p.m. It closed in January 2014 and is now a branch of Sports Direct.

HMV (West Oxford Street)

Address: 363 Oxford Street, London, W1C 2LA
Tube: Oxford Circus (Bakerloo, Central and Victoria Lines).

The original HMV store that reopened here in 2013 with a ceremony involving an appearance by Paul McCartney. In-store performances from The Maccabees, Frank Turner, The Darkness (all in 2015) and Kasabian (in 2014). A blue plaque celebrates The Beatles recording the sessions that got them signed to EMI in the basement of the building.

Horsehoe Hotel

Address: 264–267 Tottenham Court Road, London, W1T 7RH
Tube: Tottenham Court Road (Central and Northern Lines)

This pub in February 1967 was the venue where British folk icons Bert Jansch and John Renbourn amplified traditional songs and led to the formation of the group Pentangle. Upping the folk credentials somewhat is that John Martyn and Sandy Denny appeared together here in 1968. The folk nights ceased in 1969 and the building is now a Burger King.

Hyde Park

Address: Hyde Park Corner, Hyde Park, London, SW1
Tube: Hyde Park Corner (Piccadilly Line)
Capacity: Usually 60,000 (but can go up to 200,000)
Live release: Red Hot Chilli Peppers 'Live at Hyde Park' CD 2004, Paul Weller 'Live' DVD, Foo Fighters 'Skin & Bones' DVD

This park, created in 1536 by Henry VIII for the purpose of hunting deer, has hosted the world's biggest names to its central London green space. The Rolling Stones played a gig here on 5 July 1969, three days after Brian Jones died. The stage was, at the time, the largest ever built for an English outside concert. The Stones played an awful set, which can be relived on DVD (as can Mick's 'moving' speech for Brian). Support on the day came from King Crimson, Alexis Korner's group and Family. The Stones returned to celebrate fifty years together in July 2013.

On Saturday 2 July 2005 Hyde Park hosted the Make Poverty History Live 8 concert, where (in order of performance) Paul McCartney & U2, U2, Coldplay, Elton John (with Pete Doherty on Children Of The Revolution), Dido, Stereophonics, REM, Ms Dynamite, Keane, Travis, Bob Geldof, Annie Lennox, UB40, Snoop Dogg, Razorlight, Madonna, Snow Patrol, The Killers, Joss Stone, Velvet Revolver, Sting, Mariah Carey, Robbie Williams, The Who, Pink Floyd (reforming after more than twenty years for the gig) and Paul McCartney with everyone (on the closing Hey Jude) highlighted African poverty before the G8 summit. The Red Hot Chilli Peppers played the park on 19 and 20 June 2004, supported by James Brown and Chicks On Speed.

From 2005 to 2012 Hyde Park hosted the Wireless Festival (which was branded O2 Wireless between 05 and 08 and Barclaycard Wireless between 09 and 12). The festival featured New Order, Basement Jaxx, Keane, Rufus Wainwright, Supergrass and the Psychedelic Furs in 2005. The Strokes, Belle & Sebastian, David Gray, Massive Attack, The Flaming Lips, James Blunt, Eels, Depeche Mode, Goldfrapp and Bauhaus played in June 2006. The White Stripes, Aerosmith and Crowded House played in 2007 and Pulp performed reformed in 2011. When Wireless lost the rights to gigs in the park and moved to other London locations (Olympic Park and Finsbury Park) the British Summertime brand moved in with gigs by Elton John and Bon Jovi in 2013, Arcade Fire and The Libertines in 2014 and Blur, Kylie, The Who and The Strokes in 2015. One unpleasant aspect about the British Summertime events is the introduction of a 'Premium View'. For extra money one can buy themselves into an exclusive area with good views of the stage. Most gig-goers would be forgiven to think that this would usually be the raised seated area just to the side of the main audience, but they would be wrong. Instead British Summertime class the 'Premium View' to be the field directly in front of the stage where most music lovers would expect their standard ticket to give them (and a few thousand other fans) entry to if they arrived within a few hours of the gates opening. This left many fans angry when The Who played in 2015. Hopefully this policy will change.

ICA

Address: 12 Carlton Terrace, The Mall, London, SW1Y 5AH
Tube: Charing Cross (Northern & Bakerloo Lines)
Capacity: 350 (standing), 167 (seated)

This splendid-looking building, opened by artists, poets and writers in 1947, probably has the swankest address of any venue in London. A stone's throw away from Buckingham Palace, it is tempting to think that a young Prince Charles may have sneaked out to catch some of the gigs here. However, I doubt if he was there when The Jesus and Mary Chain played The ICA in 1984. The Mary Chain's (at the time) usual 20-minute set ended up in a riot, which resulted in the group being banned from the venue. Maybe as a reaction against the royal neighbours, the ICA has had more than its share of controversial performers. In October 1976 Throbbing Gristle's exhibition entitled 'Prostitution' was discussed in the House of Commons, as the public had funded a party consisting of beers and strippers. Also in that October The Clash played there and they made it into the newspapers when a photo from the gig was published in the press. This photo was of a young Shane McGowan (later of The Pogues) having his ear bitten off by a girl.

Adam and The Ants made their live debut here on 10 May 1977, under false pretensions – they claimed they were a country and western band. However, it took the management a few minutes to realise that Adam Ant wasn't crooning country songs and throw The Ants off stage (at least he stood and delivered). The industrial delight that must have been Concerto for Voices and Machinery (consisting of Genesis P Orridge and Frank Tovey) caused the management more concern in 1984 when they started destroying the stage with chainsaws. The Smiths played their tenth London gig at the ICA on 5 October 1983. Suede played six nights in a row here in September 2003 – performing one of their albums in full each night. American singer-songwriter Liz Phair made a very rare UK appearance at the ICA on 7 October, 2003.

On 3 November 2004 the ICA hosted the first live gig to be broadcast to mobile phones (at the cost of £5 to the viewer) by boy-band rockers Rooster. The ICA consists of a theatre, where the gigs are held, cinemas and galleries.

The box office is in the foyer entrance and the venue is located to the right of it. The venue is a fairly compact room painted black. Sometimes there is seating in a tiered layout; otherwise it is all standing.

The ICA continues to host gigs by established artists and up and coming groups alike.

Imperial College
Address: Beit Quadrangle, Prince Consort Road, Kensington, SW7 2BB
Tube: South Kensington (Circle, District and Piccadilly Lines)
Capacity: 450

Imperial student Brian May's group Queen played early gigs at the college in 1970 and a PRS plaque was erected at the site in 2013 to commemorate the first gig. Others who have played include The Jimi Hendrix Experience in May 1967, Hawkwind in 1971, Manfred Mann in 1972, The Brilliant Corners, Diesel Park West in 1988, Jesus Jones in 1989 and The Webb Brothers in 1999.

Infinity Address: 10 Old Burlington Street, Mayfair, London. Tube: Piccadilly Circus (Bakerloo and Piccadilly Lines). Maximo Park (Feb 2005), Amusement Parks On Fire, Clor (2004) and The Others have played here. The building has since been redeveloped.

Kings Cross Freight Depot. On 26 and 27 August 2006 Hot Chip, Sasha, Ladytron, The Research and Clor played as part of TDK's Cross Central Festival.

Leduce Contemporary Folk Club. Here at 22 D'Arblay Street, Soho, artists such as Sandy Denny (1965), Paul Simon and Al Stewart performed. The building is currently used as a dry cleaners.

London Jazz Centre. Location: 14 Greek Street. A 1950's jazz venue run by Harold Pendleton who later ran The Marquee Club.

Kings College/KCLSU

Address: MacAdam Building, Surrey Street, London, WC2R 2NS
Tube: Temple (Circle and District Lines)
Capacity: 620

Adam and The Ants played this popular student union in November 1977, while The Foo Fighters made their UK debut here in June 1995. Canadian group The Arcade Fire played the college in March 2005. Former Verve frontman Richard Ashcroft played in December 2005. Kings College was rebranded as 'KCLSU' in 2006. The gig area was on one of the upper floors of the building and was accessed by a lift.

Kings Place

Address: 90 York Way, Kings Cross, London, N1 9AG
Tube: Kings Cross (Central, Circle, Metropolitan, Northern and Victoria Lines)
Capacity: 420 (Hall 1) and 220 (Hall 2)

This modern building is home to newspaper *The Guardian* as well as Kings Place, which is a venue that specialises in folk, world and classical music. Opened in 2008, the venue was the first new public hall to be built in Central London since The Barbican in 1982. The building was designed by Dixon Jones and Arup Acoustics and has a three-layered glass façade on the York Way elevation. There are seven floors of offices above the venue and Hall 1 is three storeys tall, has an Oak Veneer interior from a 500-year-old German tree (which is also used inside Hall 2) and sits on rubber springs to improve the acoustics.

The venues offers mostly folk and classical artists. Folk lecturer and musician Fay Hield played in April 2014, and American artist Laura Cantrell also appeared in 2014.

LA2/Mean Fiddler

Address: 157 Charing Cross Road, London, WC2 8EN
Tube: Tottenham Court Road (Central & Northern Lines)
Capacity: 1,000. **Live release:** The Cranberries 'Live', video (14.1.94)

This venue was originally a ballroom under The Astoria (see entry) which became a music venue/ gay club called 'Bang' before being renamed The London Astoria 2.

The futuristic design of the entrance of the club would of mislead you down two flights into a venue that was a little dated inside, with mirrored tiles on the walls around the floor area. The venue had two levels. The first had a cloakroom, merchandise stall, male and female toilets, a bar and a balcony area, part of which was glazed and suffered from poor sound. The balcony did however offer good views down onto the stage. At the rear of the first floor were the stairs that lead down to the floor and stage area, where there was a bar at the back of the room. The venue had a decent-sized stage that would have given most groups enough room to roam. There was a raised area in front of the stage to elevate punters; however this may have been a little frustrating for shorter gig-goers behind who could struggle to see much.

The venue became prominent as the London Astoria 2 (otherwise known as LA2) but was rebranded as the Mean Fiddler when the Mean Fiddler Organisation took control of the venue (the original Mean Fiddler in Harlesden then became The Old Fiddler). As the LA2, the venue saw Suede and the Manic Street Preachers perform, and Nick Cave and The Bad Seeds played a free show for fans here on 10 May 1998 to launch their 'Best of' album. Those who have played the Mean Fiddler include John Cale and InMe.

From April 2004 to mid-2007, The Mean Fiddler had been home to The Frog club night, which had bands playing live. The venue, along with The Astoria and Metro, was demolished in 2009 to make way for a Crossrail station.

Live! On The Park at Pizza On The Park

Address: 11–13 Knightsbridge, London, SW1X 7LP
Tube: Hyde Park Corner (Piccadilly Line)

A Pizza Express restaurant and jazz venue that has featured the Pizza Express All Stars, the John Wilson Orchestra, Shakatak, Jim Diamond, Mose Allison (eleven nights in May 2007), Andy Sheppard and Curtis Stigers.

London School of Economics (LSE)

Address: Old Theatre (or The Quad), Houghton Street, London, WC2
Tube: Temple (Circle and District Lines)

Skin Games (November 1988), Faith Over Reason, Spiritulized and Boys Wonder (1990) have all played the university venue. Punks Sham 69 played on 4 February 1978 and the crowd caused £7,500 worth of damage to the venue.

Lyceum Theatre

Address: Wellington Street, Covent Garden, London, WC2E 7RQ
Tube: Covent Garden (Piccadilly Line)
Capacity: 2,500

Live release: Bob Marley and The Wailers 'Live' album and DVD (1975), Blondie 'Livid – 17 Greatest Hits Live' CD (November 1998)

The Lyceum Theatre opened in 1904 as an opera house on a site that had an entertainment use dating back to the mid-1700s. In the late 1960s the Marquee Club started to promote midnight gigs at the theatre, as the Marquee lacked the required late-night licence to do so. Groups that performed in the 1960s small hours include Jeff Beck, Al Stewart and Caravan. The Lyceum hosted the UNICEF charity gig 'Peace for Xmas' which the Plastic Ono Group headlined, and was famous for reuniting John Lennon and George Harrison on stage for the first time since the last Beatles gig. It would also be Lennon's last live gig in the UK. New Years Eve 1969 witnessed the first London gig by The Faces. The original Genesis played the venue in 1971, Led Zeppelin in 1969, and Eric Clapton christened his new group Derek and The Dominos backstage at the venue before taking the stage on 14 June 1970. Bob Marley played the venue and released an album of the gig that helped break him in the UK in 1975. The venue was also the first large-stage gig for the Sex Pistols on 9 July 1976. Prince made his UK debut here in 1981. The Lyceum was also an important venue for Ska bands with Madness, The Beat, Bad Manners and The Specials all playing here in 1979 and 1980. £2.50 would have got you a ticket for Generation X, The Fall and UK Subs in February 1979. The Smiths performed their sixth London gig here on 7 August 1983 and REM played an early UK show here on 2 December 1984. The theatre ceased live music a little while later. However, a reformed Blondie played two nights at the Lyceum on 21 and 22 November 1998, and tracks from the gigs were used in their live album 'Livid'.

U2 signed their contract with Island Records in the female toilets here in 1980, and played the venue twice that year. Bono and the boys returned four times in 1981 and paid their last visit in December 1982.

The Lyceum remains open staging musicals.

Madame JoJo's (see Pl.19)
Address: 8–10 Brewer Street, Soho, London, W1F 0SD
Tube: Tottenham Court Road (Central and Northern Lines)
Capacity: 25

Found in the heart of the sleaziest part of town, Soho, Madame JoJo's is squeezed in between peep shows and sex shops – no wonder that the venue usually hosts 'gentlemen's entertainment'. However, the venue did host the occasional gig now and again. In the 1990s The Jesus and Mary Chain played the venue and the Red Hot Chilli Peppers played a secret show here in 1995. Ed Harcourt, Scissor Sisters, Bloc Party and the Kings of Leon have also played here. The venue was in the basement with a sunken area with tables around the small stage. Robert Forster filmed the video for his single 'Cryin' Love' at Madam JoJo's. The venue was closed due to licensing issues (in conjunction with the local council and police) in late 2014 The Madam JoJo's building can also be seen in a wider context in the Soho Review Bar entry.

Marquee 1958–1964

Address: 165 Oxford Street, London, W1D 2J
Tube: Oxford Circus (Central Line)

The Marquee started as a purely jazz club in 1958 under the Academy Cinema, but by 1962 R 'n'B had a foot in the door, led by Blues Incorporated (including Alexis Korner, Charlie Watts and Jack Bruce). The Rolling Stones played here four times in 1963, although they had played several times (including their debut gig) in 1962 during the intervals. The Marquee owner was Harold Pendleton. The building was demolished in 1989 and was replaced by the current building.

Marquee 1964–1988 (see Pl.21)

Address: 90 Wardour Street, London, W1F
Tube: Tottenham Court Road (Central and Northern Lines)

The Marquee opened its new doors in Wardour Street in March 1964 with The Yardbirds christening the new stage. The building was previously a store for the clothes company Burberry.

Groups who played at this site include Adam and The Ants (fifteen times), The Animals, Jeff Beck, Black Sabbath (six times), Boomtown Rats, David Bowie (twenty times), The Buzzcocks, Cream (seven times), The Cure (five times), Deep Purple, Dire Straits (six times), The Fall (four times), Fleetwood Mac (nine times), Free (fifteen times), Alex Harvey (thirt-five times), Hawkwind, Human League, The Jam, King Crimson (seventeen times), Kiss (three times), Led Zepplin (four times), Moody Blues (nineteen times), Nico, Phil Ochs, Pink Floyd (five times), Sex Pistols, Simon and Garfunkel, Slade, Status Quo (eleven times), Rod Stewart (ten times), Thin Lizzy and The Who (twenty-nine times). U2 played four times in 1980. Little wonder that with a history of those names The Marquee is probably the most famous venue name in the UK.

Marquee 1988–1996 (see Pl.22)

Address: 105 Charing Cross Road, London, WC2H 0DT
Tube: Tottenham Court Road (Central and Northern Lines)
Live release: Jesus Jones 'Live at The Marquee' (DVD)

Built in 1911 as a cinema and operated by Montagu Alexander Pyke, who ran fifteen other London cinemas. It became home to The Marquee in 1988, and groups who played at this location include REM, Lone Justice, Kiss, Aerosmith and The Prodigy. Goodbye Mr McKenzie, who featured future Garbage frontwoman Shirley Manson, played here in August 1988; £2 would have got you entrance.

The building has been a JD Wetherspoons pub since 1996 (when it was called The Moon Under Water) and the interior pays due respect to its musical past.

Marquee 2002–2003 (see Islington Academy)

Marquee 2004–2007 (see Pl.23)

Address: 1 Leicester Square, London
Tube: Leicester Square (Piccadilly and Northern Lines)
Capacity: 900

The Marquee name was brought back in 2004, after the Dave Stewart flop the previous year (see Islington Academy). This Marquee was based in the former 'Home' nightclub in Leicester Square.

The ground-floor entrance was just the box office with a corridor leading to the lift that raised you to the main Marquee venue on the third floor. Inside the venue was a long, narrow black room with a bar in the right-hand side of the venue. There were tables and chairs scattered all over the room and a raised area with more seating on the left side (and is also where the DJ hangs out). A decent-sized stage was in the middle of the venue and it managed to miss being stuck in front of the support girders inside the room. A balcony area was sometimes open on the fourth level, and the impressive toilets were on the higher levels.

The Marquee here was run by Plum Promotions who also ran The Betsy Trotwood and The Water Rats. Like these venues the Marquee specialised in unsigned bands, and usually had three unsigned bands playing in one night. These nights were usually well attended by keen crowds eager to show support and ensured a great atmosphere for all bands to play in. Plum Promotions ended their association with the venue in late 2005. A few well-known groups have played gigs here including Ash, The Magic Numbers, Tom Vek, Dirty Vegas, Ed Harcourt, The Editors, Kubb, Mylo and Razorlight.

By the end of 2006 the Marquee was looking for a return move back to Soho.

Marquee 2007–2008
Address: 14 Upper St Martins Lane, London, WC2H 9FB
Tube: Leicester Square (Piccadilly and Northern Lines)

The Marquee brand was on the ropes when it moved here and lasted about a year. Unknown acts were the specialty at this location – not the right note for the Marquee legacy to end on. The building is now home to offices for Cussons Beauty.

Metro Club
Address: 19–23 Oxford Street, London, W1

Tube: Tottenham Court Road (Central and Northern Lines)
Capacity: 175

Another venue that was located close to Tottenham Court Road tube station. The ground-level entrance lead down some stairs into the basement venue. The first room area contained a pool table, cloakroom, chairs and lead to the main floor area. The stage was next to the entrance and was not raised far above the floor, which meant punters were almost eye to eye with the performers. The bar ran along the left flank of the room.

The venue attracted up-and-coming groups (such as Bloc Party in April 2004, The Killers, Kings of Leon, Yeah Yeah Yeahs, Mika, Scissor Sisters and the Kaiser Chiefs) and sometimes hosted more established artists like Ian McNab to its intimate surrounds. The Metro Club was home to The Blow Up Club from November 2001 until January 2009, when the venue closed to be demolished (along with The Astoria and LA2/Mean Fiddler) for the Crossrail project. However, the building in 2015 appeared to be still standing – although the venue had long since closed.

Middle Earth/Electric Golden

Address: 43 King Street, Covent Garden, London, WC2E 8JY
Tube: Covent Garden (Piccadilly Line)

Middle Earth moved to the Roundhouse in July 1968, but not before John Peel introduced Tyrannosauras Rex here. David Bowie once performed a mime act called 'Jetson and The Eagle' as a support for Tyrannosaurus Rex. Fairport Convention, Captain Beefheart, the Jeff Beck Group and a Gram Parsons era The Byrds also played here. Both Arthur Brown and Yoko Ono played this basement venue in 1967, when it was known as Electric Golden.

Middle Earth club nights were also held at The Roundhouse (Camden) and the Royalty Theatre on Lancaster Road, W11. The King Street building became residential accommodation (flats). The door to number 43 is to the right in the above photograph.

Mermaid Theatre. The Pet Shop Boys played a show with the BBC Concert Orchestra in May 2006 that was later released as the live album 'Concrete'. The show featured Robbie Williams and Rufus Wainwright. Also used for Radio 2's 'Friday Night is Music Night' shows, which have featured performers such as Nigel Kennedy. The future of the building is uncertain as its theatre status has been removed by The City of London and now appears to be used for conferences rather than entertainment. Address: Puddle Dock, Blackfriars, EC4U 3DB. Tube: Blackfriars (Circle and District Lines).

Natural History Museum. In the Gloucester Road Museum of Natural History The Strokes played among the fossils, dinosaurs and Blue Whale on 6 July 2006, as part of a series of gigs in unusual venues promoted by T-Mobile.

New Merlin's Cave/The Hippydrome. Address: The Hippydrome, 34–38 Margery Street, WC1. Tube: Kings Cross (Circle, Hammersmith & City, Metropolitan, Northern and Victoria Lines). An indie club that had the Blyth Power (1984), Television Personalities (January 1989) and The Go Betweens (apparently playing for their air fare back home to Australia) on stage. Run for a year by Adam Sanderson of The Jasmine Minks. In 1965 the venue was used for the annual 'Festival of Fools' which was held in the first six weeks of every New Year. Ewan McColl appeared as part of the festival in 1970. The building is long gone and the site has been redeveloped, although the building adjacent recalls a little of the sites history being called 'Merlin's Court'.

Notre Dame Hall/Ad Lib Club/Cavern in The Town (see Pl.26)
Address: 5, Leicester Place, London, WC2H 7BX
Tube: Leicester Square (Piccadilly and Northern Lines)

A French church located just off Leicester Square, the building was known as the Ad Lib Club and The Cavern in the Town in the 1960s. The Small Faces played in 1965, The Revillos debuted here in 1979, Wire (1979) and The Telescopes played the hall for two nights in December 1990. The Sex Pistols were filmed here twice – for London Weekend Television and by America's NBC News – for which Sid Vicious made his Pistols stage debut. The building was designed by Professor Hector O Corrato and won the gold medal of the Worshipful Company of Tylers and Bricklayers in 1958.

100 Club/London Jazz Club/Hymphrey Lyttelton Club (see Pl.27)
Address: 100 Oxford Street, London, W1D 1LL
Tube: Tottenham Court Road (Central and Northern Lines)
Capacity: 290
Live release: Siouxsie 'Dreamshow' DVD (2005), Jonathan Rice 'Live in London' DVD (2005)

Opened in 1942 by Victor Feldman in a restaurant called 'Macks' to put on Sunday-night jazz gigs, the venue soon became popular with visiting American servicemen such as Glen Miller. In 1948, with a change of ownership, the venue changed its name to the 'London Jazz Club'. By the 1950s the buildings lease was taken over by Humphrey Lyttelton's agent who rechristened the venue 'The Humphrey Lyttelton Club', which had Louis Armstrong playing in 1956. Others who appeared here in the 1950s include Billie Holiday, Acker Bilk, Kenny Ball and the Chris Barber Jazz and Blues Band. The club briefly changed its name to 'Jazz Shows' before finally becoming the 100 Club. Those who played the 100 Club in its early days include Muddy Waters, Bo Diddley, Jackie Wilson, B. B. King, The Who, The Kinks and The Spencer Davies Group. The Rolling Stones played the club on 31 May 1982; a few weeks later they returned to London to play two shows at the slightly larger Wembley Stadium.

The Stones returned to the venue again in sadder circumstances on 28 February 1986 when they played a private show in memory of former Stone Ian Stewart who had recently died. For the show The Stones were billed as Rocket 86 and it was their first gig together for four years.

The 100 Club will always be associated with punk. The Sex Pistols had a residency there in May 1976, and The Damned played their first real gig here in July 1976. The two-night Festival of Punk was held here on 20 and 21 September 1976 with The Sex Pistols, The Clash, Siouxsie and The Banshees, Subway Sect, Buzzcocks, The Vibrators and The Damned all taking part.

In the 1990s the club attracted the fledging Britpop scene with Oasis, Echobelly, Catatonia, Suede, Travis, Embrace, Babybird and the groups who followed in their wake: Muse, JJ72, Doves and Ocean Colour Scene. It was still a happening venue for jazz and indie groups – even pop act the Sugababes played there in 2006.

Stairs lead down into the basement venue where framed autographed pictures of some of those to have played the club are hung on the walls. The stage is long and skinny and group members have to walk through the crowd to get up on stage. A few tables and chairs are located either end of the stage, and apart from those it is a standing venue.

The venue is owned by Jeff Horton who took over the club in 1985 from his father who had run it since 1964. The venue ran into trouble in September 2010 and only some famous names lending support and a sponsorship deal with shoemaker Converse saved it from closing. One reason for the crisis was that the rent had risen from £11,000 a year to £166,000 over a twenty-five-year period.

Piccadilly Jazz Club (see Scene Club).
Playhouse Theatre. Located on Northumberland Avenue, WC2N 5DE. Built in 1905 with a 786 capacity, it became a BBC studio on 1951. The Beatles performed 'Please Please Me', 'Misery' and 'From Me To You' here for the BBC Radio show 'Easy Beat' on 3 April 1963. The group returned to the theatre in June 1963 and January 1964. Led Zeppelin played a few Radio 1 sessions here in March and June 1969. Paul McCartney played a one-off gig here in July 1989. Others to have played include Kiss, Queen, The Who and The Rolling Stones.
Pure Groove. This record shop at 6–7 West Smithfield, Farringdon, EC1A 9JX had many in-store performances by the likes of Edwyn Collins but is now closed.

The Palladium
Address: 7 Argyll Street, London, W1A 3AB
Tube: Oxford Circus (Bakerloo, Central and Victoria lines)
Capacity: 2,291 (seated)
Live release: The Divine Comedy 'Live at The Palladium' DVD (2004)

Built in 1910, although it retains its nineteenth-century façade, the renowned theatre architect Frank Matcham redesigned the internal theatre.

Hard to believe that this bastion of British establishments has hosted gigs by the likes of Duke Ellington, Marvin Gaye, Kate Bush, Pet Shop Boys, Tori Amos, Elvis Costello, Mary Coughlan and The Smiths. It was here in October 1963 that the term 'Beatlemania' was used for the first time. Morrissey returned to the Palladium's stage for three Sunday-night gigs in May 2006 in support of his album 'Ringleader of The Tormentors'. Art Garfunkel performed in 2007, as did Rufus Wainwright, who recreated his Judy Garland New York show in that February.

Paris Theatre
Address: Rex House, 12 Lower Regent Street, London, SW1Y 4PE
Tube: Piccadilly Circus (Bakerloo and Piccadilly Lines)

The Paris Theatre was a BBC venue where DJ John Peel's 'In Concert' programmes were recorded. T-Rex were captured on 10 December 1970, Hawkwind on 5 November 1970, Soft Machine and Barclay James Harvest played in 1972, Bob Marley in June 1973, Led Zeppelin in April 1971 and Simple Minds in September 1979. The Beatles recorded several BBC TV appearances here in 1962 and 1963. The building features on the cover of 'The Beatles Live at The BBC' album, when the Paris was in its full glory.

The building, originally the Paris Cinema, opened in 1939 and was designed by Robert Cromie. It was located in the basement of Rex House, to the left of the central door. The theatre closed in 1995 and remained empty until 2005 when it became a private gym.

Pigalle Club
Address: 215 Piccadilly, London, W1J 9HN
Tube: Piccadilly Circus (Bakerloo and Piccadilly Lines)
Capacity: 260

Opened in April 2006 by the former head of the Mean Fiddler empire Vince Power, this 1940s supper club attracted Van Morrison for 4 nights in its opening month. Tickets for the gig cost £100 each, whereas the gig plus meal cost £150 – a bargain in anyone's language! Van must have proved popular as he returned a few weeks later for another gig. Fellow Irish singer Mary Coughlan has also played the Pigalle, as well as Wet Wet Wet's Marti Pellow. The club put on live acts seven nights a week, 6 p.m. till 4 a.m. The venue closed in 2012 and became The Werewolf in 2014. The building is owned by Crown Estates.

The Beatles played the original The Pigalle Club, at 196 Piccadilly, on 21 April 1963, watched by an exclusively Jewish audience – due to the only advertising for the show being in the *Jewish Chronicle*. The club later became a Mod meeting place.

Pizza Express
Address: 10 Dean Street, Soho, London, W1D 3RW
Tube: Tottenham Court Road (Central and Northern Lines)
Capacity: 120
Live release: Mose Allison 'The Mose Chronicles – Live in London Vol 2' CD (2003)

The music venue part of this chain of Italian restaurants is located in the basement. The venue was refurbished in 1996 and Van Morrisson played at the relaunch of the venue. The venue hosts jazz artists and those who have played its intimate stage include Mose Allison, Diana Krall, Andy Summers (ex Police guitarist) and Amy Whinehouse. Norah Jones made her European stage debut on stage here, while Sting performed a version of 'Round Midnight' late one night.

The venue is seated with tables where you can eat a meal and watch the performers. The price range for tickets varies from £15 to £20. The Pizza Express in Maidstone also offers live jazz.

Portlands/The Pits/Green Man
Address: 383 Euston Road, London, NW1 3AU
Tube: Great Portland Street (Hammersmith & City, Circle Lines)

The Television Personalities (1988) and Inspiral Carpets (March 1987) played this mostly indie venue when called Portlands. The Meteors played 1981 when it was known as The Pits. It is now a pub called The Green Man and offers live jazz. The pub dates from 1756.

Rainbow Room/Restaurant. On 26 and 27 November 1973 the New York Dolls played here at Biba's department store in Kensington High Street. Other acts who appeared include Procol Harlem, The Pointer Sisters and Kilburn & The High Roads (featuring Ian Dury) in the glory days between 1973 to 1979. Biba's was in the former Derry and Toms department store, with the Rainbow Restaurant on the fifth floor of the seven-storey building on Kensington High Street. It is now home to offices, shops and the Kensington Roof Garden.

Regents Park Open Air Theatre. Address: Inner Circle, Regents Park, London, NW1 4NU. Tube: Baker Street (Circle, Hammersmith & City and Metropolitan Lines). Capacity: 1,200. The theatre has been established in the park in 1932 and usually has some live music events mixed in with their theatre productions during the summer months. Seth Lakeman and The Levellers performed in the open in August 2007, and Nitin Sawhney appeared in 2015.

Royal Court Theatre. PJ Harvey played a semi-acoustic gig at this 400-capacity theatre at Sloane Square in December 2004.

Royal Opera House. On 22 February 2004 Motorhead played the first rock gig at the Royal Opera House in the Vilar Floral Hall. The gig was part of an event called One Amazing Week, which had the aim of giving London international exposure. The 450-strong audience

was made up of competition winners. Snow Patrol launched their 'Eyes Open' album with a free gig here on the afternoon of 26 April 2006, which was later broadcast on Channel 4.
Royalty Theatre. Built in 1960 at Portugal Street in the basement of an office block. Bjork played this theatre and filmed the gig which was later released as the 'Vessel' video. Joy Division played on 17 June 1979, and Sandy Denny appeared in November 1977. It was renamed the Peacock Theatre in 1996 when the LSE took it over and used it for lectures etc. Capacity is 999.
Rouge. This club at 144 Charing Cross Road, WC2H, with a capacity of 1,100, had hosted a few gigs by mostly unsigned bands, or bands on a small indie label. Ladyfuzz played in April 2004. It later became a club called Sin.
Rough Trade West. Address: 130 Talbot Road, London, W1 1JA. Tube: Ladbrook Grove (Circle and Hammersmith & City Lines). The original Rough Trade shop, but the poorer sibling to Rough Trade East which attracts all the big names for in-store performances, with Talbot Road left with the small fry.

Rock Garden

Address: 6–7 The Piazza, Covent Garden, London, WC2E 8HA
Tube: Covent Garden (Piccadilly Line)
Capacity: 250

The Rock Garden opened in 1976, and while mostly hosting unsigned bands playing to friends and tourists, the Rock Garden has hosted a few gigs by named Bands. XTC were an early attraction in 1977, and The Smiths played their first London gig (and only their fifth altogether) here on 23 March 1983. U2 played the Rock Garden twice, in December 1979 and May 1980. Adam And The Ants played in June 1978. Suede performed a gig here in April 1990. The venue was in the basement of the building and later became home to The Gardening Club. As of 2015 the building was an Apple store.

The Roebuck/Adams Arms

Address: 108 Tottenham Court Road, London, W1T 5AA
Tube: Tottenham Court Road (Central and Northern Lines)
Capacity: 60

This pub was home to Alan McGee's (Creation Records boss) club The Living Room in the early 1980s, when the pub was called the Adams Arms (later changed to The Roebuck). Creation signings The Jesus and Mary Chain had their London debut here in 1984. The Living Room attracted groups and fanzine writers alike as part of the audience.

It is now a pub called The Court (part of the Scream chain), which features a large screen showing music videos, and so still retains a little of its rock spirit.

Ronnie Scotts

Address: 47 Firth Street, Soho, London, W1D 4HT
Tube: Leicester Square (Piccadilly and Northern Lines)
Capacity: 100 (standing), 300 (seated)

Opened originally at 39 Gerrard Street in 1959, Ronnie moved his club to the present address in 1965. Some of the biggest names in Jazz have played here including Sarah Vaughan and Van Morrisson. The Who's rock opera *Tommy* was premiered here in May 1969, and Jimi Hendrix gave his last performance here the night before he died. Charlie Watts Big Band played a week's residence here in 1985.

Performers in 2007 included Joan Armatrading and Tony Bennet. Roger Daltry and Pete Townsend held a press conference here on 30 June 2014 to announce the last tour of The Who, and then played a short acoustic set.

Rough Trade (Covent Garden)
Address: 16 Neals Yard, Covent Garden, London, WC2H 9DP
Tube: Covent Garden (Piccadilly Line)

The basement of the Rough Trade shop was another in-store venue. The Beastie Boys, Hole, Sonic Youth, Heavenly and PJ Harvey have all put in short sets here. A spiral staircase lead you down into the Rough Trade shop – now closed.

The Roundhouse (Wardour St)/Blues and Barrelhouse Club
Address: 83 Wardour Street, London, W1D 6QD
Tube: Leicester Square (Piccadilly and Northern Lines)

The building dates from 1892 but it was in the 1950s Alexis Korner that ran the London Skiffle Centre from this pub, later renaming it the Blues and Barrelhouse Club in the late 1950's, before live music ceased in 1964. No longer a music venue, the building is now called The O Bar.

The Roxy (Covent Garden)

Address: 41–43 Neal Street, Covent Garden, London, WC2
Tube: Covent Garden (Piccadilly Line)
Capacity: 100
Live release: 'Live at The Roxy' LP and 'Farewell to The Roxy' LP

One of *the* venues of the punk scene, The Roxy was only open for a short time in 1977 and was a former gay club called Chaguarama's. The Roxy had a punk disco that was free to members, and gigs included London, UK Subs, The Clash, Wire (their live debut was here in February 1977), The Slits, The Heartbreakers and The Buzzcocks. Chrissie Hynde's (later of The Pretenders) group The Johnny Moped Band (crap name!) and Generation X opened The Roxy. Adam and The Ants played the Roxy five times between June 1977 and January 1978. Supporting The Ants one time were Siouxsie and The Banshees with future Ant side man Marco Pirroni on guitar.

DJ and future BAD (Mick Jones group after the Clash) man Don Letts was a Roxy DJ and managed to film the going's on here and released the results as The Punk Rock Movie. Bands would often come on stage well after public transport had stopped running for the night.

The Roxy had a small ground-level reception area and bar, and the stage and dance floor were in the basement. The Roxy was run by Andrew Czezowski (who also managed Generation X). Although the capacity was 100, up to 400 punks could pile in to watch a band. The building is now a Speedo clothes shop.

Royal Albert Hall

Address: Kensington Gore, Kensington, London, SW7 2AP
Tube: South Kensington (Circle, District and Piccadilly Lines)
Capacity: 8,000 (with private boxes) 5,266 (for public sale)
Live release: Robbie Williams 'Live At The Albert' DVD (12.10.01), The Corrs 'Live At The Royal Albert Hall' DVD (1998), Culture Club 'Live At The Royal Albert Hall' DVD, Everly Brothers 'Reunion Concert' DVD (23/9/83), Eric Clapton '24 Nights' DVD (1990–91), Rod Stewart 'One Night Only' DVD, Siouxsie and The Banshees 'Nocturne' Album (1983)

Built in 1871 and part funded by the profits on the Great Exhibition of 1851, The Royal Albert Hall (RAH) was named after Queen Victoria's dead husband. The building had hosted mainly classical music events, the most notable being The Proms, until 1959. In September 1959 the first pop acts (Billy Fury and Marty Wilde) performed here. Come 1963 the groups had started to get a bit more rebellious with both The Beatles and The Rolling Stones performing at The RAH.

In May 1966 Dylan went electric here and divided his audience. It was also the scene of Jimi Hendrix's final UK mainland gig. In November 1968 Cream played their last gig here and were supported by the largely unknown YES. The venue continues to be a favourite of Eric Clayton's and he usually plays twenty-plus concerts here a year. When Cream briefly reformed, Clapton made the RAH the venue where Cream played three concerts in May 2005 and was later released on DVD.

The RAH has also welcomed left of field groups such as The Smiths, Gene and Suede. Creation Records held their tenth birthday party 'Undrugged' here in June 1994 with Oasis, Ride and the Boo Radleys performing. Classic/pop crossover babes Bond played and filmed a free concert at the RAH in 2000.

Since 2000, The Royal Albert Hall has been the location for the Teenage Cancer Trust annual series of gigs that are the brainchild of Roger Daltry. Those to have played include Noel Gallagher, Paul Weller, The Who as well as many comedians.

Royalty Ballroom
Address: Winchmore Hill Road, Southgate, London, N14 6AA
Tube: Southgate (Piccadilly Line)

The Royalty Ballroom is located at the end of and set back behind Dennis Parade on Winchmore Hill Road. The venue hosted Family (1967), Slade (1978) and Bill Haley (1979) as well as dance nights. The Ballroom was also used in the film *Quadrophenia* – where Sting jumps from a balcony. The building is currently a private gym.

Sadler's Wells. The Fall soundtracked the 1988 ballet *I Am Curious Orange* during every performance. Address: Roseberry Avenue, EC1R 4TN.

The Savoy Theatre. Reclusive live performers the Pet Shop Boys played this hotels theatre for 4 nights in July 1997, to promote their cover of the Bernstein/Sondheim song 'Somewhere'. The shows were filmed and later released as the 'Somewhere' DVD. Address: The Strand, WC2R 0ET.

Scene Club/Club 11/Piccadilly Jazz Cub. Address: 41 Great Windmill Street, London, W1. Tube: Piccadilly Circus (Bakerloo and Piccadilly Lines). Originally a jazz club called Club 11 in the 1950s, and then becoming the Piccadilly Jazz Club, the building became the Scene in the 1960s, a mod venue. The Animals played in 1963, as did The Who the following year, live music ceasing in 1965. It is now demolished and used for car parking. See Club 11 entry.

School of Oriental and African Studies. Located at Thornhaugh Street, Russell Square, WC1, Nirvana played the Students Union on 27 October 1989.

Selfridges. 9 March 2006 saw this department store hosting a gig by punk veterans The Buzzcocks and The Slits as part of the store's 'Future Punk' weekends. Babyshambles played 4 songs in the seventh-floor car park on 7 December 2006.

Seymour Hall. Located at Seymour Place, Marylebone, W1H 7TJ and adjacent to the Marylebone Swimming Pool, the hall was more use to boxing matches than gigs, but it didn't stop Pink Floyd playing there in a 'Freak Out Ethel' night. Tube: Edgeware Road (Circle and District Lines).

Shaftesbury Theatre. Dexys Midnight Runners played here in 1982 and later released a DVD entitled 'The Bridge – The Live Performance' in 2006. Address: 210 Shaftesbury Avenue, WC2H 8DP.

St Anne's. This church at 55 Dean Street, Soho, W1D 6AF, had Paul Simon in 1965.

St John's. Canadian's Arcade Fire showcased their second album, 'Neon Bible' at this Smith Square church in SW1 (Tube: Westminster) for three nights at the end of January 2007. David Gray played a couple of nights in July 2007.

St Moritz Club. Joe Strummers 101'ers played this club at 159 Wardour Street, W1F 8WH in 1975. It became home to Gaz's Rockin' Blues nights in 1995.

SW1 Club. Suede played this club at 191 Victoria Street in October 1992.

Saville Theatre

Address: 135–149 Shaftesbury Avenue, London, WC2H 8AH
Tube: Piccadilly Circus (Bakerloo and Piccadilly Lines)
Capacity: 1, 200

In 1966 'Sunday's at the Saville' would have live performances by the likes of Pink Floyd, Jimi Hendrix Experience, The Who, Fairport Convention, Little Richard, Fats Domino, The Bee Gees and Cream (supported by the Jeff Beck Group in July 1967). Beatles manager Brian Epstein was the original promoter, until he died in summer 1967. The Beatles did record some colour footage of them performing 'Hello Goodbye' here in the 1960s.

In 1973 the Saville, which was a 1930s theatre, was turned into a cinema.

Scotch of St James
Address: 13 Mason's Yard, London, SW1Y 6BU
Tube: Piccadilly Circus (Bakerloo and Piccadilly Lines)

Opened in 1965 by Louis Brown and John Bloom, the club was a favourite hangout for The Beatles and The Who's Keith Moon. Jimi Hendrix headlined his first UK stage here on 25 October 1966, although he had appeared at the club previously on 27 September 1966, jamming with future members of Humble Pie. Jimi also met his future girlfriend Kathy Etchingham at The Scotch. It closed in 1972.

Scots Hoose/Spice of Life
Address: 6 Moor Street, Cambridge Circus, London W1D 5NA
Tube: Leicester Square (Northern and Piccadilly Lines)

This pub at was home to a folk club where Bob Dylan, Paul Simon, Cat Stevens and Sandy Denny gigged. The Strawbs played in 1965. It is now called 'The Spice of Life' and still puts on live music. The Guillemots and Jamie Cullum have both played here.

Slaughtered Lamb
Address: 34–35 Great Sutton Street, London, EC1V 0DX
Tube: Farringdon (Circle, Hammersmith & City and Metropolitian Lines)
Capacity: 120 (standing)

This really quite unremarkable building/pub has mainly acoustic bands and artists playing in its basement. Those to have played include The Civil Wars (their UK debut), Kris Drever (2013), Beth Rowley (2013), King Creosote (three nights in 2013) and Lau (2011).

The Social
Address: 5 Little Portland Street, London, W1 W7JD
Tube: Oxford Circus (Central and Bakerloo Lines)

The occasional 'name' band plays downstairs here every now and again. Jack White of the White Stripes performed three songs on 27 May 2007 at the 'Sonic Cathedral' club. Jack played 'Effect and Cause', 'Sugar Never Tasted So Good' and 'The House of The Rising Sun'.

Soho Revue Bar
Address: 11 Walkers Court, London, W1
Tube: Oxford Circus (Central Line)

Opened in 1952 as the notorious 'Raymond Revue Bar', this Central London venue has seen gigs by Clap Your Hands Say Yeah (January 2007), former Sugababe Siobhan Donaghy (May 2007), Kula Shaker (2007) and The Kills (January 2008) since the name change. Currently called 'The Box Soho' and is apparently quite an 'extreme' Soho caberet club.

Somerset House

Address: Somerset House, The Strand, London, WC2R 1LA
Tube: Charing Cross (Northern and Bakerloo Lines)
Capacity: 3,000
Live release: Snow Patrol 'Live At Somerset House' DVD (8.8.04), Goldfrapp 'Wonderful Electric Live in London' DVD

Somerset House, the one-time records and tax office, now puts on slightly more interesting subjects. In the winter you can go ice skating in the square and in the summer you can catch the 'Summer Series' featuring acts such as Snow Patrol, Belle & Sebastian, Idlewild, Divine Comedy, Robert Plant, Lily Allen, Corinne Bailey Rae and Goldfrapp playing on the temporary stage in the central courtyard. In 2007 the Summer Series of gigs featuring Amy Winehouse were televised and broadcast on ITV1.

In January and February 2015 PJ Harvey became an art installation here while she recorded her album 'Recording in Progress' which was later called 'The Hope Six Demolition Project' when it was released in 2016. Fans could pay to view the recording process through a one-sided mirror – like a peep show but with music.

The Speakeasy/Bootleggers/Cameo

Address: 48–50 Margaret Street, London, W1W 8SE
Tube: Oxford Circus (Central and Bakerloo Lines)

Opened in 1966, Eric Clapton and Jimi Hendrix were some of the musicians who would just turn up and play. Pink Floyd (December 1967), Deep Purple (July 1969), Cream, Roy Harper and Joni Mitchell all played here, and Frank Zappa was known to compare –The Bee Gees, The Who and Mick Jagger watched. Thin Lizzy made their British debut here in December 1970. Hawkwind played several times in 1970. David Bowie played on 8 January 1970 and his band line-up included producer Tony Visconti on bass guitar.

The Speakeasy was a well-known music industry late-night meeting place. The Sex Pistols started a commotion one night when they got verbal with Radio 1 DJ 'Whispering' Bob Harris for not giving their records any airtime.

Both Hendrix and New York Doll Billy Murcia spent their last night alive here.

It was closed in 1978, with two shops taking up the ground floor and the space vacated by the Speakeasy now a members club called 'Beat'.

St James' Church

Address: 197 Piccadilly, London, W1J 9LL
Tube: Piccadilly Circus (Bakerloo and Piccadilly Lines)

This church, built by Sir Christopher Wren in the 1680s, hosts the occasional gig by noteworthy artists. REM played here on 16 September 2004 and Aqualung in 2004. Former James front man Tim Booth, The Divine Comedy and actress/singer Minnie Driver have also played the church. Eels played in January 2008. The church has free lunchtime recitals three times a week and evening concerts.

The artist and poet William Blake was baptised here.

St Lukes
Address: LSO St Lukes, Old Street, London, EC1V 9NG
Tube: Old Street (Northern Line)

Part of the Barbican Centre and home to the London Symphony Orchestra, St Lukes was designed by Hawksmere (who also designed Christchurch in Spitalfields). St Lukes is an eighteenth-century church and a Grade I-listed building.

St Lukes tends to be the favoured venue of BBC producers who have staged Antony and the Johnsons (in 2005) as part of BBC 4's 'Sessions', Sting (during his lute phase), Nora Jones and Rosanne Cash (all in 2006) as part of BBC 1's 'Sessions'. Brian Ferry took part in the series in 2007 while he was promoting his album of Bob Dylan covers. Crooner Tony Bennett was also recorded here in 2007.

St Pancras Old Church
Location: 191 Pancras Road, London, NW1 1UL
Tube: Kings Cross (Northern, Victoria, Circle, Metropolitan, Hammersmith & City Lines) or Mornington Crescent (Northern Line)
Capacity: 120

St Pancras Old Church is popular with the hipsters of the capital and held several gigs in 2014. Killing Jokes Jaz Coleman read chapters from his book here in 2015, and Eliza Carthy played in the same year.

Studio 51/Ken Colyers Jazz Club
Address: 10–11 Great Newport Street, London, WC2H
Tube: Leicester Square (Northern and Piccadilly Lines)

This club started in 1951 as a basement jazz club that doubled as rehearsal rooms. In the 1960s The Rolling Stones practiced and gigged here often, playing to 1,000 people on a Sunday afternoon. Van Morrison decided to form an R&B group after watching Downliners Sect –Them was the result. The Yardbirds became the resident band here, and the Boomtown Rats made their UK mainland debut here. It was also known as Ken Colyers Jazz Club.

2i's

3 Savile Row. On the roof of Apple Corporation The Beatles played their last gig on 30 January 1969. The gig lasted only forty minutes, after the Royal Bank of Scotland, who were located opposite, got the police to stop the gig.

Tate Britain. Nick Cave played in the Duveen Gallery of this Pimlico gallery in March 2003. Location: Millbank, SW1P 4RG.

Temple Hall. Paul Simon played in 1965. Located at Middle Temple Lane, EC4Y 9AT.

Theatre Royal. Pulp played a Christmas gig at this Drury Lane theatre on 18 December 1994 – the height of their 'Britpop' fame. Kanye West played the theatre on 26 February 2006, with 100,000 fans applying for the 2,000 tickets. In January 1974 Genesis played a five-night residency.

Trafalgar Square. The first gig to take place here was R.E.M. on 29 April 2001 as part of South Africa Day, watched by 30,000 people. On 12 September 2004 the Pet Shop Boys performed their soundtrack to the classic silent Russian film *Battleship Potemkin* underneath a screen showing the film. The event was free and although raining, the square was packed. The square is also used for other one-off events such as St Patrick's Day celebrations. In March 2006 Gemma Hayes, Altan and others played here to celebrate St Patrick's Day. 'Love Music Hate Racism' held an event here on 29 April 2006 and featured Boy Kill Boy, Babyshambles and Belle & Sebastian. The Scissor Sisters played a fee gig for the charity 'Global Fund' on 16 September 2006.

Top Ten Club. A 1950s rock 'n' roll venue in Berwick Street, W1.

Tower Records. In August 1994 indie label Beggars Banquet celebrated their tenth anniversary at this Piccadilly Circus record shop (now a Virgin store) by a week of in-store gigs by its artists. Those performing included The Go Betweens who reformed to play an acoustic set.

Address: 59 Old Compton Street, Soho, London, W1D 6HR
Tube: Leicester Square (Northern & Piccadilly Lines)
Capacity: 200

2i's was a coffee bar which opened in 1956 (for a very brief time the 2i's was located at 44 Gerard Street). For many this building represented Swinging London and the birth of the British music scene. Starting off with skiffle groups and progressing to rock 'n' roll with Tommy Steele (1956), Adam Faith, Joe Brown and Cliff Richard (1958) playing the bar. Future Led Zeppelin manager Peter Grant (1960s) was a doorman while Marc Bolan (1960s) would make customers their cappuccinos. The 2i's closed in 1970 and the building later became part of The Dome restaurant chain and has remained a restaurant under various names.

The venue was recreated for the 1980s film *Absolute Beginners*, which stared David Bowie and Patsy Kensit.

12 Bar Club

Address: 22–23 Denmark Place, London, WC2H 5NG
Tube: Tottenham Court Road (Central and Northern Lines)
Capacity: 80

This venue had possibly the best location for any musician – along the street known as 'Tin Pan Alley', famed for its musical instrument shops (and very handy should the guitarist break all their strings in the soundcheck!). The part of the venue that fronts Denmark Street (pictured above) was actually a laidback café, with the stage area at the rear of the building.

The performance space was perhaps the most bizarre in London, the stage being in a tiny room (space for around twenty people seated) with a very low ceiling, which was the floor to the first level (again with space for around twenty people and two tables). The ceiling directly above the stage was cut out and the performers' heads were actually eye level with the feet of the audience on the first level. The audience on the floor level could only really see the performer by sitting down and turning their necks 180 degrees – not recommended if you suffer from stiff necks!

The stage itself was very small, and is maybe the only stage in London to have a brick fireplace on stage, which is usually where the guitar amps get put. The fireplace dates back to 1635, when the building was constructed (making it one of the oldest buildings in the live circuit in London, if not the whole of the UK) when it was used as a stables, which were later converted into a forge. The building remained as a forge until the First World War when it became a carpenter's workshop. After the Second World War it was used as a store house. However, in 1994 Andy Preston, of the nearby Andy's Guitars shop opened it as The Forge Folk and Blues Club – primarily as a staff social club where employees could perform.

The venue opened as The 12 Bar Club in 1994 and Robyn Hitchcock, Andy White, Billy Bragg, Kristen Hersh, Bernard Butler and Bert Jansch have all played the venue. Former Jesus and Mary Chain member Jim Reid played a rare solo gig here in January 2006. Others who have played the club before going onto much larger stages include James Blunt, Keane, Katie Melua, Joanna Newsom, Jeff Buckley, Adele, The Libertines and Regina Spektor.

The venue closed in January 2015 when served notice by the landowner to enable the site to be redeveloped. A 25,000-name petition against the closure failed to save the venue. Both Marc Almond and Pete Townsend signed the petition. The venue relocated to the Phibbers pub on the Holloway Road in early 2015. Meanwhile, the original venue was occupied by squatters calling themselves 'Bohemians 4 Soho' and the Alan McKee-managed band 'Alias Kid' played a gig in support of them.

229 Club

Address: 229 Great Portland Street, London, W1W 5PN
Tube: Great Portland Street (Circle, Hammersmith & City and Metropolitian Lines)
Capacity: 620/140

Opened in 1965 in the basement of the International Student House, the venue became a music venue in April 2007. Those to have appeared on stage here include The Beta Band, Razorlight, Biffy Clyro, Primal Scream, Florence and The Machine and Keane.

This venue contains two stages, the larger (620) Room 1 and the smaller (140) Room 2, both of which are underground. In 2013 the venue hosted the first C86 festival with The BMX Bandits and The Primitives headlining. The festival returned in 2014 and had The Wedding Present as the star turn.

Tiles

Address: 1 Dean Street, London
Tube: Tottenham Court Road (Central and Northern Lines)

Tiles opened here in April 1966 and closed late 1967. Pink Floyd, The Who, Manfred Mann and The Animals all played here during that short period. Tiles was also at 79–89 Oxford Street (see Beat City entry). In 2015 the building seemed to have been demolished – although the façade may have been retained.

Turnmills

Address: 63 Clerkenwell Road, London, EC1
Tube: Farringdon (Circle, Hammersmith & City and Metropolitan Lines)

Was the home to the Heavenly Social where the Chemical Brothers were the resident DJs. More recently music-press darlings The Horror's performed at Turnmills on 27 January 2007. Since then the venue has closed and the building used for other purposes before being demolished

University of London Union (ULU)

Address: Malet Street, London, WC1E 7HY
Tube: Goodge Street (Northern Line)
Capacity: 828 (standing), 320 (seated)

The University of London Union has been staging gigs since the late 1970s and it has attracted some of the most important artists of the decades since then. It was here in May 1983 that The Smiths were spotted by John Peel's producer John Walters and on the strength on their performance were booked for a Peel session, which helped the group on their way to success. Others who played the venue in the 1980s include Sonic Youth and Primal Scream. In the 1990s the ULU became the place to see American grunge bands such as Nirvana, Superchunk and Pearl Jam. Veteran punk-poet Patti Smith played the ULU on 17 March 2004, followed by another iconic New York punk/New Wave group Television on 23 June. British groups continued to play as well and included Radiohead, Ash and The Bluetones.

The venue is located up several levels of stairs, and the venue doubles as a lecture theatre for the university. The venue is mostly standing although there are a few seats near the bar area, but with no view of the stage.

UFO/Rectors Club. Address: 30–31 Tottenham Court Road, London. Tube: Tottenham Court Road (Central and Northern Lines). Capacity: 600. As the Rectors Club the building offered jazz in the 1920s, but is more famously known as the home to the first psychedelic club. In December 1966 Pink Floyd was the resident group in this basement club. Procol Harum played their second gig here in December 1967. Other groups who played here during the one year it was open included Soft Machine, Fairport Convention and Arthur Brown. During the daylight hours the UFO was an Irish club called The Blarney. The UFO closed in October 1967 and relocated to the Roundhouse. The building was later bulldozed during the 1970s and a cinema now stands there.

The Vaults. Basement Jaxx played this SE1 club in August 2006, previewing their new album 'Crazy Itch Radio'.

The Venue (Victoria). Address: 160–162 Victoria Street, Victoria, London, SW1E 5LB. Tube: Victoria (Victoria/Circle and District Lines). Nothing to do with its namesake in New Cross, The Venue Victoria put indie bands on in the early 1980s. Steve Strange ran the Venue for a short time at the start of 1981 and presented Depeche Mode, Duran Duran and The Stray Cats while he was there. The Monochrome Set (March 1981), The Raincoats (May 1982), Xmal Deutschland (1983), Pigbag, Aztec Camera and The Go Betweens also played there. It was a large, theatrical stage with one of those disgusting 1970s curtains hanging down at the back and side of the stage. The Smiths played their 10th London gig here on 15 September 1983 (supported by The Go-Betweens and Felt) all for £3 entry. The Venue was part of Richard Branson's Virgin Group. Was opposite Victoria Tube Station, but now demolished and replaced by offices and shops.

Villiers Street Theatre. Blondie played a promotional gig here to launch their 'Curse of Blondie' album on 18 September 2003. Located at The Archers, Villiers Street, WC2N 6NL. Tube: Charing Cross (Bakerloo and Northern Lines).

Victoria Apollo Theatre

Address: 17 Wilton Road, Victoria, London, SW1
Tube: Victoria (Victoria Line)
Capacity: 1,262

Victoria Apollo Theatre opened in 1930 as The New Victoria Cinema (New Victoria Cine Variety Theatre) and was designed by Lewis and Trent for the Gaumont chain, with a concrete construction. Although a cinema, it would host shows by big bands on the circuit.

It closed as a cinema in 1975 and reopened as a theatre in 1981. Shirley Bassey performed here and on 18 December 1983 Paul Weller, U2, Elvis Costello and Ian Dury all played here as part of CND's 'The Big One' peace show. Nick Cave and a slimmed-down Bad Seeds played in January 2006. Fiona Apple followed in April 2006.

It usually presents musicals such as *Starlight Express*, *Bombay Dreams* and *Saturday Night Fever* on its stage.

Virgin Megastore (Oxford Street)/Zavvi
Address: 14 – 16 Oxford Street, London W1D 1AR
Tube: Tottenham Court Road (Central and Northern Lines)

The Oxford Street Virgin Megastore offered a good many in-store performances and signings while it was open. In-store gigs were held in the basement (the musical instrument department) on a small permanent stage. In-store events were publicised at the main entrance or in the window display (if by a major group). Rufus Wainright performed in 2005; other performers include Hole, Oasis, Alkaline Trio and Suede.

Events were popular and it was worth getting to the store early to avoid the disappointment of missing out on getting in. Gigs usually started at 6 p.m. and lasted around half an hour. The Virgin chain became Zavvi's in 2007 (after a management buyout) and closed altogether a year later. The building was a Primark store in 2014.

Vortex (Wardour St)
Address: 201 Wardour Street, London, W1F 8ZH
Tube: Tottenham Court Road (Central & Northern Lines)
Capacity: 850

Vortex opened in July 1977 (after being known as 'Crackers' disco) with The Buzzcocks, Johnny Thunders and the Heartbreakers and The Fall. The Slits and Siouxsie and the Banshees soon followed, and Adam and The Ants played here three times in 1977. The Vortex closed in early 1978, but got name-checked in The Jam's 'A Bomb in Wardour Street'. After closing the building became home to Vespers Club and later Vogue. As of 2015 the building is home to Peter Stringfellow's Angels, a lap-dancing venue.

Westminister Central Hall. Located at Storey Gate, SW1H 9NH, the building is also known as The Methodist Central Hall as it was built between 1905 and 1911 to celebrate the centenary of the death of John Wesley. The hall is a working church and when gigs take place there is a limit on the amount of alcohol that can be consumed by any one person. The ticket price includes two drink tokens. Queen (with Adam Lambert) played on New Year's Eve, rocking out 2014 and bringing in 2015. Belle & Sebastian sold out two nights in May 2015.
Westminister Polytechnic (now Westminister University). Cream (1966) and Jimi Hendrix played this seat of learning on Little Titchfield Street.
YMCA. Joy Division played the Prince of Wales Conference Centre at the YMCA, 112 Great Russell Street, WC18 3NQ on 2 August 1979. Tube: Tottenham Court Road (Central & Northern Lines).

The Wag Club/Whiskey-A-Go-Go/Flamingo (see Pl.45)
Address: 35 Wardour Street, Soho, London, WC1X 8BZ
Tube: Tottenham Court Road (Central and Northern Lines)
Capacity: 500

Known as The Flamingo in the 1960s, in the early 1970s the venue was known as the Whiskey-A Go-Go. The Wag (a shorter version of the original name) opened in April 1981 and closed twenty years later in April 2001. Grandmaster Flash and Africa Bambaataa played their first UK gigs on the Wag's tiny stage. Other acts who appeared include The Pogues, Fine Young Cannibals, Bananarama, Sade and The Beastie Boys. The Wag was run by Chris Sullivan. Billy Bragg recorded 'Talking Wag Club Blues' in the 1980s and the track turned up on Volume 1 of the Bragg boxset released in 2006.

The building has been home to an O'Neils pub since 2001.

Water Rats/Monto Water Rats/Pindar of Wakefield

Address: 328 Grays Inn Road, Kings Cross, W1
Tube: Kings Cross (Circle, Hammersmith & City, Metropolitan, Northern and Victoria Lines)
Capacity: 100 (standing)

The Water Rats started putting gigs on in the 1960's when it was known as the Pindar of Wakefield and Bob Dylan played here in December 1962. Both the Pogues and Oasis played early gigs here in 1982 and 1994 respectively. In 1985 the Grand Order of Water Rats (a showbiz charity) brought the building and renamed after themselves.

The Darkness played twice in 2001, and The Kaiser Chiefs played here in March 2004 before their debut single 'Oh My God' was released. Keane, Muse, Doves and The Hives have all paid their dues here and the likes of Ash, Feeder, The Breeders and Alanis Morrissette have all played secret gigs on its stage. The Futureheads launched their second album here with a gig broadcast on Radio 1 on 1 May 2006. Michael Stipe, Paul McCartney, Liam and Noel Gallagher have all been known to have been in the crowd at The Water Rats.

The Water Rats was used for nine years by Plum Promotions for unsigned bands until 2006, featuring mainly unsigned bands who have proved successful at playing the smaller Betsy Trotwood, as well as a few better-known names (such as Tegan and Sara). When the new promoters moved in the venue became known as Monto Water Rats. Katy Perry made her UK debut here in September 2008.

NORTH LONDON

Alexandra Palace (see pl. 1)

Address: Alexandra Palace Way, Wood Green, London, N22 7AY
Tube: Wood Green (Piccadilly Line)
Train: Alexandra Palace
Capacity: 7,250
Live releases: Travis 'At The Palace' DVD (20.12.03), Faithless 'Live at Alexandra Palace' DVD 2005, Paul Weller 'Catch-Flame' CD (12.2005)

Affectionately known as the 'Ally Pally', the venue is located in the 196-acre Alexandra Park in North London. Originally burnt down two weeks after opening in 1873, the current structure reopened in 1875 as a theatre, concert venue and offices. It is most famously known as the home of the BBC and the TV studio of the first television broadcast in 1936.

From its elevated position on top of a hill, the Ally Pally offers fantastic panoramic views over London. Any visit to London would not be complete until you have viewed the city from the Ally Pally vantage point, let alone experienced this wonderful building and history.

In April 1967 the Ally Pally hosted the fourteen-hour Technicolour Dream with Pink Floyd, Soft Machine, The Move and The Pretty Things playing live. Led Zeppelin played two nights in December 1972.

In 1980 fire once again raged in the palace, destroying the Great Hall, Banqueting Suite and roller rink. The palace reopened in 1988.

The Stranglers played their last gig here with original singer Hugh Cornwell on 11 August 1990. More recently acts such as The White Stripes, Faithless, Travis, Franz Ferdinand, Embrace, The Darkness, Kaiser Chiefs, Morrissey, Marilyn Manson, Arcade Fire and The Pixies have all played in the Great Hall. On gig nights free buses usually run from the tube station to the Ally Pally. Gigs finish around 10.40 p.m. If you just want to visit the venue take bus W3 from Wood Green station and it will drop you right outside the building.

Archway Tavern

Address: Archway Close, Archway, London, N19 3TD
Tube: Archway (Northern Line)
Capacity: 500

An Irish pub more famous for being on the cover of The Kinks album 'Muswell Hillbillies' than for big names gracing its stage. The Kinks also signed their first record contract in the pub. Art Brut played the Tavern in July 2003. Home to The Tube Club and The Face Club, which both put on young hopeful bands.

Barden's Boudoir. Address: 36–44 Stoke Newington Road, N16 7XJ. Billy Childish & The Musicians of The British Empire played in May 2009. The Boudoir closed in 2010. Currently called The Nest and still has live bands. Train: Dalson Kingsland.

The Bell. Bronski Beat played this pub at 257–259 Pentonville Road, N1 in 1983. Later became a Moroccan-themed pub called 'Sahara Nights' and was called 'The Big Chill Out House' in 2014.

The Black Boy. This pub at 1446 High Road, Barnet, N20 9BS had folk icon Sandy Denny on stage in 1967.

The Black Heart. This bar in a former warehouse at 2–3 Greenland Place, Camden, NW1 0AP, has a 150 capacity and is a popular venue for unsigned acts. Tube: Camden Town (Northern Line).

Blue Opera Club/Cooks Ferry Inn. Address: River Lea Towpath, Angel Road, Edmonton, N9. The Inn was a jazz club started by Harry Randall from 1947 until the late 1960s when it became the Blue Opera Club – an R&B venue where The Who, The Animals, The Yardbirds and Led Zeppelin (March 1969), Mott The Hoople, Lindisfarne, Cream, John Lee Hooker and Fleetwood Mac all played. The club continued until the 1970s. Space rockers Hawkwind played on 24 May 1971.

Richard Thompson's 'Cooksferry Queen' took inspiration from the venue. Demolished for road widening, but was where the River Lea goes under the Lea Valley Viaduct (Angel Road) on the Chingford side of the river. The gigs took place in a hall attached to the pub.

Barfly/The Monarch
Address: 49 Chalk Farm Road, Camden, NW1 8AN
Tube: Camden Town (Northern Line)
Capacity: 200

The venue was originally called The Monarch, a venue that opened its doors in 1991 and championed up and coming bands. The Monarch became The Barfly in March 2000 and has continued to host some noteworthy gigs by the likes of The Strokes, Starsailor, Elbow, Coldplay, Juliette and The Licks and Badly Drawn Boy. James Dean Bradfield of the Manic Street Preachers played a solo gig here in May 2006 while promoting his album 'The Great Western'. The venue estimates that around 1,000 bands play the venue each year.

The Barfly was part of the of Barfly chain/Mama Group across the UK, which also had venues in Cardiff, Liverpool, Glasgow and York. Barfly believe in supporting the world's best new music by filling their venues with the stars of tomorrow. Early gigs by the then unknown The Shins and The Killers would appear to back-up their belief. More established groups have also played the intimate venue and include The Fall, Mull Historical Society and even the Pet Shop Boys (all in 2004).

The general bar area is on the street level with the main stage area upstairs, with toilets in the basement. Advance tickets are available from the venues website and from the ticket line.

Birthdays
Address: 33–35 Stoke Newington Road, Dalston, London, N16 8BJ
Train: Dalston Kingsland (from Stratford)

One of a number of venues to have sprung up in the super fashionable Dalston area around 2010. However, this trendy status fails to explain why a reformed Ordinary Boys played in 2014 – when they were definitely well past their sell by date. The slightly more hip Bloc Party and The Cribs have played the venue.

Bluesville (see Pl.3)
Address: The Hornsey Wood Tavern, 376 Seven Sisters Road, London, N4 2PQ
Tube: Manor House (Piccadilly Line)

A 1960s R&B venue where Led Zepplin played in March 1969, billed as 'Led Zeppelin Back From Their Sensational American Tour'. Other groups who played the venue include Jethro Tull (August 1968), Cream (February 1967) and The Jimi Hendrix Experience (May 1967). A sister venue opened at The Manor House, 316 Green Lanes. The Bluesville became a bar and restaurant called the Alexandra before being demolished sometime after 2005 and was replaced by housing.

Boogaloo Bar

Address: 312 Archway Road, London, N6 5A
Tube: Highgate (Northern Line)

Opened in Christmas 2002, this bar has a strong Irish feel. Bands who have appeared here sporadically since opening include Bright Eyes, Dirty Pretty Things, Shane MacGowan, Yeti, Paddy Casey and former Sex Pistol Glen Matlock. Babyshambles have played a few gigs at the Boogaloo.

The Boston Arms/The Dome

Address: 178 Junction Road, Tufnell Park, London, N19 5QQ
Tube: Tufnell Park (Northern Line)
Capacity: 800

The Boston Arms was built in 1899. The Boston music room is attached to the pub and The Dome covers both the pub and music room and was originally built in 1884 as the Stanley Halls and Baths (also known as the Tufnell Park Palais).

Home to the Dirty Water Club, The Boston has staged gigs by the likes of The Kills, The Triffids, The Parkinsons, Bradford, The White Stripes, Chelsea, The Exploited, Curved Air and Blyth Power. Cult artist Billy Childish has played the venue many times and the Boston was the venue for Billy's The Buff Medways final gig in 2006. Noel Gallagher performed on 2 February 2015 to promote his album 'Chasing Yesterday', and Florence and The Machine played The Dome on 4 March 2015.

As well as being the regular pub for the local Irish community, the Boston is an Arsenal supporter's club local (hint: don't go in wearing a shirt of another team!).

The Brecknock
Address: 227 Camden Road, London, NW1 9AA
Tube: Camden Town (Northern Line)

Ex-Sex Pistol Glen Matlock's band The Rich Kids played this pub in 1977, helped out on guitar by the Clash's Mick Jones and also featuring a pre-Ultravox Midge Ure. Elvis Costello's early band Flip City played here in the 1970s. It later became The Pickled Newt and is now known as The Unicorn. The pub is situated on the corner where Camden Road crosses Brecknock Road. Like most pubs that used to feature live music, the pub now offers satellite football instead.

Buffalo Bar
Address: 259 Upper Street, Islington, London, N1 1RU
Tube: Highbury & Islington (Victoria Line)
Capacity: 150

Situated on the doorstep of Highbury and Islington underground station, The Buffalo opened in 2000 and hosted The Libertines (March 2003), Magic Numbers (August 2004), The Pipettes (November 2004), Futureheads (June 2003), Dirty Pretty Things (January 2006), Bat For Lashes

(January 2006), along with Bloc Party, Keane, The National, Stereolab and Bombay Bicycle Club. Hope of The States played a special show in October 2005 as Thee Hope of the States Wooden Electrik Arkestar. New York legends Suicide played in 2007.

The Buffalo Bar staged the Art Rocker (Tuesdays) and Goo Music (Wednesdays) club nights. Forward Russia! and Acoustic Ladyland both played the Artrocker club nights in 2006. Since 2006 the Buffalo Bar hosted the Artrocker Festival.

The venue was under threat in November 2014 when the owners, Stonegate Pub Company, announced plans to redevelop the building. The Buffalo Bar eventually closed shortly afterwards in December 2014. Live music continues in the building as it is part of the pub above – The Famous Cock Tavern.

Bull and Gate (see Pl.6)
Address: 389 Kentish Town Road, London, NW5 2TJ
Tube: Kentish Town (Northern Line)
Capacity: 150
Live release: Timebox compilation album

Like most venues the Bull and Gate had a varied history, although it is perhaps the only one to have formerly been a launderette! The building dates back to the seventeenth century, and apart from being a pub and launderette the building has also been a snooker hall and theatre.

The pub became a prominent music venue in 1979. During the 1980s the larger than life promoter Jon 'Fat Beast' Driscoll kick-started the careers of the Primitives, Voice of the Beehive and Half Man Half Biscuit here. Fat Beast, along with the Timebox label, released the Timebox compilation album in 1986 and showcased many regular acts who went on to do great things. After the 1980s, groups such as Blur, the Manic Street Preachers, Daisy Chainsaw, the Cranberries, PJ Harvey and Suede all graced the venues small stage before heading off in the direction of the Astoria and larger venues.

In its heydays the venue hosted mainly gigs by new, unsigned bands who played original material. There were usually three or four bands playing in one night, who were all encouraged to bring at least twenty-five paying friends with them. The last promoters seemed refreshingly honest in their booking approach and would accept raw rehearsal recordings on cassettes or CDs, the reasoning being that if the songs and groups are good then it will shine through.

The future of the venue looked uncertain when the landlord retired and sold it in June 2005. Keane gave the venue a show of support when learning of its potential fate by playing a gig there on 24 February 2005. However, it was all in vain as the venue closed shortly afterwards to become a gastro pub.

Closure was a sad fate for a venue that was still at its peak with The Libertines, Muse, British Sea Power and Coldplay playing important breakthrough gigs there in the late 1990's and the new Millennium.

Camden Centre. Located on Euston Road, WC1H 9JE, Terry Callier, De La Soul and Secret Affair played in 2009. Part of Camden Town Hall.

Camden Palace. (see Koko).

Camden Workers Social Club. Located on the ground floor in Lyndhurst Hall Athlone Street/ Warden Road, Kentish Town, NW5, the club had Felt and Lush in 1989 and The Sugarcubes in 1987. Morrissey shot his video for 'Sing Your Life' here in 1991. The building was demolished in 2006 and was replaced by flats.

Cross Kings. A venue in Kings Cross that closed in 2010.

The Country Club. Address: 190A Haverstock Hill, Hampstead, NW3 2AL.

Tube: Belsize Park (Northern Line). Here in the grounds of the Globe Tennis Club, the Country Club offered rock and pop gigs from 1963 until 1974. The Rolling Stones (1964), Mott the Hoople (1969) and Elton John were some of the acts who played the club. Located down an access opposite the Everyman Cinema.

Cecil Sharpe House

Address: 2 Regents Park Road, Camden, London, NW1 7AY
Tube: Camden Town (Northern Line)
Capacity: 500 (standing)

Cecil Sharpe House is a venue/resource centre dedicated to English folk music run by the English Folk Dance and Song Society. The building was built in the 1930s and is a Grade II-listed building. I suspect the listing is due to the cultural significance of the building, which houses the Vaughan Williams Memorial Library, the national folk music and dance archive, rather than for the handsome local authority design of the building. The building was part destroyed by German bombs in September 1940, but was rebuilt and extended, reopening on 5 June 1951 with a ceremony led by Princess Margaret.

Those to have played include Martin Simpson (2014), Eliza Carthy, Bellowhead, Mumford and Sons, Laura Marling, Goldfrapp and Graham Coxon. Folk supergroup The Full English (whose songs came from the building's archive) played their last gig together here in May 2015. The main gig space is Kennedy Hall which has integral benches around the walls, and a sprung floor.

The building is named after Cecil Sharpe who started the early twentieth-century revival in the dance and songs of the British Isles. Cecil collected hundreds of traditional songs in 1903 while in Somerset and in 1911 founded the English Folk Dance Society. This in turn merged with The Folk Songs Society in 1932, and The English Folk Dance and Song Society was formed.

Clissold Arms

Address: 105 Fortis Green, East Finchley, London, N2 9HR.
Tube: East Finchley (Northern Line)
Capacity: 160

In 1960 Ray and Dave Davies (The Kinks) played their first gig in this, their local pub. The brothers lived opposite the pub at 6 Denmark Terrace and their father was a regular customer. The front room of the pub has been called 'The Kinks Room' and is filled with Kinks memorabilia although the brothers actually played in the main bar area. Both Ray and Dave returned in June 1996 and played their last gig together for many, many years. The pub gets mentioned in Dave's song 'Fortis Green'.

Coliseum (Harlesden)
Address: 25 Manor Park Road, Harlesden, London, NW10 4JJ
Tube: Harlesden (Bakerloo Line)

Built in 1912, this former cinema put on gigs in the Punk days, with The Clash, The Slits, Buzzcocks and Subway Sect playing in 1977. Like so many other former cinemas, the Coliseum became a JD Wetherspoon pub, although it has not remained with them. Still a pub, but called The Misty Moon, the building retains it cinematic feel inside, with a curved ceiling and film memorabilia on the walls.

Diorama Theatre. Located at 15–16 Triton Street, Regents Place, London, NW1 3BF (Tube: Warren Street), the Manic Street Preachers played here in 1991. Has a tiny capacity of eighty.
The Dome (see The Boston Arms).
Duke of Clarence. 140 Rotherford Street, London, N1 3DA. Train: Canonbury. The Libertines and Babyshambles have played this unlicensed pub, which was later offered for sale on eBay but did not manage to sell.
Edmonton Regal/Sundown. Address: Junction of Silver Street and Fore Street, Edmonton, N9. Built in 1934 as a 3,000 capacity cinema, Bill Haley (1957), Rolling Stones, The Beatles, The Who, Frank Sintara and The Everly Brothers (1963) played here. Jerry Lee Lewis made his UK debut here in May 1958 and the gig was supposed to be one of a planned thirty-seven gigs in the country for him. However, it soon emerged in the press that The Killer had married his thirteen-year-old cousin and of the planned thirty-seven gigs only three were played. Became The Sundown in 1968 and saw T-Rex, Desmond Dekker and Bob Marley on its stage. The building was used as a cinema until 1972 when it became a bingo hall. The building was demolished in 1986 and a supermarket now stands on the site. Also see the Sundown entry.

Dingwalls/Lock 17

Address: 11 East Yard, Camden Lock, Chalk Farm Road, Camden, NW1 8AB
Tube: Camden Town (Northern Line)
Capacity: 500
Live release: Alex Chilton 'Live in London' LP (1980), Selector 'Live From London' DVD

Opened in June 1973 as Dingwalls Dance Hall, Dingwalls was at the centre of London's music scene in the 1970s and `80s, with gigs by The Clash, Ramones, Thin Lizzy, Ian Dury and Dire Straits. Blur (then known as Seymour) played their first London show here and ended up with the venues security spraying the group with mace! Such gentle behaviour was merely a reflection of the venue's past, when in August 1976 Paul Simimon (The Clash), Jean Jacques Brurnel (The Stranglers), Johnny Rotten and Sid Vicious (The Sex Pistols) had a fight outside the venue. In May 1977 Joe Strummer was arrested for spray-painting 'The Clash' on the venue's outside wall. Blondie played two nights at Dingwalls in January 1978 and REM played their first UK gig here on 19 November 1983. U2 played on 14 December 1979, making their first visiting assault on the capital when they played London ten times in December 1979.

In the 1990s the venue focused on comedy nights, hosting Jongleurs comedy club although the occasional gig slipped in. The Jongleurs nights remain, although the venue is now known as Lock 17 (although the Dingwalls name continues to stick) and puts on groups and singer songwriter's on their first rung of success, rather than big names. After a young Coldplay were shafted by a promoter at Dingwalls in 1998 (they thought they were the headline act with three supports but found out they were on fifth out of eight groups and they would only get 10p for each Coldplay flyer handed in on the door), the group pulled out of the gig and hired the venue themselves for the following night, playing to 400 fans. The venue is in the basement with four tabled and seated tiers leading onto the main standing area. Views of the stage are pretty good from each tier. Toilets are down a corridor beside the right-hand side of the stage.

Other performers include Laura Viers and Erin McKeown (2005), Fionn Regan (2007) and Pink, who played a secret show here on 22 March 2006 to an audience of competition winners and press. The exterior of the building was illuminated pink, with Pink's name projected onto the building.

Drummonds

Address: 73–77 Euston Road, Kings Cross, London, NW1 2QS
Tube: Kings Cross (Circle, Hammersmith & City, Metropolitan, Northern and Victoria Lines)

Drummonds, opposite St Pancras station, would put on indie bands in the late 1980s. Television Personalities (October 1988), Motorcycle Boy (May 1988) The Jazz Butcher, Jesus Jones and Benny Profane (October 88) all played here. It is now part of the O'Neills chain of Irish pubs with traditional Irish sessions on offer.

Dublin Castle (see Pl. 8)

Address: 94 Parkway, Camden, London, NW1 7AN
Tube: Camden Town (Northern Line)
Capacity: 134

This pub in the centre of Camden Town is one of Camden's best known music venues and has held gigs since 1974. It is in this venue that local boys Madness played most of their early gigs in the late 1970s. Even now the venue has an irresistible charm to the nutty boys, as in 2004 Madness secretly played the venue five times – billed as The Dangermen. Other groups that have played this small venue before fame came knocking include Gene, Space, Cast, Travis and The Cardigans. The Dublin Castle did get a scoop in 1995 when Blur played a secret gig here at the height of their Britpop fame. Babyshambles played the Castle on 11 January 2007 and The Vaccines appeared on 16 February 2015.

Apart from the odd secret gig by a big-named group, the venue caters mainly for unsigned bands on the London gig circuit.

Inside the Dublin Castle the walls are covered with signed posters of Madness, Amy Winehouse and other Camden-based acts who have spent time drinking and performing at the pub.

Electric Ballroom/The Buffalo

Address: 184 Camden High Street, Camden, NW1 8QP
Tube: Camden Town (Northern Line)
Capacity: 1,100
Live release: Kelly Osbourne 'Live in London' DVD, Wire 'Document & Eyewitness' (album)

One of the legendary Camden venues, the Electric Ballroom, came into being in July 1978. Previously a Masonic Lodge with a swimming pool and steam baths, it opened originally as a ballroom, called 'The Buffalo', for the Irish community in the 1930s. The ballroom was extended in 1941 when Camden Town tube station, which is adjacent to the ballroom, was bombed. The Ballroom's owner, Bill Fuller, bought the whole site and built a new dance floor on the side of the original ballroom. Acts who played the Buffalo include the Joe Loss Band and the Van Morrison fronted Manhattan Showband (in March 1964). Early in the 1970s Paul McCartney, Gary Glitter and Led Zeppelin rehearsed here. On 22 August 1978 Sid Vicious gave his last ever public performance on the Electric Ballrooms stage, aided by The Damned's Rat Scabies and another former Sex Pistol, Glen Matlock. The night was called 'Sid Sods Off' as he was off to the USA.

Shortly after opening in 1978 the Electric Ballroom briefly closed after local residents complained about noise. However, after being sound-proofed the Ballroom reopened in July 1979 with The Specials, Madness and Dexy's Midnight Runners. Joy Division played two gigs here – one in August and one in October 1979. Others who played here in the late 1970s/early 1980s include Adam and the Ants, The Clash, The Cramps, U2 (on the 7 and 8 December 1979 supporting Talking Heads and OMD) and The Sisters of Mercy. Later in the 1980s the Jesus and Mary Chain, The Mission, The Smiths and Public Enemy played. Recent gigs include performances from Blur's Graham Coxon, Hard-Fi, Athlete, Go-Team!, Dizee Rascal, The Automatic and Boy Kill Boy. Richard Ashcroft played three nights at the Ballroom in 2006. Paul McCartney played a Low-key gig at the Ballroom on 7 June 2007 to promote his album 'Memory Almost Full'. Prince played several gigs here in February 2014.

At the time of writing and throughout the past few years the venue has been under threat of closure and redevelopment from London Underground. The proposal is to redevelop Camden Town underground station and would see the Electric Ballroom and nearby Camden Market demolished to make way for a retail development that would form part of the station. However, Camden Market has commissioned a rival alternative plan that would keep the market and venue intact.

Once inside the venue stairs lead down into a bar area which follows onto the main floor area. A balcony area looking into the Main Hall and various rooms is above ground level, but is a bit of a maze. The Main Hall holds 800 while the upstairs area holds 300. The VIP bar fits accommodates 100.

The Enterprise
Address: 2 Haverstock Hill, Chalk Farm, London, NW3 2BL
Tube: Chalk Farm (Northern Line)
Capacity: 100

Dan Treacy of Television Personalities ran The Room At The Top club here in the 1980s and had indie bands such as The Mighty Lemon Drops playing. Ian Brodie (Lightening Seed and top producer) played the venue in January 2005 to promote his solo album. I Am Kloot and The Crimea have also played The Enterprise. Gemma Hayes played four sold-out nights here in February 2006 and was joined on stage by My Bloody Valentine's Kevin Sheilds. It was home to Barfly Acoustic@ The Enterprise.

Fabric. Located at 77a Charterhouse Street, Farringdon, EC1, Bloc Party played a charity gig at this club in March 2006.
Finsbury Park Empire. This theatre built in 1910 had a capacity of 2,000. Duane Eddy, along with others, played it before the venue closed in May 1960. The Empire was demolished in 1965.

Finsbury Park Astoria (see Rainbow)
Finsbury Park Hotel. Address: 336 Green Lanes, London, N4 2AW. Tube: Manor House (Piccadilly Line). A 1980s venue that had mainly unsigned groups playing throughout the week.
The Flowerpot. See The Verge entry.
Folk Barge. Located somewhere in Kingston, this is the floating venue that had many early gigs by local boy John Martyn from 1967 onwards. The barge became derelict and has been long removed and assumed broken up. Possibly also the Kingston venue called the Jazz Barge.
Fopp. Address: 220–224 Tottenham Court Road, London.
Tube: Goodge Street (Northern Line). A record shop that held some in-store gigs by the likes of Larrakin Love in 2006. The gigs usually took place in the coffee shop area in the rear basement of the store, and purchasing the artist's latest product from the store was usually the requirement for entry. There was also a Fopp store at 287 Camden High Street, Camden (just before the lock) that also had some in-store gigs. The Fopp chain closed in June 2007, although a few stores have been revived since then. However, in-store gigs seem not to have been resuscitated.
Four Aces. Address: 12 Dalston Lane, Dalston, E8 3BQ. Built in 1886 as the North London Colosseum and Amphitheatre it became the Dalson Theatre in 1898. In the early 1960s it became known as The Macador, then The Rambling Rose before becoming The Four Aces in 1966. Artists who played here include; Stevie Wonder, Bob Marley, Percy Sledge, Prince Buster, Ben E King, Desmond Dekker and Madness. Later became the Labyrinth (see entry) before being demolished in 2007. The CLR James Library and housing now occupy the site.
Fox and Goose Hotel. An Ealing hotel at Hanger Lane (A4005), W5 1DP, where The Who played in 1963. Remains a hotel/pub. Tube: Hanger Lane (Central Line).

The Falcon

Address: 234 Royal College Street, Camden, London, NW1 9NJ
Tube: Camden Town (Northern Line)
Capacity: 150

The Camden Falcon will forever go down in musical folklore as the spiritual home of Britpop. In late 1989, early 1990 Food Records saw an unknown band called Seymour at the Falcon. The record company signed the band but changed the name to Blur, and the rest is Britpop history. Lush played the back room of this pub on 29 April 1989; Inspiral Carpets played in August 1988, and Morrissey cast his eyes over Suede here in 1992. Suede played the venue five times during the very early nineties. The Barfly promoted gigs here from late 1996 and the Stereophonics played several early shows here, as well as Feeder, Doves, PJ Harvey, Travis and Muse. Coldplay gigged here on 7 December 1998 and it led to them being signed by Fierce Panda who were watching them perform. Also in the crowd was DJ Steve Lamacq.

Select magazine once described the venue as being 'seemingly held together only by the staples affixing flyers to the walls'. The site has been redeveloped as flats but the original façade of the Falcon is still clearly recognisable. The photograph shows The Falcon in March 2007 with the upper floors redeveloped as flats.

Fiddlers Elbow
Address: 1 Malden Street, Camden, London, NW5 3HS
Tube: Chalk Farm (Northern Line)

The Fiddlers Elbow now offers traditional Irish music but was the home to the club 'Come down and meet the folks' which specialised in singer-songwriter/Americana types. Former Rockingbird Alan Tyler played here in 2005 when the club was based at the pub. The occasional 'rock' gig is still put on here.

The pub, which dates back to 1845 and was originally called The Old Mother Shipton, is a Grade II- listed building.

Finsbury Park
Address: Seven Sisters Road, Finsbury Park, London
Tube: Finsbury Park (Piccadilly and Victoria Lines)
Capacity: 75,000
Live release: Pulp 'Live in the Park' DVD (1998), Madness 'Madstock' DVD (1992), Sex Pistols 'Filthy Lucre Live' CD (1996).

An 111-acre public park opened in 1869. It was here in 1992 that Madness staged 'Madstock', which has gained notoriety as the place where support act Morrissey's career took a nosedive. Wrapping himself in the Union Jack (a good few years before Oasis were able to pull the stunt off) in front of a crowd that included some racist skinheads (who Madness have sadly always attracted), Mozzer incurred the wrath of the *NME* as they took it as the final evidence that Mozzer was himself racist.

Finsbury Park was also home to the Fleadh festival (started in 1988) which attracted Bob Dylan, Van Morrisson, The Cranberries, James, The Corrs, Suzanne Vega, Shane MacGowan, The Divine Comedy and Kirsty MaColl to its stage.

On 31 December 1990 a New Year's Eve party in a heated big top tent was staged in the park and featured The House of Love, Ride, Lush and Ocean Colour Scene. The Sex Pistols reformed here on 23 June 1996 and were supported by Buzzcocks and Iggy Pop. Later, Paul Weller, Kiss (1997), Pulp (1998) also played in the park. The Stone Roses played two reunion shows here in 2013 and The Arctic Monkeys played in May 2014.

When gigs are held in the park there is usually a good selection of food from catering vans, and sometimes even a fun fair.

Fishmongers Arms/Village of The Damned
Address: 287 High Road, Wood Green, London, N22 8HU
Tube: Wood Green (Piccadilly Line)

The Fishmongers Arms was 1960s R&B and Blues club where Pink Floyd, Led Zeppelin (December 1968) and Fleetwood Mac played. The venue changed its name in the 1970s, becoming the Village of The Damned and later became an Irish pub called O'Rafferty's.

The building was being redeveloped in 2006 and is now a community police station.

The Forum/Town and Country Club (see Pl.10)

Address: 9 17 Highgate Road, London, NW5 1JY.
Tube: Kentish Town (Northern Line)
Capacity: 2,110 (standing)
Live release: The Pogues, 'Live at The Town & Country' DVD (1988), Starsailor 'Love Is Here Live At The Forum' DVD (1/11/04), The Wonder Stuff 'Live' DVD (2000).

The Forum was originally a cinema designed in the Art Deco style that showed films from 1934 until 1970. A short spell saw the building used as a dance hall before becoming the Town and Country Club music venue in 1986. Groups who have played the Town and Country stage include Throwing Muses, Go Betweens, The Pogues, The Triffids, REM and Voice of The Beehive. Debbie Harry played three nights in November 1989 on her 'Def, Dumb and Blonde' tour. The Town and Country Club shut up shop in 1993 with Van Morrission closing the curtain. The venue reopened in May 1993 as The Forum under the Mean Fiddler Group and the first gig was by Van Morrission. In April 1997 Suede played a gig consisting only of 'B' sides. Other visitors to the Forum include Oasis, Black Rebel Motorcycle Club, The Magic Numbers, Air, Cat Power and the reformed Velvet Underground and Sex Pistols. Catatonia played the Forum on 5 April 1999 supported by Coldplay who described the gig as being a landmark event as it was their first big support slot. The venue became part of The MAMA group of music venues in 2007.

The venue has a standing only ground floor with a lowered dance floor area in front of the stage, and a first level (Circle) seated area which is unreserved. There is a bar on each level and a cloakroom on the ground floor near the entrance.

A plaque by the box office credits the building's design to Architects Stanley Beard and WR Bennett. The venue was identical to another cinema in Ealing and when that building was demolished some of its architectural features were salvaged for the Forum.

The Galtymore. This club at 194 Cricklewood Broadway, Cricklewood, NW2, can boast that some of the most tedious comedians on TV have appeared on its stage. However, The Fall played here on 14 and 15 September 2006, and returned in late 2007.
G Lounge. Aussie rockers Wolfmother played here at 18 Kentish Town Road in April 2006 as part of the 'Camden Crawl'.
The Good Ship. Located at 289 Kilburn High Road, NW6 7JR. Opened in 2005 and hosts mostly unsigned bands on the Capitals circuit.
Heath Street Baptist Chapel. Located at 84 Heath Street, Hampstead, NW3 1DN, this religious building has hosted sensitive folk artist Lucy Rose several times. Tube: Hampstead (Northern Line).

The Garage/Upstairs at The Garage/T&C2

Address: 20–22 Highbury Corner, London, N5 1RD
Tube: Highbury and Islington (Victoria Line)
Capacity: 900 (standing), Upstairs at The Garage, 200
Live release: The Fall 'Live at The Garage' CD (April 2002)

The exterior of the Garage is not inviting; it is shabby and derelict with its windows and doors seemingly forever boarded up, weeds growing out of the gutters and in desperate need of a lick of paint. So, at first sight the venue appears to have closed down years ago. However, the venue usually has a pretty full line-up on most nights and supplements the main Garage venue area by also offering a smaller, more acoustic venue – Upstairs at The Garage – above the venue (entrance is gained to the left of the Garage entrance door).

The building was originally an engine shed and then a bingo hall. Its original name was the Town and Country II (T&C2), home of the Twang Club, until it became the Garage in 1993. The Red Hot Chilli Peppers played in 2002; Beth Orton (1996), Cinerama, My Chemical Romance, Ari Upp's The Slits, The Dickies (all 2004) and John Cale (2006) have all appeared at the Garage.

The Garage was closed for a much needed refurbishment in July 2006 with an advertised reopening in 2007, however the venue reopened much later than that and there was even some speculation that it would remain closed. Kasabian played one of their smallest gigs for many years at the venue on 29 January 2015 as part of the 'Make Some Noise' charity campaign.

Golden Lion Camden
Address: 88 Royal College Street, Camden, London, NW1 0TH
Tube: Mornington Crescent (Northern Line)

Cambridge Americana group the Broken Family Group have played this Camden pub. The Golden Lion was home to the 'Come down and meet the folks' events, which were organised by Steve from The Arlene's. The 2001 Christmas party featured The Rockingbirds, Boz Boorer (Polecat and Morrissey's co-writer/guitarist) and Adam Ant. The 'Come down and meet the folks' gigs later moved on to the Fiddlers Elbow and The Apple Tree.

Granada (Harrow)
Address: Sheepcote Road, Harrow, HA1 2JN
Tube: Kenton (Bakerloo Line)

Designed by J. Owen Bund and opened in 1937, the cinema was made a Grade II-listed building in 1988, although it is now used as a private gym (called Golds). However, as a cinema the

building hosted some very noteworthy gigs. Gene Vincent played in 1960, 1962 and 1964, Little Richard in 1962 and 1963, Roy Orbison in 1963 and 1964, Bobby Vee (1962), Del Shannon, The Kinks (1964) and The Hollies (1964). From the exterior I must admit that I struggle to understand why the building was listed when the Granada in Greenford has a more striking presence and is not listed. However, the interior detail seen in the foyer shows the quality of the finish cannot be questioned.

The Green Note
Address: 106 Parkway, Camden, London, NW1 7AD
Tube: Camden Town (Northern Line)

Opened in the Summer of 2005 by two friends (Immy and Rifa), the Green Note attracts mostly roots, acoustic, folk and world music performers. Folk legend Martin Carthy has performed as well as Irish troubadour Andy White.

The Green Note also offers hungry punters a healthy, organic food selection.

Hippodrome (Golders Green)

Address: North End Road, Golders Green, London, NW1 7RP
Tube: Golders Green (Northern Line)
Capacity: 3,000

Built in 1913, the Hippodrome was taken over by the BBC as a studio to record concerts. Those who played include Queen (the first group to have played the venue, in 1973), Status Quo, The Kinks, AC/DC and Roxy Music. Located opposite Golders Green tube and bus station, the Hippodrome is now known as the El-Shadou International Christian Centre.

Hope and Anchor

Address: 207 Upper Street, Islington, London, N1 1RL
Tube: Angel (Northern Line)
Capacity: 80

Built in 1880, the Hope and Anchor started hosting gigs in 1972 and continues as a live music venue, putting on up-and-coming signed and unsigned groups. However, the tough economic times have meant that instead of bands playing seven nights a week they have reduced bands to three nights a week.

Joy Division played their first two London gigs at this pub venue in 1979. Dexys Midnight Runners also made their London debut here in June 1979. U2 played their third London gig here on 4 December 1979, with tickets costing 75p! U2 returned in May 1980. This Victorian pub was also Madness's local, where the band watched other Ska band The Specials perform in 1979. The pub's basement is rather bizarrely where Frankie Goes To Hollywood made their videos for Relax and Two Tribes, in 1982. During its heydays the venue had a 200 capacity, although licensing has reduced this to 80 (in 2014). The current stage is also in the opposite end of the basement to that of the hacylon days of the 1970s. Since late 2013 the first floor has been used as a theatre.

The pub's folklore has it that Joey Ramone caught Sid Vicious shooting up in the toilets. The venue gets a few brief mentions in Nick Hornby's book 'A Long Way Down'.

Opposite the pub at 8 Compton Terrace is where Madness played their first gig at a house party.

Islington Assembly Hall (see Pl.17)

Address: Upper Street, Islington, London, N1 2UD
Tube: Angel (Northern Line)
Capacity: 150 (balcony seated) 250 (main area)

Opened in 1930 as a venue for dancing and variety shows, the hall was closed in 1980 due to lack of use. From this time up until 2009 the building was used for storage for the town hall next door. It started to get noticed on the gig circuit in 2010 when Islington Council refurbished and reopened the building as a music venue. The hall has an Art Deco interior and is a Grade II-listed building. The Foo Fighters (as The Holy Shits) played a gig here on 12 September 2014. Other performers in 2014 included Throwing Muses, Thurston Moore and Wishbone Ash.

Islington Carling Academy/The Marquee (2002–03)

Address: 16 Parkfield Street, N1 Shopping Centre, Islington, London, N1 0PS
Tube: Angel (Northern Line)
Capacity: 800

The Islington Academy originally opened its doors in September 2002, when it was launched as The Marquee Club and was backed by the Eurythmics Dave Stewart and entrepreneur Mark Fuller. Costing £4 million and situated in the upmarket N1 Shopping Centre, The new Marquee offered big-name acts with an additional Michelin restaurant for punters to dine in. No wonder that come January 2003 the venue was up for sale because of cash problems. However, on 5 September 2002 the future still looked rosy with Primal Scream playing on the opening night, followed by Jimmy Cliff, UK Subs, Badly Drawn Boy, Ms Dynamite and Joe Jackson. Reopening as The Islington Academy, having been bought by the MacKenzie Group Ltd, the venue continues to hold gigs by the likes of Belle & Sebastian, Jonathan Richman and The Mendoza Line. Rufus Wainwright played here in 2005 and Sparks played a twenty-night residency in April 2008.

The venue is situated just off the shopping centre in a rather dark walkway. Once inside the venue stairs lead up to the main area where there are two bars at the rear on opposite sides of the room. There are lots of industrial air-conditioning ducts on show above the stage which when working can really interfere with quiet songs, so much so that the venue suddenly solves the problem by quickly turning them off! In front of the stage is a slightly sunken floor – although you can still be struggling for a decent view from the middle of the room.

There is an additional venue, The Islington Bar Academy, joined to the main venue. This is used for smaller, more intimate gigs, which are usually acoustic affairs. Inside there is a small bar, tables and seats. Potentially off-putting for performers are gaming machines to the right of the stage. The stage is small but not tiny and is raised around a foot off the ground. Entrance to the Bar Academy is gained on the shopping centre's first-floor box office entrance.

Jazz Café

Address: 5 Parkway, Camden, London, NW1 7PG
Tube: Camden Town (Northern Line)
Capacity: 400 (standing), 250 (seated)

The Jazz Café opened in December 1990. Although called The Jazz Café, the venue hosts gigs by many different styles of music including jazz, funk, soul and rock. Artists who have played the venue include Roy Ayers, Georgie Fame, Omar, Amy Winehouse, Vonda Shepherd, De La Soul, Nanci Griffiths, Jimmy Cliff and Jonathan Richman. It is worth noting that the big names that play the venue often play a short run of two or three nights. As a member of the Jazz Passengers, Debbie Harry (of Blondie) played five nights in February 1996 here and returned for a further three gigs in July 1997.

Upon entering the venue's door there is a small box office on the left where tickets can be bought in person for upcoming shows. Directly in front of the entrance there is the bar, which divides the bar area from the main gig area. Through the bar there are views of the stage and main floor area. On the entrance side of the bar there is seating and a doorway that leads through to the main floor area and stairs to the first-floor balcony restaurant, where you can sit and eat while watching. Downstairs is standing only.

Kalamazoo Club

Address: 2 Crouch End Hill, Crouch End, N8 8AA, moving to the Great Northern Railway Tavern at 67 High Street, Hornsey, N8 7QB

An acoustic club originally founded at the Kings Head pub in 1995 with Bert Jansch playing the opening night. The club later moved to the Great Northern Railway Tavern and has gigs on the third Saturday in the month. Noteworthy performers include Martin Carthy, John Renbourne, Martin Stephenson and Bert Jansch with Bernard Butler. The club also hosts events at the Union Chapel.

Kenwood House. Hosted a series of 'Live by The Lake' gigs including Suede and Keane in 2013. Address: Hampstead Lane, Hampstead, NW3 7JR.

Kilburn Empire. Address: 256 Belsize Park, Kilburn, London. This music hall opened in 1906 and later became known as the Essolda Cinema, The Classic and The Broadway. The building was demolished in 1994 and a Marriot Hotel now occupies the site. However, the building was of note as on 13 and 14 July 1974, The Rolling Stone's Ronnie Wood played some solo gigs here aided by fellow Stone Keith Richards and ex-Face Ian McLagan.

Kings Cross Freight Depot. On 26 and 27 August 2006 Hot Chip, Sasha, Ladytron, The Research and Clor played as part of TDK's Cross Central Festival.

Kings Head, Crouch End. The Fatima Mansions played this pub at 2 Crouch End Hill, N8 8AA, in 1991. The pub continues to hold occasional gigs, although it is more known for comedy. Train: Crouch Hill.

Kingston Polytechnic. The Main Hall, Cambury Park Campus, Penrhyn Road, KT1 2EE, has hosted The Smiths (1983), U2, Barclay James Harvest and John Martyn (1970).

Kingston Tavern. Elvis Costello's early group Flip City played this pub on Russell Garden's W14, in the early 1970s.

Kilburn National Ballroom

Address: 234 Kilburn High Road, Kilburn, London, NW6 7JG
Tube: Kilburn (Jubilee Line)
Capacity: 1,200
Live release: The Smiths 'Rank' CD (1986), Blur 'Starshapped' DVD

The Kilburn national Ballroom was built in 1914 and was designed by E. A. Stone in the Baroque style. It has a stunning copper dome on its roof above the entrance. It was originally called The Grange Cinema and was taken over by the Gaumont chain in 1929. The cinema closed in 1975.

The building became a club called Butty's in the 1970s and later The National Ballroom. As the Kilburn National Ballroom, the venue put on groups such as The Smiths and The Triffids in the 1980s. The Smiths released their live album 'Rank' from their 23 October 1986 show here. David Bowie's Tin Machine played in June 1989, and Loop played in December 1990. In 1992 the Manic Street Preachers caused controversy when Nicky Wire made a comment about Michael Stipe and AIDS – not very thoughtful from a supposedly intelligent/politically sound group. Suede performed for two nights in October 1996. The original incarnation of The Pixies played two nights here on 5 and 6 of July 1989. The venue closed in 1999 and is Grade II-listed building.

The building is now home to the Universal Church of the Kingdom of God (UCKG) and is a Christian spiritual centre offering lectures and one-to-one spiritual advice. The UCKG must like former music venues as they also operate from the former Rainbow Theatre in Finsbury Park – which was also designed by E. A. Stone.

Kings Place

Address: 90 York Way, Kings Cross, London, N1 9AG
Tube: Kings Cross (Central, Circle, Metropolitan, Northern and Victoria Lines)
Capacity: 420 (Hall 1) and 220 (Hall 2)

This modern building is home to newspaper The Guardian as well as Kings Place which is a venue that specialises in folk, world and classical music. Opened in 2008, the venue was the first new public hall to be built in Central London since The Barbican in 1982. The building was designed by Dixon Jones and Arup Acoustics and has a three layered glass façade on the York Way elevation. There are seven floors of offices above the venue and Hall 1 is three stories tall, has an Oak Veneer interior from a 500 year old German tree (which is also used inside Hall 2) and sits on rubber springs to improve the acoustics.

The venues offers mostly folk and classical artists. Folk lecturer and musician Fay Hield played in April 2014, whilst American artist Laura Cantrell also appeared in 2014.

Koko/Camden Palace/Music Machine (see Pl.18)
Address: 1a Camden High Street, Camden, London, NW1 7JE
Tube: Mornington Crescent (Northern Line)
Capacity: 1,410 (gigs), 1,500 (clubs)
Live release: Snow Patrol 'You're All I Have' limited CD single (2006)

Built in the late 1800s as the Palace Theatre, and designed by WGR Sprague (who architecture guru Nikolaus Pevsner called 'the most interesting theatre architect of his time'). Charlie Chaplin was one of the theatre's founders. The building became one of the homes of BBC radio, and throughout the 1950s it was the studio for the Goon Show. During the 1960s the theatre became a cinema, but come the 1970s it changed again, this time into a music venue called The Music Machine, staging gigs by fledging Punk and New Wave groups such as the Sex Pistols and The Clash. The Clash, in fact, played a benefit gig for the deceased Sid Vicious in December 1978 here.

The venue became the Camden Palace on 21 April 1982 and soon became the place to be seen by any New Romantic worth their mascara. The dandy's could dance the night away in the club run by the New Romantic figurehead Steve Strange of Visage and catch the first performance of the Eurythmics. So notorious was the venue as a New Romantic hangout that The Pogues referenced the clientele in the song 'Transmetropolitan'. Madonna played her first (and for a long time only) London gig at the Palace in June 1983 when she was promoting her first single 'Everybody'. Madonna returned to Koko on 15 November 2005 to play to 1,500 fans who had won tickets to watch her perform five songs, promoting her new album 'Confessions on the Dancefloor'. Madonna closed her set with 'Everybody', as a nod towards her first UK appearance. In 1988 Prince held one of his famous aftershow parties at the venue and performed with the Stones' Ronnie Wood and Eric Clapton.

The Palace name survived, hosting the Feet First indie club nights and rave events until early 2004 when the doors were closed. The venue reopened in September 2004 as Koko with a multi-million- pound facelift which included restoring the original nineteenth-century theatre features. The interior of the venue is fantastically lush, with a red and gold colour scheme. A massive glitter ball hangs from the ceiling – which has more plasterwork on it. In fact, the glamour only stops at the toilets when beige tiles and stainless-steel bowls take over. The Koko's venue is used for comedy, award shows, cabaret, clubs and intimate gigs. The venue hosted the NME club nights where DJs are mixed in with live bands.

Upon entering the venue you walk into a lush foyer with chandeliers and fine ceiling roses. The box office is located here with three windows – one for pre-paid ticket collection, one for the guest list and one for ticket sales. A covered walkway leads to the first floor/circle, which is where the sound desk and stairs to the ground floor are. The ground floor holds the main stage and main bar, both at opposite ends of the venue. The bar has male toilets to the left of it and female toilets to the right. The bar area is rather cool, laidback hangout with comfy sofas in the corners and sparkling chandeliers hanging above a red-lit bar. A half-height wall separates the bar area from the main floor, which is slightly lowered from the bar. Another comfy sofa is placed in the centre at the back of the floor, under the sound desk. More sofas and tables are spread around the dance floor in alcoves with plaster Hercules pillars supporting the first-floor boxes. At the back of the stage is a giant, empty picture frame.

The first floor/circle is a tiered floor area with bars and a VIP area that can accommodate up to 250 people. The private boxes are found here along with some floor-standing lamps that look attractive. The upper level/circle is almost invisible from the ground and can hold 200 people. Koko is a lovely building that only suffers one fault – the sound quality at the front of the stage. Because the PA system is suspended from the ceiling in front of the stage, anyone standing around 15 feet from the stage is in a sound vacuum.

Koko was the venue used in ITV's *The Album Chart Show* where artists like Jarvis Cocker, The Magic Numbers and Amy Winehouse have appeared.

Lady Owen Arms. A pub at 285 Goswell Road, Islington where Blur (1990) and Snuff (1988) were notable performers. Demolished in 1998 and replaced by flats.
The Laurel Tree. This pub at 113 Bayham Street, Camden is noticeable for being the first stage performance of Coldplay in early 1998. Now (2014) a pub run by Brew Dog.
LMS. Address: 10 Church Road, Hendon, London, NW4 4EA (Tube: Hendon Central). Demented Are Go appeared at this pub in August 1989, when some of the Klub Foot groups moved here from the closed Clarendon Ballroom. UK Subs played in 1988 and Snuff have also gigged here. Now an Irish pub called The Claddagh Ring.
Lock 17 (see Dingwalls).
Lord Nelson. Location: 100 Holloway Road, N7 8JE. Had gigs by Elvis Costello's Flip City. Later renamed The Ashburton and currently called 'Horatia' and still has gigs by unknowns. Tube: Highbury and Islington (Victoria Line).
Loyola Hall. The Who played this Stamford Hill venue on 7 August 1965.

The Lexington

Address: 96–98 Pentoville Road, London, N1 9JB
Tube: Angel (Northern Line)

The Lexington was run by Stacey Thomas who also ran the Buffalo Bar. Bands play on the first floor and a very rock 'n roll gig postered staircase leads to the gig area. The ground floor has a very relaxed feel to it with fancy old sofas scattered around. The Primitives played two nights in April 2014 and VV Brown appeared in May 2014. Hollywood actress Juliet Lewis has also played the venue.

The Luminaire

Address: 311 Kilburn High Road, Kilburn, NW6 7JR
Tube: Kilburn (Jubilee Line)
Capacity: 300

The Luminaire opened in March 2005 in the former Late nightclub and attracted acts such as My Drug Hell, James Yorkston and Television Personalities. Ex-Libertine Carl Barat's group Dirty Pretty Things made their live debut here in February 2006. Scritti Politti also played in February 2006, breaking a twenty-six-year hiatus from playing live – due to stage fright – to promote the album 'White Bread, Black Beer'.

The venue, which was above McGoverns pub and run by Andy Ingis and John Donnelly, closed in March 2011, although it had been a popular venue with music fans and had won several 'venue of the year' awards in *Time Out* (2006) and *Music Week* (2007).

The Macbeth
Address: 70 Hoxton Street, Shoreditch, London, N1 6LP
Tube: Old Street (Northern Line)

The pub is over 100 years old and has hosted various forms of musical entertainment during this time; it is one of the most well-known venues in the super cool Hoxton scene. For four months from September 2014 the venue became 'Jack Rocks The Macbeth' when Jack Daniels hosted gigs and question and answer sessions with the likes of La Roux. Carl Barat and The Jackals brought in 2015 with their second gig in two venues on New Year's Eve 2014; the other gig was at The Amersham Arms.

Majestic Ballroom (see Pl.20)
Address: 10 Stroud Green Road, Finsbury Park, London, N4 2DF
Tube: Finsbury Park (Victoria Line)
Capacity: 2,800

The ballroom was originally two buildings that became one and had a 2,800 capacity. The Beatles played in 1963. Later became a bingo hall and then a bowling alley before one of the original buildings was demolished.

Mean Fiddler/Old Fiddler (Harlesden)

Address: 24–28a High Street, Harlesden, London, NW10
Tube: Willesden Junction (Bakerloo Line)
Capacity: 1,500

The venue that spawned the monster of live music venues and festivals – The Mean Fiddler Organisation – started in these humble origins, opening in December 1982. The building had previously been a drinking club owned by boxer Terry Downes. The Mean Fiddler was operated by Irish man Vince Power who wanted a venue to indulge his love of country music. Although originally conceived as a Nashville country club, other styles soon crept in. By 1984 The Pogues and Bo Diddley had played there. In the mid-1980s indie and rock groups started to dominate the stage: That Petrol Emotion, Sonic Youth, The Pixies, Voice of the Beehive and Red Hot Chilli Peppers (making their UK debut) had all played the Mean Fiddler. However, Johnny Cash, Paul McCartney, Rory Gallagher, John Martyn, Robert Cray and Roy Orbison (making his last ever UK appearance) still played here.

The smaller Acoustic Room was located, rather unsurprisingly, above the main venue, where acts such as Beverly Craven, The Levellers and Kevin Coyne played.

The Mean Fiddler building remains and has several uses: as retail space, office space and a as homeless hostel. The building is located opposite Tavistock Road.

The Mean Fiddler name later took over the LA2 club in central London, with the original Harlesden venue becoming the Old Fiddler. (Also see LA2 entry.)

The Moonlight Club/Klooks Kleek (see Pl.24)

Address: The Railway Hotel, 100 West End Lane, West Hampstead, NW6 2LU
Tube: West Hampstead (Jubilee Line)
Live Release: John Mayall Plays John Mayall (Live at Klooks Kleek) album (1965)

The pub/hotel started putting bands on in the 1960s when it was known as Klooks Kleek. It was renamed The Moonlight Club in the 1970s and had a brief spell in the late 1980s when it returned to being called Klooks Kleek. It was then was taken over by the Rat and Parrot chain before reverting back to an independent pub. Decca recording studios were almost next door and so may explain why so many big 1960s names played there, such as Led Zeppelin (1969), The Who, Rod Stewart and John Mayall. When Mayall recorded his 1965 live album here, John McVie (who later joined Fleetwood Mac) played bass in Mayall's band.

The Soft Boys and Television Personalities were lined up here in September 1980. U2 played on the Moonlight's stage on 1 December 1979 supporting girl group The Dolly Mixtures. The future stadium Gods returned in May 1980, July 1980 (with 200 fans outside unable to get in) and in November 1980. Joy Division played three nights in a row in April 1980 – as part of a Factory Records showcase – and the Damned played there in April 1979 (with recordings from the gig featuring on the live album 'Eternal Damnation'). However, Adam and The Ants may win the record for playing the most times – six times in 1978! The Stone Roses played what Ian Brown said was the group's first gig at the Moonlight on 23 October 1984, at an anti-heroin benefit organized by Pete Townsend. PJ Harvey played her first London gig at the Moonlight in August 1991. Other groups who played include The Jam, The Cure and Suede.

Moth Club

Address: Old Trades Hall, Valette Street, Hackney, E9 6NN
Train: Hackney Central

Housed in an ex-servicemen's club (Moth stands for Memorable Order of Tin Hats), the Moth Club opened in August 2015 and is operated by the team who run The Shacklewell Arms and The Lock Tavern. The inside has a rather wonderful glitter ceiling and an eccentric mix of music, comedy and quizzes.

Manor Hill School. The original line-up of The Damned played this school in 1977. Now called The Compton School and located at Summers Lane, Friern Barnet.

Market Tavern. Address: 2 Essex Road, Islington, London, N1. An indie club that hosted gigs by The Jasmine Minks, My Life Story, The Rockingbirds and Popinjays, all lined up in November 1988 for a £2 cover charge. Still open as a pub although with a name change to The Winchester.

Mazenod Church Hall. The Who played in 1963, located at Mazenod Avenue, Kilburn, NW6 4LS.

Monarch (see Barfly).

Music Machine (see Koko).

New Pegasus. Address: 109 Green Lanes, London, N16. Tube: Manor House (Piccadilly Line). Carter the Unstoppable Sex Machine, the Television Personalities and Drug Free America played in 1989.

North London Polytechnic. See University of North London entry.

Nambucca

Address: 596 Holloway Road, North London
Tube: Holloway Road (Piccadilly Line)
Capacity: 200

This pub, which was originally called 'The Cock Tavern' and was built in 1881, had Babyshambles performing on 5 December 2004, the same night the group also played at Infinity. Confirming the building's rock credentials, above the pub lived indie groups The Holloways and We Smoke Fags. The pub had a severe fire in December 2008 but did reopen. The Enemy played a gig at Nambucca in 2015.

Northwood Hills

Address: 66 Joel Street, Northwood, Middlesex, HA6 1LL
Tube: Northwood Hills (Metropolitan Line)

This pub is where Elton John made his first public appearances in 1962 when landlord George Hill booked the young (fifteen-year-old) Reg Dwight to play. A PRS plaque has been erected on the building to mark the occasion. The building is now a restaurant called Namcaste Lounge and is located opposite the tube station.

Old Welsh Harp. This pub at Hendon was rebuilt in 1937 and had a pre-Faces Ronnie Wood band, The Thunderbirds, in 1965. The pub was demolished in 1971 for the Staples Corner road.

Parliament Hill Fields. This park at Hampstead Heath hosted The Camden Festival in the late 1960s. In 1968 Jefferson Airplane and Fairport Convention played whilst in 1969 Pink Floyd and Fleetwood Mac performed to 25,000 fans. Moving forward to 2009 ABBA's Benny Andersson played ABBA songs in the bandstand to celebrate Sweden's presidency of the European Union.

Pentonville Prison. Dirty Pretty Things and The Enemy played in the prison's 180 capacity chapel on 27 August 2007 as part of the 'Wasted Youth' campaign to highlight suicide in prison. Famous musicians who have spent time behind bars here include; The Stranglers Hugh Cornwell (1980), Pete Doherty (2005), Boy George (2009) and George Michael (2010). Located on Caledonian Road, N7 8TT.

Portlands/The Pits/Green Man
Address: 383 Euston Road, London, NW1 3AU
Tube: Great Portland Street (Hammersmith & City, Circle Lines)

The Television Personalities (1988) and Inspiral Carpets (March 1987) played this mostly indie venue when called Portlands. The Meteors played 1981 when it was known as The Pits. Now a pub called The Green Man and offers live jazz. The pub dates from 1756

Powerhaus (1996–2004)/Sir George Robey (see Pl.30)
Address: 240 Seven Sisters Road, Finsbury Park, London, N4 2HX
Tube: Finsbury Park (Piccadilly and Victoria Lines)
Live Releases: Steve Marriott 'Live at The Sir George Robey 23.10.85' album

The Sir George Robey's place in the music history books is assured as it was the local pub to the young John Lydon (Johnny Rotten). As the Sir George Robey it hosted gigs by Fairport Convention (October 1985), Steve Marriott, The Las and They Might Be Giants (both in September 1987).

Called the Sir George Robey until March 1996 when it became The Powerhaus, rechristened when the original Powerhaus moved here from its Islington address. Run by The Mean Fiddler Organisation, bands such as Salad, Die Cheerleader and The Butthole Surfers played the Powerhaus at this location. Powerhaus closed in 2004.

The building had fallen on hard times – empty, up for sale and crumbling. Boarded up and unused for a good few years, the building had only become more derelict, appearing to have all internal floor removed, and its future appeared to be uncertain (although it is a listed building). The building was demolished in late 2015. The venue was located opposite the former Rainbow Theatre close to the underground station.

Powerhaus/The Barn/Pied Bull
Address: 1 Liverpool Road, Islington, London, N1 0RP
Tube: Angel (Northern Line)

The original home to the Powerhaus, it used to be known as The Barn in the 1970s and then Pied Bull. It hosted groups such as Hawkwind in October 1970 the UK Subs in 1988. Changing to the Powerhaus in the late 1980s, groups such as Cactus World News, Buffalo Tom, Suede, BMX Bandits, Boys Wonder, Momus, Stone Roses, Jah Wobble and Wilko Johnson would play here in the same week as unsigned out of London groups in the early 1990s. In August 1989 That Petrol

Emotion, Swans, Primal Scream and Green on Red all played here. The Powerhaus moved to the Sir George Robey pub in 1996.

The venue's main area was in the basement with a raised stage. The building later became a bank.

Proud Galleries
Address: The Gin House, Stables Market, Camden, London, NW1 8AH
Tube: Camden Town (Northern Line)
Capacity: 400

A restored warehouse where The Clash rehearsed in the 1970s, the building houses a photographic gallery with heavy focus on musicians. The gallery also hosts the Year Zero Club where The Kooks, Dirty Pretty Things and Yourcodenameis:Milo played. The venue hosted Oxfam's 'Pudstock' in January 2007 with sets by Supergrass, Athlete, Graham Coxon and Ed Harcourt. Ash appeared in June 2007. The venue is 3000 square feet spread over two floors.

Fire raged through the Stables in May 2014 but the building was saved and the venue has since reopened.

Purple Turtle
Address: 61–65 Crowndale Road, Camden, London, NW1 1TN
Tube: Mornington Crescent (Northern Line
Capacity: 300

The Purple Turtle has a fairly solid schedule of gigs by unsigned or just breaking through bands. The venue is opposite Koko in Crowndale Road. The Manic Street Preacher's Nicky Wire played a solo gig at The Turtle in 2006 in support of his album 'I Killed The Zeitgeist' – the most noteworthy gig here .

The Purple Turtle is one of the venues used in The Camden Crawl gigathon.

Railway Hotel. Address: The Bridge/Station Approach, Wealdstone, Harrow. Train: Harrow and Wealdstone. A jazz and R&B venue started in the 1950s, and was home to the Bluesday club nights. The Yardbirds had a residency here in 1963 and were replaced as the house band by The Who in 1964. Famous for being the venue where Pete Townsend first (accidentally) smashed up his guitar. Roger Daltry recalls the venue being tiny with a very low ceiling with an easy load in of gear from the back door straight onto the stage (*Mojo* magazine, March 2014). Destroyed by a fire in 2000. Not to be confused with the Railway Hotel in Kilburn that was home to Klooks Kleek & The Moonlight Club.

Regents Park Open Air Theatre. Address: Inner Circle, Regents Park, London, NW1 4NU. Tube: Baker Street (Circle, Hammersmith & City and Metropolitan Lines). Capacity: 1,200. The theatre has been established in the park in 1932 and usually has some live music events mixed in with their theatre productions during the summer months. Seth Lakeman and The Levellers performed in the open in August 2007 and Nitin Sawhney appeared in 2015.

The Rochester. This pub at 145 High Street, Stoke Newington, N16, had The Jam play twice in March 1977 and also was punk band London's first gig. Now part of the Wetherspoons chain.

Royal Dance Hall/Tottenham Royal/Tottenham Palais. Address: 413 High Road, Tottenham, N17 6QH. Built in 1910 as a roller skating rink next to The Palace Theatre, the building was converted into the Canadian Rink Cinema just a year later in 1911. In 1925 the cinema became the Tottenham Palais and got on the jazz circuit. Later the Palais was renamed

The Tottenham Royal/Royal Dance Hall where The Dave Clarke Five were the resident band in the 1960s. Others to have played in the `60s included The Troggs, The Who and The Animals. David Bowie rehearsed his Ziggy Stardust show here in early 1972. Other 1970s gigs were by Desmond Dekker and Gregory Isaacs. The 1980s saw a host of new names for the building – The Mayfair Suite, The Temple, and United Nations Club. In 2004 the building was demolished and was replaced by housing.

The Roxy (Harlesden). Address: Craven Park Road, Harlesden, London, NW10 8SH. The Roxy Odeon Cinema had the Sex Pistols and The Clash rehearsing on its stage in December 1976. Later, The Clash, supported by The Slits and Subway Sect, debuted new drummer Topper Headon here on 11 March 1977. Opened in 1937 as an Odeon cinema with a 1,719 capacity, the cinema closed in 1972, although it reopened as a Liberty cinema before becoming The Roxy. The building went on to be used as a nightclub called The Tara. The building was demolished in 1989 and flats called 'Odeon Court' were built on the site.

The Rainbow/The Finsbury Park Astoria (see Pl.31)

Address: 232 Seven Sisters Road, Finsbury Park, London, N4 3NP
Tube: Finsbury Park (Victoria Line)
Capacity: 2,802
Live release: Eric Clapton 'Rainbow Concert' album (1973), Van Morrison 'Its Too Late To Stop Now' album (1974), Spirit 'Spirit Live' (1978), Ramones 'Its Alive' (1979)

The Finsbury Park Astoria was one of the places where in 1967 Jimi Hendrix had ignited his strat on the first night of The Jimi Hendrix Experience's first tour. Also on the bill that night were Cat Stevens, the Walker Brothers and Englebert Humperdinck, so I guess Jimi had to do something to retain the rock 'n' roll spirit! The Beatles played two shows a night for sixteen days here in December 1963.

The Rainbow opened in 1971. Frank Zappa, played that year, and Pink Floyd premiered 'The Dark Side of The Moon' here over four nights in February 1972.

Can played a rare UK date in 1973 .The Clash brought their White Riot tour to the venue in 1977, supported by The Jam, Buzzcocks and Subway Sect, all for a whopping £2.20 including VAT! However, the gig ended up in a riot as the audience ripped out the seats egged on by The Clash, who won a victory as the venue's management had refused to remove the seats before the gig. Blondie visited the venue on their second British tour on 15 November 1977. The Damned played their 'goodbye bash' here in April 1978. Former Sex Pistol John Lydon's new band Public Image Limited (PiL) played The Rainbow on Christmas Day 1978 – which was also the group's live debut. Boy George appeared here as a brief member of Bow Wow Wow in the early 1980s. For the gig the band's manager Malcolm McLaren filled the venue out with carousels and other carnival rides – probably to distract the audience from how bad the band were!

The venue closed in the 1980s as a result of the building being in very poor condition. The building was eventually sold to the Universal Church of the Kingdom of God (UCKG) who at the time were trying to buy the Brixton Academy (they failed). The UCKG currently own another former music venue – The Kilburn National Ballroom.

The building was built as a theatre in 1930 and has several Art Nouveau features on the exterior (consisting of white faience and green faience dressings), which is dignified and understated and does not really prepare you for the interior. The foyer has retained the original fountain, although a green plastic knee-high hedge has been added around the pond. However, the main hall itself is simply stunning – full of colour and detail in a Hispano-Moresque-fantasy style. The UCKG should be commended for working with the original fabric of the theatre.

The Roundhouse (Camden) (see Pl.33)

Address: 100 Chalk Farm Road, Camden, London, NW1 8EH
Tube: Camden Town (Northern Line)
Capacity: 3,300 (standing), 1700 (seated)
Live release: Hawkwind 'Silver Machine' single (February 1972), Dresden Dolls 'Live at The Roundhouse' DVD (2007)

Built in 1820 as a steam-engine repair building, the Roundhouse was turned into a gin warehouse in 1869. In 1964 it was bought by Centre 42, a cultural organisation that promoted the arts, and the building was reopened in 1966 after having £750,000 spent on improvements.

The first gig was on 11 April 1966 when Manfred Mann and The Yardbirds played a private gig for CND, and it was then that the venue really took off. By the end of the 1960s Pink Floyd, Soft Machine, Cream, The Who, Jimi Hendrix and The Doors (their only UK gig in 1968) had all played here; Led Zeppelin even made their London debut here in November 1968. Hawkwind played the Roundhouse four times in 1970 and took part in a benefit gig called 'Greasy Truckers' with Man and Brinsley Shwarz on 13 February 1972. An album of the event 'Greasy Truckers Party' was released with each group getting a side dedicated to them.

The Roundhouse became a major punk venue in the 1970s and The Ramones made their UK debut at the venue on 4 July 1976. Patti Smith played two nights in May 1976. The Clash played their first gig at the Roundhouse in September 1976. X-Ray Spex and Adam and The Ants played there on 14 May 1978 with a show starting at 5.30 p.m. and costing £2 to get into. Blondie played their sixth London show at the Roundhouse on 5 March 1978.

The Roundhouse closed in 1983 and remained empty until a brief resurgence in 1996 when a short brace of gigs by Elvis Costello, Billy Bragg and Suede blew the spiders' webs away. When Suede played three nights in December 1996 they were joined on the last night by Neil Tennant of the Pet Shop Boys.

In 1998 The Roundhouse Trust was established to redevelop the building. The phrase 'redevelop the building' is usually a cause for concern, but The Roundhouse Trust thankfully did not turn the Roundhouse into offices and actually restored it sympathetically in line with the cultural hub of London. The restored Roundhouse opened in 2006 and is available for music, theatre, dance and digital media, and is a creativity centre for young people. The trust hoped to raise £28,000,000 to rebuild The Roundhouse.

Among the first gigs to take place were The Divine Comedy, The Dresden Dolls, Jarvis Cocker and The Zutons. George Michael played a special 'nurses only' concert here in December 2006 as a thank you for the help given to his ill mother while in hospital. James Brown played his last UK gig here in December 2006 as part of the BBC's Electric Proms. The Beastie Boys played an instrumental gig at The Roundhouse in September 2007. Morrissey played almost a week's residency at The Roundhouse in January 2008 as part of the lead up to the release of his new 'Best Of' album.

The Manic Street Preachers filmed the video for their single 'A Design for Life' here when The Roundhouse was still in its abandoned state. The band have played the venue many times since then including two three-night runs. One run was for the release of 'Journals for Plagued Lovers' and the other run was in December 2014 for a performance of the classic album 'The Holy Bible', which was celebrating its twentieth anniversary.

Although The Roundhouse is a lovely venue and is well designed, it is difficult to exit the building after the show. Slow, crammed and boring is the only way to describe the long journey out of the gig area and down the stairs until you finally reach the street – and that is without the wait for the cloakroom.

Royalty Ballroom

Address: Winchmore Hill Road, Southgate, London, N14 6AA
Tube: Southgate (Piccadilly Line)

The Royalty Ballroom is located at the end of and set back behind Dennis Parade on Winchmore Hill Road. The venue hosted Family (1967), Slade (1978) and Bill Haley (1979) as well as dance nights. The Royalty Ballroom was also used in the film *Quadrophenia*, where Sting jumps from a balcony.

The building is currently a private gym.

Scala (see Pl.35)

Address: 275 Pentonville Road, Kings Cross, London, N1 9NL
Tube: Kings Cross (Northern, Victoria, Circle, Hammersmith & City and Metropolitian Lines)
Capacity: 375
Live release: The Alarm 'Live In The Poppyfields' DVD (1.3.04)

The Scala is housed in a former cinema which has also spent time as a snooker hall. Built in 1920 it was known as The Gaumont, The Odeon and the Kings Cross Cinema. The Scala put gigs on in the 1970s, including the only UK gig of Iggy Pop's Stooges (until the 2005 performance of 'Funhouse' at the Hammersmith Apollo) and Lou Reed – both in July 1972. The album cover to Iggy And The Stooges 'Raw Power' and Lou Reed's 'Rock 'n' Roll Animal' were both shot on stage at the Scala by photographer Mick Rock.

The Scala is now a permanent music venue and club (after closing as the Scala Cinema in 1993), after disappearing from view after the 1970's gigs and now features regularly in tour itineraries. Foo Fighters, Moby, The Killers, Suede and Maria McKee have played the venue. The Scala is home to the 'Chalk' club that puts on live bands and DJ sets.

Coldplay played in June 2000 and encored with a cover of the Bond theme song 'You Only Live Twice'. Rapper Lady Sovereign appeared in February 2007 followed by indie group The Long Blondes in March. The Police (no, not the group) forced Kano to cancel a gig here in October 2005 due to concerns over public safety.

Screen on The Green

Address: 83 Upper Street, Islington, London, N1 0NP
Tube: Highbury and Islington (Victoria Line)
Capacity: 300

The Screen on The Green was built as a cinema in 1913, and still is an arts cinema, which in the 1970s hosted gigs by the up-and-coming punk groups. The 29 August 1976 saw an all-nighter at the venue with the Sex Pistols headlining, supported by The Clash (making their stage debut) and The Buzzcocks (playing their first gig outside Manchester). Tickets to this historic gig would have cost you £1; doors opened at midnight and chucking out time was dawn.

The Screen on The Green was namechecked in the Adam and The Ants B-side to 'Antmusic', 'Fall-in' in 1980.

The Screen on The Green no longer puts on gigs, although it does form part of the road that is the music venue trail from Angel (to the south) to Highbury and Islington (to the north) where you can take in The Garage, The Buffalo Bar, Union Chapel, Hope and Anchor, Islington Assembly Hall and the Islington Academy.

Shaw Theatre
Address: 100 Euston Road, Kings Cross, London, NW1 2AJ
Tube: Kings Cross (Northern and Victoria Lines)
Capacity: 446

The current Shaw Theatre is a modern 1990's building that along with the adjacent Novotel replaced the original theatre (built in 1971). The original theatre hosted occasional gigs and included a four- night residency by Australian group The Triffids who were promoting their album 'The Black Swan' in April 1989. One of these gigs was broadcast on Radio 1 as part of their 'In Concert' programmes.

Toyah played the venue in December 1990 and Tori Amos launched her 'Little Earthquakes' UK tour in the original theatre in 1992. Queen rehearsed their Live Aid performance on the Shaw's stage in 1985.

The new building continues to host sporadic gigs with Tori Amos returning to play the venue to promote her 'Tales of a Librarian' CD on 8 November 2003. The gig was part conversation and part song, with tickets only being available on the morning of the gig. Indie rockers Idlewild played the Shaw in early 2005 and were quickly followed by Van Morrisson promoting his 'Magic Time' album. Dionne Warwick played a residency at The Shaw in 2006, and Eartha Kitt played five nights in February 2007.

The theatre hosts mainly money-spinning business conferences associated with the Novotel hotel next door and classical concerts.

Silver Bullet (see Pl.36)
Address: 6 Station Place, Finsbury, London, N4 2DH
Tube: Finsbury Park (Victoria Line)
Capacity: 200

The Silver Bullet was a pop-up venue that opened up in May 2010 and ended up staying put thanks to delaying of redevelopment plans. It has mostly free gigs, so it doesn't attract big names, although performers of note include Slow Club, James Walsh (of Starsailor) and John Newman. Laura Marling appeared in January 2015. The venue takes its name from the pub that inhabited the building previously, which was itself named after the *Silver Bullet* train that used to pass by on the rail tracks. It is located opposite Finsbury bus station.

Sobell Sports Centre/Michael Sobell Sports Centre
Address: Hornsey Road, Holloway, N7 7NY
Tube: Finsbury Park (Victoria Line)

This sports hall opened in 1973 and was named after the benefactor who donated the money to build it. The building has a somewhat harsh cast-concrete exterior. Ian Dury played in 1980 and was joined on stage by Wilko Johnson. Banarama supported The Jam in December 1981. Rainbow appeared in 1983 and were followed in 1985 by New Order.

The State Theatre/Gaumont State Theatre

Address: 195 Kilburn High Road, Kilburn, London, NW6
Tube: Kilburn (Jubilee Line)
Capacity: 8,000

When The State opened in December 1937 it was the world's largest theatre with a total capacity of 8,000 (4,000 seated and 4,000 standing). Designed by George Coles, the 100-foot-high tower had a BBC TV-approved broadcasting studio inside of it. The Marble Hall entrance had a candelabra replica of one inside of Buckingham Palace.

The State had a long history of attracting the cream of the jazz world with Django Reinhardt (1939), Louis Armstrong, Sarah Vaughan, Frank Sinatra (1953), Dizzy Gillespie (1961) and Dave Brubeck (1963) all appearing. In March 1953 Jazz at the Philharmonic played here and included Ella Fitzgerald in its ranks. Ronnie Scott's Sextet supported.

The State was also important in the 1950s rock 'n' roll scene with Buddy Holly and Jerry Lee Lewis playing in 1958. The Rolling Stones (1963) The Beatles (1963 and 64), Petula Clark (1950), David Bowie (1973) and The Who (1977) also performed here.

The State became a bingo hall and is currently a church. The building still retains the State name on its tower and is a local landmark. The theatre was restored in 1985 and it is a Grade II*-listed building. It is also known as The Gaumont State Theatre.

St Pancras Old Church (see Pl.37)

Location: 191 Pancras Road, London, NW1 1UL
Tube: Kings Cross (Northern, Victoria, Circle, Metropolitan, Hammersmith & City Lines) or Mornington Crescent (Northern Line)
Capacity: 120

St Pancras Old Church is a church popular with the hipsters of the capital, with several gigs in 2014. Killing Jokes Jaz Coleman read chapters from his book here in 2015, while Eliza Carthy played in 2015.

<u>St Michael's Hall.</u> Fairport Convention made their live debut at the hall on The Riding, Golders Green on 22 May 1967.

<u>Stoke Newington Eye.</u> Address: 79–81 Stoke Newington High Street, London, N16 0PH. Train: Stoke Newington. Opened around 2004. Called The Spot in 2014.

<u>Sundown.</u> A small London-based chain of live music venues operated by Rank around 1972 (and closed soon after opening). There were three Sundowns all in Ranks cinemas. In Brixton the Sundown was opened by a gig from Deep Purple and the building is what later became The Brixton Academy. In Mile End, the Odeon at 401 Mile End Road became a Sundown and had Slade in September 1972, Fleetwood Mac in November 1972 and John Martyn and Sandy Denny also played that year. It closed as a music venue in 1973 and reverted back to a cinema, although it was demolished in 1984. The Who played the Edmonton Sundown venue four times in December 1973 and this was apparently the most successful of the Sundown venues. Steppenwolf also played here. (See Edmonton Regal entry.)

Surya
Address: 156 Pentoville Road, London N1 9JL
Tube: Kings Cross (Northern, Victoria, Circle, Metropolitan and Hammersmith & City Lines)
Capacity: 225

Opened in 2012 and is a venue that plays on its eco credentials and specialist beers. Those to have played include Mark Morris (from The Bluetones) and former Sex Pistol Glen Matlock.

12 Bar Club (Holloway Road) (also see entry in Central London section)
Address: 203 Holloway Road, London, N7 8DL
Tube: Holloway Road (Piccadilly Line) or Highbury & Islington (Victoria Line)

Evicted from its Central London site the 12 Bar Club moved here in early 2015, in a building that was previously The Phibbers pub. Spread over three floors the club brought plenty of memorabilia from the original venue with it. The stage is on the ground floor and just like the original venue there is a first-floor balcony that looks right into the stage below.

Tinkers Folk Club
Address: The Three Horseshoes, 28 Heath Street, Hampstead, NW3 6TE
Tube: Hampstead (Northern Line)

In the 1960s the upstairs theatre had Ralph McTell and Paul Simon singing and strumming. The building became part of the Wetherspoons chain, but was later sold off. It remains a pub called The Horseshoe and is still an operational theatre (accessed at the side of the building from Oriel Place) called The Pentameters Theatre.

Torrington Arms
Address: 4 Lodge Lane, North Finchley, London, N12 8JR
Tube: Woodside Park (Northern Line)

This pub started hosting gigs, live jazz in the late 1960s, and later became a key venue on the pub-rock circuit with Brinsley Schwarz and Dr Feelgood playing along with Shakin' Stevens. It closed around 2004 and is now a Starbucks coffee shop and restaurant. The promoter in the early days was George Blevins and in the later days Pete Feenstra had that duty.

The Underworld

Address: 174 Camden High Street, Camden, London, NW1 ONE
Tube: Camden Town (Northern Line)
Capacity: 500

This Camden venue is a stone's throw from Camden Town tube station and is situated in the cellar of the Worlds End pub. The Flaming Lips played here in October 1992, years before they found mainstream success in 2003. Other groups who have played include Zodiac Mindwarp and The Love Reaction, The Cranberries, Hole, Frank Black, Offspring, Placebo, Radiohead and Sheryl Crow. The Foo Fighters played a warm-up show on 16 June 2006 in preparation for their much larger booking at Hyde Park.

The venue has a triangular shaped stage in the corner of the underground dance floor.

Union Chapel (see Pl.40)

Address: Compton Terrace, Islington, London, N1 2UN
Tube: Highbury and Islington (Victoria Line)
Capacity: 1,000 (seated)
Live release: David Byrne DVD, Marc Almond 'Live at the Union Chapel' DVD (December 2000)

A working church that opened its doors to live music in 1991. Patti Smith played a benefit gig here for the venue on 2 August 2002. Other performers include Bjork, Tori Amos, The Pretenders, Beck, Sigur Ros, Polyphonic Spree (August 2002), Beth Orton (March 2001), Low (February 2003), Damien Rice (2003), Kathryn Williams (October 2006), Brett Anderson (July 2007), John Cale, David Byrne and Goldfrapp (May 2001).

In November 2007 the venue hosted Mencap's 'Little Noise Sessions' which included a surprise set from U2's Bono and The Edge who performed four acoustic songs on 23 November. The set comprised of 'Stay', 'Desire', 'Angel of Harlem' and a new song, 'Wave of Sorrow'.

The Union Chapel is a Grade II-listed building, as well as being a place of worship that has four halls which can accommodate between 150 and 1,000 people. The chapel is open to the public to look around on Wednesdays and is simply breathtaking.

<u>**University of North London/North London Polytechnic.**</u> Address: Holloway Road, London. Tube: Holloway Road (Piccadilly Line). Live release: Jesus and Mary Chain 'Riot' single. In the days when every university, polytechnic or college could muster an Ents Society to put on gigs, this venue (known then as North London Polytechnic) hosted the Jesus and Mary Chain in March 1985. At the time famous for playing twenty-minute sets, the Mary Chain kept the audience waiting an hour and when they finally made it on stage a riot ensued. It probably did not help that the gig had sold out and the crowd outside were let in by the group. The group's equipment was wrecked and the PA knocked over. A recording of the gig was later released and called 'Riot'. Other groups who have played here include Ace (1973) and Chilli Willi & The Red Hot Peppers (1975).

<u>**Village Inn.**</u> Japan and Squeeze played in 1977. Location: 529 High Road, Wembley.

<u>**The Waiting Room.**</u> 175 Stoke Newington High Street, N16 0LH. Located under the Three Crowns pub. Active from around 2014.

<u>**Westfield College.**</u> Both John Martyn and Elton John played here in the early 1970s.

The Verge/Bullet Bar/The Flowerpot/Heros
Address: 147 Kentish Town Road, NW1 8PB
Tube: Kentish Town (Northern Line)

The Verge was the stage for an early outing for Bloc Party (then known as The Angel Range), The Darkness (2001) and Art Brut (2003). The Verge later became the Bullet Bar and continued to offer live music. The venue became The Flowerpot in 2009, although it closed in 2010, but not before The Drums, Mumford and Sons (May 2009) and Florence and The Machine had played. The Flowerpot was also the venue for The Vaccines first London gig. The venue closed when the lease was sold and it briefly became known as Heros where The Libertines' Carl Barat played a solo gig. The building closed yet again and there were rumours that it would be demolished. However, in 2015 planning permission was granted for an additional floor to be added to the building, which would be used as flats, while the original building would become offices. The building dates from 1849.

Vortex (Dalston) (see Pl.44)
Address: Dalston Cultural House, 11 Gillett Street, London, N16 8JH
Train: Dalston Kingsland (from Stratford)
Capacity: 90

This jazz venue was at 139 Stoke Newington Church Street, N16, for seventeen years until leasing problems caused the venue to move to this present site in 2005. Acoustic Ladyland and Polar Bear were some of the acts who played the original venue.

Wembley Arena/SSE Arena/Wembley Empire Pool (see Pl.47)
Address: Empire Way, Wembley, Middlesex, HA9 0DH
Tube: Wembley Park (Metropolitan Line)
Capacity: 12,200 (standing), 11,000 (seated)
Live release: Christina Aguilera 'Stripped Live In The UK' DVD, Atomic Kitten 'Greatest Hits Wembley Arena' DVD, Blue 'Guilty Live From Wembley' DVD, T-Rex 'Born To Boogie' DVD

Opened in 1934 for the British Empire Games and originally called the Wembley Empire Pool, the venue hosted the annual NME poll-winners concerts in the 1960s, where line-ups would include The Beatles, Bob Dylan and The Rolling Stones. The venue is also noteworthy for being the last venue The Beatles played. Changing its name to the Wembley Arena in 1977, the arena continues to host some of the biggest acts in the world as well as the latest pop sensations.

Pl. 1 Alexandra Palace.

Pl. 2 The Astoria.

Pl. 3 Bluesville.

Pl. 4 Brixton Academy/
Brixton O2 Academy/
Fair Deal/ Sundown.

Pl. 5 Academy detail.

Pl. 6 Bull and Gate.

Pl. 7 Bush Hall looking down from the rear balcony with the stage in the distance.

Pl. 8 Dublin Castle.

Pl. 9 Earls Court.

Pl. 10 The Forum/
Town and Country Club.

Pl. 11 Granada
(Kingston-upon-Thames)

Pl. 12 Granada (Tooting).

Pl. 13 The Grand.

Pl. 14 The Half Moon
(Putney).

Pl. 15 Hammersmith Odeon/
Apollo.

Pl. 16 Hammersmith Palais/
Palais de Danse.

Pl. 17 The stage of the Islington
Assembly Hall.

Pl. 18 koko/Camden Palace/Music Machine.

Pl. 19 Madame JoJo's.

Pl. 20 Majestic Ballroom.

Pl. 21 Marquee, 1964–88.

Pl. 22 Marquee 1988–96.

Pl. 23 Marquee 2004–07.

Pl. 24 The Moonlight Club/
Klooks Kleek.

Pl. 25 Nashville Rooms.

Pl. 26 Notre Dame Hall/Ad Lib Club/
Cavern in The Town.

Pl. 27 100 Club/London Jazz Club/
Hymphrey Lyttelton Club.

Pl. 28 The O2/Indigo Matter.

Pl. 29 The Old Blue Last.

Pl. 30 Powerhaus/Sir George Robey.

Pl. 31 The Rainbow/
The Finsbury Park Astoria.

Pl. 32 Rough Trade East.

Pl. 33 The Roundhouse
(Camden).

Pl. 34 The Roundhouse
(Dagenham/Upney)/
Village Roundhouse.

Pl. 35 Scala.

Pl. 36 Silver Bullet.

Pl. 37 St Pancras Old Church.

Pl. 38 The Troubadour.

Pl. 39 The Troxy.

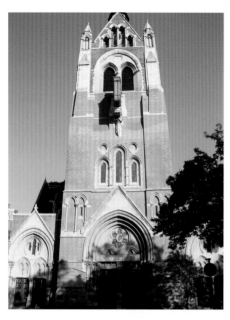

Pl. 40 Union Chapel.

Pl. 41 The Venue (New Cross).

Pl. 42 Village Underground.

Pl. 43 Village Underground, Great Eastern Street elevation, and roof detail.

Pl. 44 Vortex (Dalston).

Pl. 45 The Wag Club/ Whisky-A-Go-Go/ Flamingo.

Pl. 46 Walthamstow Assembly Rooms.

Pl. 47 Wembley Arena.

Pl. 48 Wilton's Music Hall.

Pl. 49 The Witchdoctor/Savoy Rooms/
Mr Smiths.

Pl. 50 The Windmill.

Refurbished during 2005, the makeshift marquee, Wembley Pavilions, was erected to deputise for the arena. The image below shows the Arena before the £32 million refurbishment which reoriented the entrance and upgraded facilities to modern specifications while remaining sympathetic to the original 1930s architecture. Depeche Mode were the first group to play the refurbished arena when it reopened on 2 April 2006. Other who played in 2006 include Muse (four times in November), New Order (October on their 'Singles Collection Live' tour), Snow Patrol (December), Jay-Z (September), Scissor Sisters (November), Placebo (December), Richard Ashcroft (December) and Paul Simon (November). Country legend Willie Nelson played in January 2007 and Dolly Parton played twice in March the same year. Others who came to the Arena in 2007 were The Killers, The Who and Pearl Jam. When Bob Dylan played two nights in 2007 it brought his grand total of performances at the arena to twelve times since he first played in 1987.

Blondie appeared twice in 1999 on their 'No Exit' tour – in June and November. U2 brought their 'Joshua Tree' tour to the arena on 2 June 1987 when they threw in a cover version of 'C'mon Everybody' into their set. Pet Shop Boys played in December 1999 on their 'Nightlife' tour. Blink-182 played in December 2004.

The arena operated since 2013 by AEG Facilities and rebranded the SSE Arena in April 2014 under a ten-year deal.

Wembley Arena Pavilions

Address: Empire Way, Wembley, Middlesex
Tube: Wembley Park (Metropolitan Line)
Capacity: 10,000

This temporary marquee was erected in 2005 while Wembley Arena was being refurbished. Heated and seated inside, the Pavilion hosted gigs by Alice Cooper (supported by Twisted Sister) in November 2005 and UB40 played twice in December 2005. The Pavilion was made redundant by April 2006 when the arena was reopened. It was located to the left of the front of the new Wembley Stadium and cost £4 million to build.

Wembley Stadium

Address: Empire Way, Wembley, London, HA9 0WS
Tube: Wembley Park (Metropolitan Line)
Capacity: 90,000 (seated), 120,000 plus standing
Live release: 'Live Aid' DVD (1984), Queen 'Live At Wembley Stadium' DVD, Genesis 'Live At Wembley Stadium' DVD (1–4/7/87)

Wembley Stadium's (the national stadium) original twin towers overlooked some of the most famous British sporting events as well as the biggest acts in the world. Sport had been played on the site since the 1880s and was a golf course until 1918 when work started on The Empire Stadium. Built by Sir John Simpson and Maxwell Ayerton, the stadium took only 300 days to build and cost £750,000. The stadium was opened in 1924.

On 13 July 1985 Wembley Stadium was the British venue for Live Aid where acts such as Queen, U2, Adam Ant and Status Quo rocked the world. The original stadium also hosted the final Wham! gig as well as gigs by Prince, Oasis, Tina Turner, Bruce Springsteen, Genesis and The Eagles. The original capacity was 74,000. Bon Jovi was the last group to play the stadium before the bulldozers moved in to demolish it in 2003.

Michael Jackson played the stadium an amazing fifteen times; The Rolling Stones 12 times; U2 and Madonna both played eight times. Elton John played seven times and Bon Jovi five times. U2 played on 12 and 13 June 1987 on their 'Joshua Tree' tour with support from The Pogues, Lou Reed, The Pretenders, along with other groups. U2 returned on 11, 12, 20 and 21 August 1993 with their 'Zoo TV – Zooropa' tour, and the boys were joined on stage by author Salman Rushdie on the eleventh of that month. Tickets for the twentieth were poor sellers, and U2 consequently let the unemployed in for free if they had their UB40 card as proof. Apart from Live Aid the original stadium also had events like the Nelson Mandela Tributes (1988 and 1990), Freddie Mercury Tribute (1992) and Amnesty International (1989).

Bon Jovi was to be the first group to headline the at the new stadium in 2006, but delays in construction meant cancellations for all gigs scheduled in 2006. Robbie Williams, The Rolling Stones and the reformed Take That were also due to play the stadium in 2006. The Stones moved to Twickenham and Take That took their fans to the Milton Keynes Bowl instead. The actual first headline act at the new stadium was George Michael on 9 June 2007 who was fined £130,000 for over-running his show by thirteen minutes (£10,000 a minute) into the venue's curfew. Gigs followed by Muse who played two nights in June 2007 and Metallica in July 2007. The stadium was the venue for the Diana and the Live Earth concerts in July 2007.

The new stadium has a 133-metre-high arch and a more amazing 2,600 toilets. The stadium cost £757 million to build and completion was over six months late. Ed Sheeran has been the only act to play the stadium completely solo (just him and his guitar), playing three nights in July 2015.

The White Horse (Hampstead)
Address: 154 Fleet Road, Hampstead Heath, London, NW3 2QH
Tube: Belsize Park (Northern Line)

Stereolab, The Divine Comedy, Suede (supported by The Auteurs), Lush and PJ Harvey played here in the 1980s. Suede played their first ever live gig on 10 March 1990 on this pub's stage, and the band returned a further three times in 1992. The venue must have held fond memories as it was also the venue for a Suede fan club party/gig in March 2000.

From 1989 to 1993 Too Pure Records held their club, The Sausage Machine, at the White Horse. The venue has now returned to being a pub, concentrating on food and drink.

EAST LONDON

Barking Broadway
Address: The Broadway, Barking, London, IG11 7LS
Tube: Barking (District and Hammersmith & City Lines)
Capacity: 850

The building dates from 1936, although it appears more contemporary due to a refurbishment in 2004. The Bard of Barking, Billy Bragg, played a hometown gig here on his 'Hope Not Hate Tour' on 1 May 2006, however the Broadway usually attracts less interesting performers – such as groups from the 1960s that may have one original member in them (if you are lucky!).

Blackheath
Address: Dartmouth Field, Goffers Road, Blackheath, SE3 0UA
Train: Blackheath

The On Blackheath festival started in 2014 with Frank Turner, Grace Jones and Massive Attack headlining. Moving forward to 2015, the acts of note were Elbow, Madness and Manic Street Preachers while 2016 had James, Belle & Sebastian and Squeeze.

<u>Ace Hotel.</u> Location:100 High Street, Shoreditch, E1 6JQ. Hosts up-and-coming indie bands as well as jazz acts. In operation from around 2013. Train: Shoreditch High Street.
<u>Arts Café.</u> Situated in Toynbee Hall at 28 Commercial Road, E1. The Broken Family Band played in June 2003.
<u>Bricklayers Arms.</u> Razorlight played a guerrilla gig on the roof of this Shoreditch pub to launch their debut album in 2004. Located at 63 Charlotte Street, EC2A 3PE. Tube: Old Street (Northern Line).

Bridgehouse 2
Address: Bidder Street, Canning Town, London, E16 4ST
Tube: Canning Town (Jubilee Line)
Capacity: 200

Of all the lost venues of London, why o why did someone decide to bring back the Bridgehouse? Located in perhaps the roughest part of the city, surrounded by car breakers, garages and waste transfer stations, bands and punters alike must wonder what they are doing here. The road has pot holes the size of vicarage ponds and the concrete paths are broken and veer upwards as if they were a mountain range thrown up by the convergence of tectonic plates. The venue is located in a garage and has a capacity of 200.

Bridge House. Address: 23 Barking Road, Canning Town, London, E16. Located under a flyover near the East India Dock, U2 played their sixth London gig at this pub on 11 December 1979. Electronic groups Blancmange and Depeche Mode (December 1980) were both 'discovered' by their future labels here. Billy Bragg entered a talent contest at the pub in 1982 but failed to win. Iron Maiden practically lived on the pubs stage, playing eight times in 1977 and a total of thirty-five times in all. Others who appeared at the Bridge House include Rory Gallagher (1978), Tom Robinson Band (1977), Squeeze (1977), Ronnie Lane (1981) and Chas and Dave (1981). The pub was central to the Oi! Movement with many of those bands playing the Bridge House. The pub stopped putting on live music in 1982 and the building was later demolished in 2001.

A book by the venue's promoter details the venue's history. *The Bridge House, Canning Town: Memories of a Legendary Rock and Roll Hangout* by Terence Murphy was published in July 2007.

Café Oto. Located at 18–22 Ashwin Street, E8 3DL. Opened in April 2008 in a former printers. Part of the super cool Dalston scene, the café hosted the first gig by the Thurston Moore Band, the band formed by the former member of Sonic Youth and Debbie from My Bloody Valentine, in August 2014. Martin Carthy appeared in 2015. The venue promotes what it calls 'experimental sounds'.

Central Hotel. Located at 150 Barking Road, East Ham, E6 3BD (Tube: Upton Park), Sandy Denny performed here in 1967.

City of London Polytechnic Student Union (CLPSU). Fairholt House, 102–105 Whitechapel High Street, E1, had punks Chelsea (1981) and indie act The Bodines (late 1980s).

Cabot Hall

Address: Cabot Place West, Canary Wharf, London, E14 5AB
Tube: Canary Wharf (Jubilee Line & Docklands Light Rail)
Capacity: 400

Situated in the heart of Thatcher's metropolis, Cabot Hall offered some culture on the doorstep of commerce. The Waterboys played an acoustic gig in the venue in 2004, and others who have graced the stage include June Tabor. The venue also offered comedy and visual-art events. It opened in 1991 but closed in 2006 when the hall was converted into retail units and restaurants. Maybe those City traders did not fancy some evening entertainment when they could be pursuing markets in Asia instead? Commerce 1, Culture 0.

Cargo

Address: Kingsland Viaduct, 83 Rivington Street, Shoreditch, EC2A 3AY
Tube: Old Street (Northern Line)
Capacity: 500

Situated inside a Victorian railway arch, Cargo actually has a modern feel to it once you pass through some heavy wooden entrance doors. There is a yard to chill out in the evening air on some nice benches. The venue, although housed in an industrial structure from another century, has a very contemporary feel to it with some hip furniture, exposed air ducts and bar area.

The bands who play Cargo are of the up-and-coming variety, although Cargo does occasionally host well-known groups such as Coldcut (January 2006), Fields (2006) and Tom McRae (February 2007) live.

Cart and Horses

Address: 1 Maryland Point, Stratford, London, E15 1PF.
Train: Maryland (from Liverpool Street)

This Stratford boozer must have had Iron Maiden living next door, as the group played the pub ten times in 1976 and continued to play loads of gigs here throughout 1977. The pub makes the Iron Maiden connection very clear to this day with the legend 'birthplace of Iron Maiden' sign written all over its elevations. Inside is what amounts to a shrine to the group with posters, photographs and records of the group all over its walls. If you don't like Heavy Metal and you don't like Iron Maiden there's not a lot for you here.

Catch

Address: 22 Kingsland Road, Shoreditch, London, E2 8DA
Tube: Old Street (Northern Line)

Unsigned bands sometimes played for free in this suddenly popular live music area of London. 'On the Rocks', '333 Club', 'The Legion', 'Old Blue Last' and 'Cargo' have all appeared on the scene since around 2002. The venue image on the left is from 2005 and the right is from 2014.

Docklands (London) Arena

Address: Limeharbour, London, E14 9TH
Tube: Crossharbour and London Arena (Docklands Light Rail)
Capacity: 12,500 (standing), 11,500 (seated)
Live release: Erasure 'Wild, live at The London Arena' (video) and Slipknot 'Disasterpeices' (video)

Possibly one of the most uninspiring-looking and soulless venues in London, the Docklands London Arena has failed to deliver on its early promise to host the capital's biggest and best gigs when it opened in 1989. The major reason for this must be its location – stranded somewhere down the arse end of the DLR.

It became more known as a sporting venue (and home to an ice hockey team). The very few live acts that turned up include Erasure (1989), Duran Duran (1991), and Slipknot. A reformed Blondie and INXS played together here on 17 December 2002. The Arena was demolished in 2006 and housing now occupies the site.

ExCeL. This docklands exhibition hall saw A-Ha, Van Morrison, UB40, Roxy Music (with Brian Eno), Simple Minds, Katherine Jenkins and Jools Holland perform during the British International Motor Show (20–30 July 2006). It's been pretty quiet on the gig front since then.
Four Aces. Address: 12 Dalston Lane, Dalston, E8 3BQ. Built in 1886 as the North London Coliseum and Amphitheatre, it became the Dalson Theatre in 1898. In the early 1960s it became known as The Macador, then The Rambling Rose before becoming The Four Aces in 1966. Artists who played here include Stevie Wonder, Bob Marley, Percy Sledge, Prince Buster, Ben E King, Desmond Dekker and Madness. Later became called Labyrinth (see entry) before being demolished in 2007. The CLR James Library and housing now occupy the site.
General Havelock. This pub at 229 High Road, Ilford, ID1 1NE, had a few gigs by John Martyn in 1969. The building remains. Train: Ilford.

The George. This pub at 375 Commercial Road has hosted three gigs by Baby shambles – 24 and 27 January 2005 and 1 February 2005.

Granada (East Ham). Address: 281 Barking Road, London, E6. Phil Everly performed by himself here whilst his brother Don was tripping on speed. The Beatles played in March and November 1963. Now demolished and the site used for car parking for a mosque.

Hackney Attic. Found on the top floor of the Hackney Picturehouse (former Ocean building), 270 Mare Street, E8 1HE, the venue hosted The Darkness in 2002. See Ocean.

Hippodrome Theatre (Ilford). Built in 1909, this theatre at Ilford Lane, Ilford had Gracie Fields, Vera Lynn and George Formby on its stage. Damaged in 1945 when a V2 rocket took out part of the building (and killing fifteen people) the theatre was demolished in 1957, replaced by offices and an Iceland store at the site.

Granada (Walthamstow)

Address: 186 Hoe Street, Walthamstow, London, E17 4QH
Tube: Walthamstow Central (Victoria Line)

The Granada here dates from 1930 and is a Grade II-listed building. Although a cinema, it had practically every important artist of the early years of rock 'n' roll including The Beatles, Roy Orbison (both in 1963), Jerry Lee Lewis, Gene Vincent (1962), Scott Walker, Buddy Holly, The Who (1967) and The Kinks. The Godfather of soul, James Brown, made his UK debut here in March 1966. Gigs stopped in 1973. The building later became a Cannon cinema in 1989, then an Odeon for a short spell in 1990 when it was sold to EMD Cinemas (with a clause from the Odeon chain preventing it from screening English language films). The cinema closed in 2009 and was sold to the United Church of The Kingdom of God, who tried, unsuccessfully, to turn the cinema into a church. This is the church that currently occupies the former Rainbow and Kilburn National venues and had previously attempted to buy the Brixton Academy.

Hackney Empire
Address: 291 Mare Street, Hackney, London, E8 1EJ
Train: Hackney Central

Built in 1901 for Oswald Stoll's Empire music hall chain, the building was designed by Frank Matcham. This East End theatre has had some noteworthy appearances: Rolling Stone Ronnie Wood played a benefit for Homerton Hospital in February 1991 and Billy Bragg and Kirsty MacColl played together in December 1991. The Hackney Empire was also the venue for early pop television program *Oh Boy* where Cliff Richard, Billy Fury, Adam Faith, Marty Wilde and

Eddie Cochran performed in their black-and-white glory in the late 1950s and early 1960s. The venue underwent restoration around 2004 and Pete Doherty has played several times since. A reformed King Crimson played in 2015.

Hoxton Bar and Kitchen
Address: 2–4 Hoxton Square, London, N1 6NU
Tube: Old Street (Northern Line)
Capacity: 300

This venue is in super fashionable Hoxton and its small gig room, located at the rear of the building, has hosted some very interesting bands on its compact stage. Vampire Weekend, Jessie J, Laura Marling, Florence and The Machine, Mumford and Sons and Rita Ora are some of the diverse acts to have appeared. The venue was taken over by MAMA (who also run The Borderline, Barfly, Jazz Café, The Forum and The Garage) in 2013.

Hoxton Hall
Address: 130 Hoxton Street, Shoreditch, London, N1 6SH
Tube: Old Street (Northern Line)
Capacity: 120

Built in 1863 as a music hall, by 1893 the building had been taken over by the Quakers to be used as a meeting room and was later used as an air raid shelter in the Second World War. Thanks to the Shoreditch/Hoxton area being 'the place to be' for artists and musicians in the early part of the millennium, the hall became a noted venue for the darlings of the London music scene to play. The building is a Grade II*-listed building and has a wooden interior with two levels with cast-iron balconies.

Island (Ilford)

Address: 300–310 High Road, Ilford, IG1 1QW.
Train: Ilford (from Liverpool Street)
Capacity: 1,964

Opened in 1937 as The Regal Cinema for the ABC chain, it became part of the ABC brand in 1962. The cinema closed in 1984 and reopened as a bingo hall. The bingo stopped in 1989 and became The Ilford Island nightclub in 1992 that hosted gigs by George Clinton, Morrissey (1995), Oasis (1994), The Prodigy (1994 and 1995), The Damned (1993) and Squeeze (twice in December 1993). The club closed after a bouncer was shot and it is now an Indian restaurant – the foyer area is a pub. The Island was well named, being encircled by roads, and is next to the police station.

Ilford Palais. The Who appeared at The Palais Des Danse in 1967. The Palais was demolished in 2007 and has been replaced by housing.

Labyrinth. Essex ravers The Prodigy made their live debut in this Hackney club (former Aces High club) on Dalston Lane, E8 3AZ. In the 1990s the club extended into the Gaumont cinema behind it. In 1997 the cinema was purchased by the council and was demolished in 2007 to make way for housing and a library.

Leyton Swimming Baths. The Beatles played these baths in High Road, Leyton on 5 April 1963. Demolished and the site now occupied by a Tesco store.

Mile End Stadium. On 17 June 1995 at the very height of their Britpop fame Blur played to 27,000 fans here (maybe to add to their mockney credentials). The gig was the first time that the band played 'Country House', the song that would latter go head to head in the charts with bitter rivals Oasis. Address: 190 Burdett Road, E3 4HL. Tube: Mile End (Central, District and Hammersmith & City Lines.

The Legion
Address: 348 Old Street, London, EC1V 9NQ
Tube: Old Street (Northern Line)

From 2005 The Legion was home to shoegazing club night 'Sonic Cathedral', which put on gigs by the likes of Ladytron, Telescopes, Engineers, Amusement Parks on Fire, Sonic Boom, Jim Reid (of The Jesus and Mary Chain) and Ride's Mark Gardner. Used occasionally by Plum Promotions (see Betsy Trotwood, Plan B, Water Rats) as another springboard venue for new bands. Take Exit 2 from Old Street tube station.

93 Feet East
Address: Truman's Brewery, 150 Brick Lane, London, E1 6QL
Tube: Liverpool Street (Central, Circle, Hammersmith & City and Metropolitan Lines)
Capacity: 260 (Main Hall) 220 (Pink Bar)

Housed in part of the former Truman's Brewery in Banglatown's Brick Lane, 93 Feet East has a pretty busy schedule with bands on most nights of the week. James Blunt played the venue in early 2005, The Darkness (2001), Joy Zipper in 2004 and The Fall played two nights in 2006. Gigs tend to finish around 11 p.m.

Oscars. A club at Green Gate, Eastern Avenue, Newbury Park, Ilford that had Adam and The Ants in January 1978. The club continued with live bands into the late 1980s.

Oval Space. Address: 29–32 The Oval, E2 9DT. A strange place located in an almost forgotten part of Bethnal Green. The building appears to be a multi-media centre with gigs taken place by the young, mostly experimental bands of London. The 5,000 sq foot of floorspace is spread over two floors and a large glass window gives views to the near-by gasworks. Guests in 2015 included Micahu and The Shapes, The Orb and Mercury Rev.

The Plough Inn. Located at 173 Wood Street, Walthamstow, E17 3NU, this pub dates from 1875. Notable gigs include Wreckless Eric and John Otway, both in 2007. Closed in 2010 and has been converted into apartments.

Power Lunches. Address: 446 Kingsland Road, E8 4AE. One of the many small venues to have appeared around the Shoreditch area.

Ocean/Hackney Attic

Address: 270 Mare Street, Hackney, London, E8 1HE
Train: Hackney Central (from Liverpool Street)
Capacity: 2,100
Live release: Stiff Little Fingers DVD (2004)

Housed in the former Hackney Library and Methodist Hall (opened 1907), Ocean was one of the larger venues to have appeared on the gig circuit in recent times. The venue opened in March 2001 after a £23m input of public money with Soft Cell performing together for the first time in seventeen years over two nights. Calexico, Ash, Sharon Shannon, Fun Lovin' Criminals and New Model Army all followed in the venues first month of opening doors.

The venue's greatest drawback was its size and location, stranded in Hackney some considerable distance from the nearest underground station and a large audience who would need to travel to get there. By 2006 Ocean seemed to have hit calm waters with every indication that its remote location had forced its closure. Hackney Council took over the building in 2006, when the trust set up to run Ocean (Ocean Music Trust in 1999) folded. The building was taken over by Picturehouse Cinemas in 2011 and Ocean turned into a four screen, 550 seat cinema. However, the top floor is a small venue called Hackney Attic, where The Darkness and Lesley Woods of The Au-Pairs (2014) have played.

The Old Blue Last (see Pl.29)
Address: 39 Great Eastern Street, London, EC2 3HY
Tube: Old Street (Northern Line)
Capacity: 120

The Old Blue Last pub dates from 1876. Irish performer Simple Kid played a four-night residency here in March/April 2006, whilst Clor and Do Me Bad Things have also played in the pub. The Artic Monkeys played a low key gig at the Old Blue Last on 25 May 2006 – breaking in new bassist Nick O'Malley before an overseas tour, while original bass player Andy Nicholson was unable to tour (and was later replaced permanently by O'Malley). Pop princess Kylie played a few songs here in February 2014. Other significant acts to have played include Hotchip (2005), Lily Allen (2006), Florence and The Machine (2007), The La's (2011) and Mumford and Sons (2007).

The Old Blue Last is owned by *Vice* Magazine. Sometimes offers free gigs by new groups.

On The Rocks
Address: 25 Kingsland Road, Shoreditch, London, E2 8AA
Tube: Old Street (Northern Line)
Capacity: 300

Unsigned bands are a specialty at this venue located in the fashionable area of Shoreditch. Almost opposite the venue is the 'On the Rocks' rehearsal room. Closed in 2010 and now called Basing House and has electronic music. The Darkness played in 2001.

Oslo

Address: 1A Amhurst Road, Hackney, London, E8 1LL
Train: Hackney Central (from Stratford)
Capacity: 375

Located next to Hackney Central station, the Oslo has a reputation for Scandanvian dining and live bands. The venue is on the first floor and has had Sean Lennon (Ghost of a Saber Tooth Tiger) perform in May 2015 and Mumford and Sons played on 9 and 10 March 2015, showcasing their new album 'Wilder Mind'. Run by DHP who also own Rock City and Bogeda in Nottingham.

The Pleasure Unit
Address: 359 Bethnal Green Road, London, E2 6LG
Tube: Bethnal Green (Central Line)
Capacity: 150

Former Libertine and Babyshambles frontman Pete Doherty played two acoustic shows at The Pleasure Unit in August 2004. Billy Childish's Buff Medways played in January 2006 and returned in March 2006.

The Pleasure Unit had pretty full weeks of bands playing and offered a spring board to unsigned groups. However it closed and a bar called The Star of Bethnal Green now occupies the building.

Red Lion (Leytonstone)/Chez Club
Location: 640 High Road, Leytonstone, London, E11 3AA.
Tube: Leytonstone (Central Line)

This pub hosted The Who (three times in 1964 and once in 1965), Jethro Tull, Tyrannosaurus Rex (1968), Led Zeppelin, Genesis, Roxy Music and Fleetwood Mac. The Chez Club relocated to The Red Lion from the Chestnut Tree (on Lea Bridge Street) briefly in 1971, and hosted Hawkwind, Slade, Barclay James Harvest and Pink Friaries in its time here.

The Red Lion is where members of Iron Maiden meet Paul Di'Anno for the first time in 1978 and later auditioned him to be the group's lead singer.

Although it had been dormant for a while, not attracting 'name' bands, the pub continued to host live music. Damon Albarn – who spent the first part of his childhood in Leytonstone – popped in in 2014 and performed a version of 'Parklife' (for a TV crew of course!). Although the pub has been open, there have been restoration works carried out on the exterior of the building for two years and when the scaffolding is removed a beautifully detailed building should be revealed.

Rex (Stratford)
Address: 361–375 High Street, Stratford, London, E15 4QE
Tube: Stratford High Street (DLR)
Capacity: 3,000

The Rex opened in 1896 as the Frank Matcham-designed Borough Theatre and Opera House, closing in 1933. The front corner facade was resigned by George Coles and the building reopened in 1934 as The Rex.

Manfred Mann appeared in 1972 and was followed on stage some years later by The Prodigy (1997), Lil' Wayne (2008), Foo Fighters (2000) and Queens of The Stone Age (2000). A doorman was shot dead in 1999 at a Beenie Man gig. The venue was run for a while by Vince Power, but the building stood empty for a while until becoming a nightclub called Sync in 2014. The building is owned by the local Newham Council.

Rhythm Factory
Address: 16–18 White Chapel Road, London, E1 1EW
Tube: Aldgate East (District and Hammersmith & City Lines)
Capacity: 400

The Rhythm Factory opened in February 2004 and offers a mixed menu. On one hand they have up- and-coming London groups with a battle of the bands competition, whilst on the other they have gigs by Selfish Cunt and other breakthrough signed bands. The Libertines played many gigs here in 2003.

At the front of the venue is a small bar/café where you can relax by watching a musician or a poet perform. Behind the café area are two stage areas where the main attractions play.

Former Libertine Pete Doherty's Babyshambles were booked to play the venue in early 2005, but it was another gig that they infamously cancelled at the last minute. However, the band returned in January 2007 to play three nights here, and one those was a solo acoustic performance by Pete Doherty. Pete returned to the venue in December 2007 to play another solo set.

Rough Trade East (see Pl.32)
Address: Dray Walk, Brick Lane, London, E1 6QL
Tube: Liverpool Street (Central, Circle and District Lines)

To the far end of this record shop, past the racks of CDs, past the shelves of books and magazines and beyond the sales counter is the discreet Rough Trade Stage where a fairly regular schedule of in-store performances take place. The Manic Street Preachers played a set here in 2014 to promote their latest album – Futurology. The Rough Trade website details all their forthcoming in-store events. A wristband is needed to gain entry to the show.

The Roundhouse (Dagenham/Upney)/Village Roundhouse (see Pl.34)
Address: Junction of Lodge Avenue with Porters Avenue, Dagenham, London, RM1 2HY
Tube: Upney/Becontree (District Line)

The Roundhouse was active between 1969 and 1975 when it hosted The Village Blues Club and was known as the premier East London music venue where Led Zeppelin, Genesis, Thin Lizzy, Pink Floyd, Queen, Status Quo and Deep Purple played. The building was a former bingo hall that had a 2,000 capacity and two stages – one being no more than a wooden board on beer crates. Behind the venue is a new residential development called Bragg Close, which was named after local boy Billy Bragg. The venue is located between Upney and Becontree Underground stations and still has occasional gigs – usually by 1960s bands that have reformed.

Red Lion (Barking). This pub at 66–68 North Street, IG11 8JD, was built in 1899 and hosted Paul Simon in 1965. Closed in 2008 and converted into flats. Tube: Barking.

Ruskin Arms. Iron Maiden played a few gigs here at 386 High Street North, Manor Park (Newham), E12 6PH, in the 1970s. The Small Faces rehearsed here possibly because the pub was run by the father of original Small Faces keyboardist Jimmy Winston. Although it closed briefly in 2008 it has since reopened as a pub and hotel. Tube: East Ham (District and Hammersmith & City Lines).

Servant Jazz Quarters. Located at 10a Bradbury Street, Dalston, in what appears to be a terraced house. Train: Dalston Kingsland (from Stratford).

Shoreditch Town Hall. 380 Old Street, EC1. Had Flowered Up live at the height of their brief Baggy powers. Genesis played in 1972.

St John's at Hackney. Address: Lower Clapton Road, Hackney, E5 0PD. This is a 1,400 standing capacity church that was built in 1792, designed by James Spiller and is a Grade II*-listed building. The roll call of bands playing the venue is very impressive and includes; Coldplay (2015 and 2011), Bloc Party, Cat Power, Jamie XX (all in 2015), Bonnie 'Prince' Billy, Jessie Ware (both in 2014), Keane, Richard Hawley, Gary Barlow (both in 2012). Train: Hackney Central.

St Nicks Hall. Iron Maiden made their live debut on 1 May 1976 and got paid £5 to cover their expenses. Appears to have been renamed Langley Hall and is at Aberfeldy Street, Poplar, E14 0QD.

Stratford Town Hall. The Who played on 16 May 1965. On the Broadway, Stratford.

Strongroom. At 120–124 Curtain Road, EC2A 3SQ, this bar is next to Strongroom Studios and Richard Boote is the owner of both. The bar hosts mainly unknown London rock groups.

Sundown. A small London-based chain of live music venues operated by Rank around 1972 (and closed soon after opening). There were three Sundowns all in Ranks cinemas. In Brixton the Sundown was opened by a gig from Deep Purple and the building is what later became The Brixton Academy. In Mile End, the Odeon at 401 Mile End Road became a Sundown and had Slade in September 1972, Fleetwood Mac in November 1972 and John Martyn and Sandy Denny also played that year. Closed as a music venue in 1973 and reverted back to a cinema although it was demolished in 1984. The Who played the Edmonton Sundown venue four times in December 1973 and this was apparently the most successful of the Sundown venues. Steppenwolf also played here. (See Edmonton Regal entry.)

Sebright Arms
Address: 31–35 Coate Street, Bethnal Green, London, E2 9AG
Train: Cambridge Heath (from Liverpool Street)

The Sebright Arms is a pub built on the site of the former Sebright Music Hall. In the 1970s the pub was a Heavy Metal pub. The pub closed in 2009 and was set to be demolished, however the wrecking ball never made and instead it reopened in 2012, attracting more of an indie crowd. Those to have played include Ash, Foxes, Grant Nicholas, Kate Nash, Maximo Park, Lucy Rose,

The Fat White Family, Jim Jones Revue, The Vaccines and Viv Albertine. Palma Violets played on 31 January 2015. The pub also operates The Miller venue/pub at London Bridge.

The Shacklewell Arms
Address: 71 Shacklewell Lane, London, E8 2EB
Train: Dalston Kingsland (from Stratford)

The pub, dating from the 1870s, had previously been a St Lucian-focused establishment (and a bit of a crack den with a very bad reputation locally). Taken over by new management in 2011, the new landlords started putting on gigs. It probably helped that the new owners were both well-known London promoters (Tom Baker of Eat Your Own Ears and Dan Crouch of the Lock Tavern) and had Jamie XX, Solange (Beyonce's sister), Erin McKeowen (2013) and The Horrors playing the pub (promoting their 'Skying' album in 2011). The pub retains its St Lucian tropical décor inside and its homespun exterior.

The Spitz
Address: Old Spitalfields Market, 109 Commercial Street, London, E1 6BG
Tube: Liverpool Street (Central/Circle Lines)
Capacity: 250 (standing)

Located in the historic Spitalfields Market and close to Brick Lane, The Spitz offered gigs on most nights and included jazz, techno, funk, pop, indie and rock acts. Erin McKeown and Paul Kelly are notable names who have played the venue. Beth Orton played three gigs here in December 2005 and returned to join folk legend Bert Jansck onstage in 2006.

Spitalfields Market was designed by Horner in 1887 in an Arts and Craft style and is known as a left of centre shopping area, with market traders and independent shops. Part of the market was demolished and rebuilt in 2003 and attracted new tenants who paid higher rents. As a result the tenants in the original building saw their rents increase, which lead to The Spitz closing in October 2007.

As well as being a music venue, The Spitz was also a gallery, bar and bistro. The venue part of the Spitz was upstairs and had perhaps the most colourful interior of any venue in the capital. The stage was compact and slightly raised with a small yet functional bar in one of the corners of the room. The floor had a traditional picque wooden-block flooring.

The Spitz was part of The Dandelion Trust charity and there was rumoured to be a replacement home for the Spitz during the lead up to the closure – however, nothing has ever materialised.

The Standard Music Venue
Address: 1 Blackhorse Lane, Walthamstow, London, E17 6DS
Tube: Blackhorse Road (Victoria Line)

The Standard Music Venue specialises in tribute bands, so expect to see T-Rextasy, Gunz to Roses and others imitating their heroes. Very occasionally had an act who had seen better times (and larger stages) appear, such as Jayne County, John Otway (1986), Girlschool (1987), Samson (1988), Bad Manners (1987), The Sweet (1990), Glen Tilbrook (1995) and Wilko Johnson (2008). The venue closed in 2011 and has been unoccupied since then.

St Lukes
Address: LSO St Lukes, Old Street, London, EC1V 9NG
Tube: Old Street (Northern Line)

Part of the Barbican Centre and home to the London Symphony Orchestra, St Lukes was designed by Hawksmere (who also designed Christchurch in Spitalfields). St Lukes is an eighteenth- century church and a Grade I-listed building.

St Lukes tends to be the favoured venue of BBC producers who have staged Antony and the Johnsons (in 2005) as part of BBC 4's 'Sessions', Sting (during his lute phase), Nora Jones and Rosanne Cash (all in 2006). Brian Ferry took part in the series in 2007 while he was promoting his album of Bob Dylan covers. Crooner Tony Bennett was also recorded here in 2007.

333 Club/333 Mother/London Apprentice
Address: 303 Old Street, Shoreditch, London, EC1V 9LE
Tube: Old Street (Northern Line)

Another venue in the fashionable Hoxton area and a former gay bar until taken over by Vicky Pengill in 1990. The Mother Bar opened in 1999. The 333 specialised in unsigned bands doing the rounds in the capital, although Razorlight, Pete Doherty and Groove Armada have played. It was called the London Apprentice in 2014.

The Troxy (see Pl.39)
Address: 490 Commercial Road, Stepney, London, E1 0HX
Tube: Limehouse (DLR)
Capacity: 3,100

Built in 1933 as an Art Deco cinema designed by George Coles with an original 3,500 capacity and a revolving stage. Even way back then The Troxy hosted gigs by the likes of Vera Lynn, Gracie Fields, The Andrews Sisters, Petula Clark and Cliff Richard. The venue closed in November 1960, partly as a hangover from the damage sustained during World War Two and partly due to the general decline of this part of London. However, it did not stand idol for too long as from 1963 to 1977 it was the home to The London Opera Centre. By the 1980's the centre had left the building and it was being used as a bingo hall until 2005. The building was made a Grade II

Listed Building in 1991. The Troxy is owned by Ashburn Estates and has been used for gigs when the bingo hall called its final 'house!'. Those to have played include; Morrissey, The Jesus and Mary Chain (performing 'Psychocandy' 2014), The Pixies, The Gaslight Anthem (2013), The Specials (2014) and London Grammar (2014).

Turnmills
Address: 63 Clerkenwell Road, London, EC1
Tube: Farringdon (Circle/Hammersmith & City and Metropolitan Lines)

Was the home to the Heavenly Social where the Chemical Brothers were the resident DJs. More recently music press darlings The Horror's performed at Turnmills on 27 January 2007. Since then the venue has closed and the building used for other purposes before being demolished.

The Upper Cut
Address: Forest Gate Centre, Woodgrange Road, Forest Gate, E7
Train: Forest Gate (from Liverpool Street)

Jimi Hendrix played the Upper Cut on Boxing Day 1966, but not before writing Purple Haze in the dressing room beforehand, and then performing it for the first time that night. The Who (1966), Pink Floyd (Jan 1967), The Troggs (May 1967), The Easybeats, The Animals, Otis Reading, Pretty Things, Spencer Davies Group and Gong/Daevid Allen (June 1989) have also played here. The venue was run by former boxer Billy Walker. It later became a disco called Ace of Clubs and is now demolished with only a plaque on some gates to remember it by.

Tower of London. The Tower Music Festival was in June/July 2006 and featured The Pet Shop Boys, Jamie Cullum, Dionne Warwick and others. Previously in May 2006 The Princes Trust stage an event featuring The Sugababes and Embrace among others.

Trinity Boat Wharf. The Streets played a secret gig here on 21 March 2006 for competition winners.

The Victoria. 451 Queensbridge Road, Dalston, E8 3AS. Run by Jaguar Shoes Art Collective and Ben Heath (who ran Catch between 2001 and 2009), this 150-capacity pub has had Franz Ferdinand (2013) and Slaves (2014) on its stage. Train: Dalston Junction (from Stratford). The gig space is accessed through a secret bookcase door beside the main bar.

Victoria Park. Address: Victoria Park, Approach Road, Hackney, London, E3. Tube: Mile End (Central Line). Capacity: 10,000. Tom Robinson, X-Ray Spex, The Ruts and The Clash played the first Rock Against Racism gig in Victoria Park in April 1978. In 2005 the Lovebox Weekender moved to the park and had Groove Armada and Mylo perform on stage. Returning in July 2006 with Jamiroquai, Hot Chip and The Feeling playing. In July 2007 Lovebox had Blondie and The B-52's as the major draws. Radiohead played a headline gig in the park on 24 June 2008. By 2015 Victoria Park had become the go to park for an outdoor festival in London and hosted the Citadel festival (Ben Howard, Bombay Bicycle Club), Lovebox (Rudimental and Snoop Dogg) and Field Day. The park is a five-minute walk from the tube station and there is no car parking in the area. The park was opened in 1845 and is also known locally as Vicky Park and The People's Park.

Walthamstow Technical College. Address: Forest Road. This college hosted Deep Purple, America, Jeff Beck Group (1967), Pink Floyd (1969), Love (1970), Fleetwood Mac (1971), Sandy Denny (1971), The Kinks (1972) and Taj Mahal.

Walthamstow Youth Centre. Joy Division played this centre in Mark House Road E17 on 30 March 1979, with a 50p entrance fee. The youth centre was part of a school and has since been demolished.

Whitechapel Gallery. Alex James, Blur's bassist, played a solo gig here as part of 'Art Plus Music' fundraiser on 31 March 2006.

Village Underground (see Pl.42)

Address: 54 Holywell Lane, London, EC2A 3PQ
Tube: Old Street (Northern Line)
Capacity: 450

Village Underground is warehouse dating from around 1900, now with four London Underground tube carriages on its roof. Jarvis Cocker had a week's residency here in November 2009. The Pixies played a gig here to promote their Minotaur boxset, whereas Laiback, Roni Size, Joan As Policewoman, Bob Mould and Albert Hammond Jr have played standard gigs here in Spring 2014. Julian Cope played in early 2015.

The venue is owned by Auro Foxcroft.

Walthamstow Assembly Rooms (see Pl.46)

Address: Forest Road, Walthamstow, London, E17 4JD
Tube: Walthamstow Central (Victoria Line)
Capacity: 1,150

70p in November 1976 would have brought you a ticket to see Iron Maiden at the Hall. Others to have played include The Sex Pistols (1976) and New Order (1981). A Grade II Listed Building from the 1940s with Art Deco stylings, located next to the equally stunning Walthamstow Town Hall.

What's Cooking Club

Address: upstairs at Leytonstone Ex-Serviceman's Club, Harvey Road, E11

The club offers acoustic gigs on Wednesdays and Saturdays. Tube: Leytonstone (Central Line).

Wilton's Music Hall (see Pl.48)

Address: Graces Alley (off Ensign Street), London, E1 8JB
Tube: Tower Hill or Aldgate West (District/Circle/Hammersmith & City Lines)
Capacity: 300 (seated)

Dating from 1858 this beautiful old music hall is a treasure down a London back alley. At its most popular during the music hall heyday of the mid-1800s the well-known song 'Champagne Charlie' was written inside these decaying walls. Closed for entertainment in 1880 after a fire damaged the hall, the London Wesleyan Mission soon moved in. The hall was used as an air raid shelter during the Second World War, but closed as a Methodist mission in the 1950s and was reused as a warehouse for rags. A campaign led by no other than Sir John Betjeman got the hall a Grade II*-listed building status saved it during the slum clearances of the 1970s. It was opened in 2004 by the Wilton's Music Hall Trust and has had performances by Marc Almond and KT Tunstall. Annie Lennox filmed the video for 'No More I Love You's' at Wilton's, as did Suede for 'Attitude'. Duran Duran appeared here on 19 February 2015 as part of the Warchild 'Back to The Bars' series of gigs.

XOYO

Address: 32–37 Cowper Street, London, EC2A 4AP
Tube: Old Street (Northern Line)

Based in a former printworks, Xoyo was opened in 2010 by London promoters Eat Your Own Ears and Bugged Out. Swedish band The Shout Out Louds performed in these early years. Sold in August 2012 to Andy Peyton, Xoyo is now pretty much just for clubbers rather than gig-goers, although the occasional gig still occurs.

SOUTH LONDON

The Albany Empire
Address: Douglas Way, Deptford, SE8 4AG
Train: Deptford (from London Bridge)

Originally a theatre in Creek Street (until it was demolished in the early 1980s) where Punk and New Wave groups played, the Albany moved to Douglas Way in 1981. The building is totally unremarkable and appears as an oversized bungalow with glazed box dormers.

A wide range of artists have played at the Albany and include; Alternative TV, Charlie Watts Big Band, Elvis Costello, Burning Spear, Bo Diddley, Sade, The Chieftains and The Fall.

Amersham Arms (New Cross)

Address: 388 New Cross Road, New Cross, London, SE14 6TY
Tube: New Cross (East London Line)

The pub dates from 1858 and was previously called the Amersham Hotel. Notable performers have included Suede, who played on 12 February 1992, and fellow Britpoppers Menswear in 1994. Professional Cockney's Chas and Dave appeared in February and May 2007, and Wilko Johnson played in March 2007. Jonathan Richman took to the Amersham's stage in 2010. Steve Craddock (Paul Weller's axeman) bought his band here in 2014. Carl Barat and The Jackals played on New Year's Eve 2014 before moving onto their second gig of the night at The MacBeth.

The venue is popular with indie band members who have a sideline in being a DJ and often spin their wheels of steel here. The pub is located close to Goldsmiths College, which goes some way to explain the appeal of the venue to bands.

Ambulance Station. Address: 306 Old Kent Road, Borough, London, SE1. A venue that the Jesus and Mary Chain trashed on 25 November 1984. The Butthole Surfers also played here, as did The Membranes, Television Personalities and the June Brides in 1984. Now demolished and a car park occupies the land. The site is next door to the Thomas A Beckett pub.

Battersea College. The Animals played here on 11 February 1966.

Battersea Park. The Strangers played this South London park on 16 September 1978 and caused a storm when during 'Nice 'N' Sleazy' the band were joined on stage by a group of strippers (and one naked male as well).

Battersea Power Station. For a week in 1994 this most iconic London landmark hosted a series of gigs that included one by Morrissey. The Prodigy (supported by Placebo) played in December 1997.

The Bedford. The Finn Brothers played here on 8 November 2004 and the gig was broadcast on Radio 2. Video footage of the gig later turned up on the 'Edible Flowers' DVD single. The Bedford had regular gigs sometimes with 'name' artists. The Bedford is at 77 Bedford Hill, Balham, London, SW12 9HD.

The Black Cat. An R&B club at 5 Vincent Road, Woolwich, SE18 6RF, that had Sonny Boy Williamson on stage in December 1964. Currently called The Bull Tavern.

Black Sheep (Croydon). Address: 68 High Street, Croydon, CR0 1NA. Train: East Corydon. Offered live music from every genre, although the Cosmic Rough Riders are the only act of note to have played this Croydon venue. Opened between 1997 and 2013.

Blue Horizon. This club, which ran upstairs in the three-storey Nag's Head pub at 205 York Road, Battersea, SW11 3SA, had Free performing their first gig in May 1968. Fleetwood Mac also played here. The building has been demolished.

Brixton Prison. This South London Gaol was the bizarre location for Simon and Garfunkel's first UK gig in 1965. Located at Jebb Avenue, SW2 5XF.

Burgess Park. 'London United' took place here on 16 July 2005 to defy the terrorist who bombed London on 6 June 2005. Madness frontman Suggs, along with Billy Bragg, were among those to perform at this free festival.

Broadway Theatre (see Lewisham Theatre).

Bunch of Grapes. This pub at 2 St Thomas Street, SE1 9RS had Japan in April 1975. Tube: London Bridge (Jubilee and Northern Lines).

Butler's Wharf. The Sex Pistols played a warehouse party here (near Tower Bridge) at the home of artist Andrew Logan in 1976. Footage of the gig appears in the film *The Great Rock 'n' Roll Swindle* during lesson three.

Blackheath Halls

Address: 23 Lee Road, Blackheath, London, SE3 9RQ
Train: Blackheath (from Charing Cross)
Capacity: 1,000

This rather nice Grade II-listed building is located close to Blackheath train station. The Fabulous Thunderbirds played in 1996, and the Kim Deal (Pixies) fronted The Breeders graced the Halls stage in November 2005. Former Giant Sand front man Howie Gelb played in 2006, as did former Icicle Works frontman Ian McNabb. The venue has a stronger focus on music with a classical bias, although folk artists Kate Rusby and Cara Dillon both appeared in May 2014.

Borough Hall (Greenwich)

Address: Royal Hill, Greenwich, SE10 8RE
Tube: Greenwich (DLR)

A PRS plaque marks the Borough Halls as being the first venue that Squeeze played live in 1975. The building was part of the civic centre that was opened in 1938. The Hall is still standing and now houses the Greenwich Dance Agency.

Brixton Academy/Brixton O2 Academy/Fair Deal/Sundown (see Pl.4)

Address: 211 Stockwell Road, Brixton, SW9 9SL
Tube: Brixton (Victoria Line)
Capacity: 4,921.
Live release: Motorhead '25' DVD (2000), Franz Ferdinand DVD (2005)

The Brixton Academy was built in 1929 as The Astoria Theatre Cinema, designed by E. A. Stone, and was hailed as one of the finest buildings in the country to view films. The Astoria remained as a cinema until July 1972 when it closed. The Astoria reopened in September 1972 as a live music venue called the Sundown Centre. The original stalls were removed to make a large dance floor; the circle the seats were left. The Sundown Centre did not last long and closed in January 1973.

In 1974 there was a proposal to demolish the Astoria and build a car showroom in its place, but thankfully planning permission was not given to knock down the Grade II-listed building. Instead the building was used as a massive storeroom by the Rank Organisation. The building was reopened as a music venue again in 1981, this time called The Fair Deal, but come 1982 the Fair Deal had closed. However, the building refused to lay idle and in 1983 The Brixton Academy was open for business. Notable acts that played in its early years include The Clash, who in 1985 played three nights, The Smiths played twice in 1986 (and was the venue for their last ever gig on 12 December). During this period the venue had a daytime job as rehearsal space for the major recording artists of the day (The Police, Dire Straits etc) and as a pop-video location (as seen in the Pet Shop Boys 'What have I done to deserve this?' and Billy Ocean's 'When the going gets tough…').

In 1995 The Academy was bought by Break For The Border group (who already had The Borderline and Shepherds Bush Empire). The Academy has since been bought by The McKenzie Group and then sold to the Academy Music Group.

Many major artists have played the Academy including The Rolling Stones, Madonna, Radiohead, The Ramones, Bruce Springsteen, Morrissey and Eminem. Bob Dylan played five nights in a row here in December 2005, and the £35 tickets were being sold on eBay for close to £300. The Academy continues to attract major groups as well as bands of the moment who are enjoying success. Others who have played here include Debbie Harry (in June 1990 on her 'Dirty Harry' tour), The Kaiser Chiefs, The Pogues (practically every December) and the Pet Shop Boys (on their 'Release' tour in July 2002).

The Academy has retained many of its original features including its proscenium arch over the stage and its Art Deco features. The building was designed to give the illusion of an Italian garden – hence the trees and statues in alcoves either side of the stage while stars sparkle on the ceiling. A slightly sloping floor leads down to the stage area and ensures a good view from the entire floor area. Sound quality down at the front is pretty good. The Academy is often voted the 'Best Live Venue' by the readers of the *NME*.

The controversial Michael Winterbottom film *9 Songs* was set in the Academy. The full capacity is 4,921, with 3,760 standing downstairs, 1,083 seated and 78 standing in the upper circle.

A book about the venue *Live at The Brixton Academy, A Riotous Life in the Music Business* by Simon Parks was published by Serpent's Tail in 2014. Simon Parks started The Brixton Academy and we learn the following:

– it was built as an Atmospheric Cinema and designed by TR Somerford and Edward Albert Stone and was the showpiece cinema of the Atmospheric chain (which also included The Rainbow in Finsbury Park).
– the design theme was 'Mediterranean Nights' and that the half-cupola on the exterior entrance to the proscenium arch is modeled on the Rialto Bridge in Venice.
– that Parks brought the building's lease for £1 from Watneys Brewery (who had subleased it from Rank who then charged £150,000 for their lease) and that the lease has no rent reviews from when it was built to 2029. The rent is set at £2,600 a year.
– the building is owned by an old, landed family who have no other interest in the building.
– Parks saw the Hammersmith Odeon (operated by Rank) as his main rival and was convinced gig crowds would prefer to stand at a gig rather than be seated like at the Odeon.
– the first gig under the Academy name was by Eek-A-Mouse. The first rock gig was by The Cult.

The book is a good read, although it suffers the same fate by many books about venues – a strong focus on the violent/criminal elements that are attracted to venues.

Brooklyn Bowl

Address: The O2, Building 5, Entertainment Way, London, SE10 0DX
Tube: North Greenwich (Jubilee Line)
Capacity: 800

Located inside The O2, this bowling alley-cum-restaurant also has occasional gigs. Those to have played include The Roots, Gomez, Elvis Costello, Lady Antebellum and Lauryn Hill (2014). The Charlatans played here on 20 February 2015 shortly before performing at The Brit Awards.

Charlton Athletic Football Club. Address: The Valley, Floyd Road, Charlton, London, SE7 8BL. Train: Charlton. Capacity: 50,000. The Who headlined here on 18 May 1974 supported by Lou Reed, Humble Pie, Bad Company, Lindisfarne and Maggie Bell. The Who returned in May 1976 and became the loudest live band in the world (according to the *Guinness Book of Records*) racking up 120 decibels. Elton John played The Valley on 4 July 2006 and was quieter.

Clapham Bandstand. Dire Straits played the bandstand at Clapham Common on 10 September 1977 as part of Charlie Gillet's Honky Tonk Radio Show. Built in 1890, the bandstand is a Grade II-listed Building. Address: Windmill Drive, SW4 9DE.

Clapham Common. Address: Clapham, London, SW4 9BS. Tube: Clapham Common (Northern Line). A park that occasionally hosts the gigs a couple a times a year. In 1986 the Anti-Apartheid Movement held a concert here featuring Sting and Peter Gabriel. The Happy Mondays and Billy Bragg have also turned up on the Common. Now hosts 'Ben and Jerry's Summer Sundae', which has featured acts like The Brakes, Kate Nash, The Bees (all in 2007), Badly Drawn Boy and Echo and The Bunnymen since 2005. Home to The Calling Festival since it left Hyde Park and has had Aerosmith as a headline act.

The Crypt (Deptford). Address: Under St Paul's Church, Diamond Way, Deptford, SE8 3DS. Tube: Deptford Bridge (DLR). Television Personalities (July 1985) and Ozric Tentacles (1985 & 86) played this Thomas Archer-designed English Halienate Baroque church as well as other groups.

The Crypt (Camberwell). Address: St Giles Church Crypt, 81 Camberwell Church Street, SE5 8RB. Train: Denmark Hill. Capacity: 150. A jazz venue. Denmark Hill train station is approximately 1 mile away from the venue.

Crystal Palace Bowl. Address: Crystal Palace Park, Norwood, SE19. Train: Crystal Palace (from Victoria and London Bridge). Built in 1961 by the Greater London Council (GLC), groups such as Pink Floyd, Bob Marley, The Beach Boys, Yes and Elvis Costello gigged here. Later, indie groups like The Cure, Depeche Mode, Ride and The Pixies (June 1991) played here as well. A new concert platform was built in 1997.

Crystal Palace National Sports Centre. Address: Ledrington Road, Crystal Palace, London, SE19 2BB. Train: Crystal Palace. A reformed Sex Pistols played here, supported by The Libertines in July 2002. The National Sports Centre had M People play on 16 June 1996. Located next to the main entrance of Crystal Palace train station. Site has 1,000 car parking spaces and is off the A214.

Cartoon (Croydon)
Address: 179–183 London Road, Croydon, CR0 2RJ
Train: West Croydon (from London Bridge)

Both unsigned and up and coming indie bands have played the Cartoon, Art Brut being one of the more noteworthy. The Fall played a short residency here in 2006. The Cartoon was open between 1976 to 2006. The building is currently a restaurant.

The Castle

Address: The Castle, 38 High Street, Tooting, London, SW17 0RG
Tube: Tooting Broadway (Northern Line)

This pub, which dates from 1832, had Mott The Hoople (April 1970), Status Quo and Free playing when the groups were lean and hungry. The then unknown The Darkness played in November 2001. The Castle is now a bog-standard pub with a better chance of seeing large-screen football matches than bands earning their chops.

Coronet (Elephant and Castle)

Address: 28 New Kent Road, Elephant and Castle, London, SE1 6TJ
Tube: Elephant and Castle (Northern Line)
Capacity: 2,200
Live releases: Peter and the Test Tube Babies 'Keep Britain Untidy' DVD (2004).

This allegedly Art Deco building, which is unfortunately wrapped in rather horrible blue panels, was opened in 1879 as the Elephant and Castle Theatre, becoming a cinema in the 1920s. The ABC cinema closed in 1999, and then opened as The Coronet, a multi-media venue, in Easter 2003. The auditorium has 572 seats.

Primal Scream played the Coronet on 24 January 2004 and were joined on stage by Shane MacGowan for two songs: 'Loaded' and 'Born to Lose'. Babyshambles played the Coronet in October 2004, and Oasis played in May 2005, followed later in the year by The Bees. Dirty Pretty Things played a benefit gig for the 'Make Roads Safe' campaign in September 2006.

The Coronet is a venue that often hosted gigs especially for 'under 18's' and groups with a Myspace following, although established artists, such as Patrick Wolf (in early 2007), have played 'under 18' gigs here.

In July 2014 the venue operators expressed concern that the landlords Delancey and Southwark Council had not begun discussions over the future of the Coronet, and that as such it could close in November 2015 when the lease expires. In their plea the venue stated that it employed over 100 people, had more than 250,000 customers every year, was a community asset and had £2 million ready to make improvements to the building. A petition was started to save the building. To get to the venue, take the 'shopping centre' exit from the tube station.

Coronet (Woolwich)

Address: Gateway House, John Wilson Street, Woolwich, London, SE11 6QJ
Tube: Woolwich Arsenal (DLR)
Capacity: 1,828 (seated)

The Coronet opened in 1937 as an Odeon cinema and designed in the Art Deco style by George Coles (who also designed The Troxy in Stepney and The Gaumont State Theatre in Kilburn, as well as many more).

The Damned played the Coronet in July 1985, The Fall in November 1986, New Order (1987), Squeeze (1987), Level 42 (1985) and Hawkwind (June 1989). The Coronet became a bingo hall that eventually closed in 2000 and was reopened as a church in 2001. The Coronet is a Grade II-listed building and is located opposite the Granada, which is also a church (see Granada Woolwich entry) and is next door to The Mitre Pub, which was home to Tunnel Club (see Tunnel Club entry).

Crawdaddy/Station Hotel

Address: Station Hotel, 1 Kew Road, Richmond, TW9 2NQ
Tube: Richmond (District Line)
Capacity: 320

Dave Hunt's R&B Band were the first R&B group to play the Station Hotel, which soon became known as the Crawdaddy. The Rolling Stones played gigs here in 1963. The Yardbirds replaced the Stones as the Crawdaddy's resident band at the end of 1963. The Crawdaddy club later moved to the nearby Richmond Athletic Association when the Station Hotel's landlord, Ind Coope, alarmed at the club's popularity, gave the club notice to leave. However, this move had the benefit of the new premises being 1,000 capacity – three times that of the Station Hotel's.

Russian-born Giorgio Gomelsky was the promoter of the Crawdaddy.

The Station Hotel is still standing, although it is now a restaurant called One Kew Road, and is located opposite the Richmond tube station.

The Cricketers

Address: 17 Clayton Street, Kennington, Oval, London, SE11
Tube: Oval (Northern Line)

Situated behind the Oval cricket ground on the corner of Clayton Street, the Cricketers had its gigging heyday in the late 1980s when indie groups like Carter The Unstoppable Sex Machine, Dave Graney and The Coral Snakes, John Otway and poet John Cooper Clarke played.

It is currently closed and has been that way for over ten years. The site will probably be redeveloped, losing this pink-and green cottage-style pub for good.

Crossfield Estate (Deptford)
Address: Farrier House, Deptford Church Street, Deptford
Tube: Deptford Bridge (DLR)

Here on this residential housing estate in Deptford, the band that would change its name to Dire Straits made their live debut playing outside a block of flats in the garden area. A PRS plaque has been erected on the north side of Farrier House (outside flat No.1) to mark the event. The estate dates from the late 1940s and is located by the A2209/Deptford Church Street. The estate originally had twelve housing blocks, but two have been demolished. Members of Dire Straits and Squeeze lived in the estate.

> **Davies Theatre.** This theatre, built in 1928 at 73 High Street, Croydon, had a world-class line-up of stars from the Golden Age of entertainment. Those to have played here include Frankie Laine (1954), Gracie Fields (1954), Liberace (1956), Bill Haley and His Comets (1957), Mario Lanza (1958) and Buddy Holly (1958). The theatre has since been demolished and replaced by an office block called 'Davies House'.
> **Electric Brixton.** See The Fridge.
> **Eltham Baths.** Located on the Eltham Hill/Eltham High Street and Shepherds Road junction, the baths were built between 1938 and 1939. The Who played on 28 February 1966 and others to have played include The Yardbirds, The Pretty Things and The Kinks. The Kinks made a live return to the baths in 1985 playing one of their last gigs together here before splitting up. The baths were closed in 2008 and were demolished for housing in 2011.
> **Folk Barge.** Located somewhere in Kingston, this is the floating venue that had many early gigs by local boy John Martyn from 1967 onwards. The barge became derelict and has been long removed and assumed broken up. Possibly also the Kingston venue called the Jazz Barge.

Dirty South/Rose of Lee

Address: 162 Lee High Road, Lewisham, SE13 5PR
Tube: Lewisham (DLR)

Babyshambles played this Lewisham pub in July 2006, and Dodgy appeared in 2010. The pub is the former Rose of Lee (see entry) where Kate Bush played in the KT Bush Band. The pub appeared to be closed in early 2015, the upper floors used as bedsits (called Rose House).

El Partido

Address: 8 – 12 Lee High Road, Lewisham, London, SE13 5LQ.
Train: Lewisham (from London Bridge).

Bo Diddley and Jimmy Cliff played this club's small stage in the 1960s. The venue was spread over two floors. As of 2015 it was an NHS dental clinic.

Fairfield Hall
Address: Park Lane, Croydon, CR9 1DG
Train: Croydon (from London Bridge and Victoria)
Capacity: 1,550 (seated)

The complex opened in 1962 and comprises of the Hall, The Ashcroft Theatre, The Arnhem Gallery and The David Lean Cinema. Elton John played on 9 May 1976 as part of his 'Louder Than Concorde but Not Quite as Pretty' tour. David Bowie brought his Ziggy Stardust tour here in 1973, and Cliff Richard, Status Quo and Eartha Kitt played in the 1970s. Tyrannosaurus Rex played in early 1970. Ray Davies played in October 2012.

Captain Sensible worked as a toilet cleaner here before fame came knocking with The Damned.

Fellowship Inn/Railway Tavern
Address: Ranesdown Road, Catford, London, SE6 3BT
Train: Bellingham (from Blackfriars or Elephant and Castle)

This pub was the first public house built on a London housing estate (which was built as a 'home for heroes' for veterans of the First World War and their families).It was designed by F. G. Newnham as an 'improved' public house for the Barclay Perkins and Company Brewery and building became a Grade II-listed building in 2013. The large hall at the rear of the pub (photo below) was used for gigs by The Yardbirds and The Blues Breakers. Fleetwood Mac

appeared twice in 1968, although it is more known for being where British boxer Henry Cooper lived and trained. In 2014 the hall was given £3.8 million of Lottery funding to restore the hall to a community pub, a cinema and live music venue. The hall is in separate ownership from the pub (the local council is believed to own it). The building is located next to Bellingham train station.

Fighting Cocks
Address: 56 Old London Road, Kingston, KT2 6QA
Train: Kingston (from Waterloo)

The Fighting Cocks has a long history of gigs going back to the 1930s when touring jazz acts use to play. More recently the venue attracts a punkier crowd with Frank Turner, Gallows and The Stupids playing the venue.

The Fridge/Ace Cinema/Electric Brixton

Address: 1 Town Hall Parade, Brixton Hill, Brixton, London, SW2 1RJ
Tube: Brixton (Victoria Line)
Capacity: 1,100
Live release: Gong Maison 'Live At The Fridge' DVD (5/5/91)

Originally opened in 1914 as the Palladium Cinema, the building was one of an amazing nine cinemas that opened in Brixton between 1910 and 1915. Sadly the original Edwardian stone frontage has long since gone, along with the domed tower from the roof. The building became the Brixton Ace in the late 1970s and put on punk/new wave bands such as The Clash, New Order and The Sisters of Mercy. The Smiths played their third and fourth London gigs at The Ace (on 4 and 29 of June 1983). The building became The Fridge in 1984 (moving from its original site at 390 Brixton Road – see Ram Jam entry) and was relaunched as The Fridge in 1985 by Soul II Souls' Jazzy B. The Pet Shop Boys made their live debut here in September 1984. As The Fridge it had rows of fridge doors fixed onto the frontage, which were very eye catching. The Fridge moved away from gigs and instead had DJs playing reggae, soul, R&B, house, techno and hip hop over the venue's two floors. It became the Electric Brixton in 2011 and started hosting gigs again.

The Gaumont (Lewisham). This cinema was at 1–5 Loampit Vale, Lewisham, SE13. Those to have played the cinema include Sarah Vaughan, Chuck Berry, Nat King Cole, Johnny Cash, Ray Charles, The Beatles (1963), The Who, Adam Faith (1960) and The Bay City Rollers. Became an Odeon in 1962. The cinema has been demolished.

Goldsmith Tavern (New Cross). Address: 316 New Cross Road, New Cross, London, SE14 6AF. Tube: New Cross (East London Line). The Inspiral Carpets played the Tavern in June 1989. Closed in March 2003 and reopened in August that year after being refurbished. By 2011 the building was a bar/restaurant called The New Cross House. Located almost opposite The Venue (New Cross).

Granada (Sutton). Address: Carshalton Road West, Sutton. Located on the corner of Carshalton Road and Manor Park Road, the cinema opened in 1934 as The Plaza Cinema, becoming a Granada in 1942. The cinema was designed by Robert Cromie and had a 2,390 capacity. However, the stall of this Granada appear to only have witnessed Johnny Ray performing here, way back in 1957. The cinema closed in 1975 and has since been demolished and an office block now occupies the site.

The Green Man (SE). This pub at the top of Blackheath Hill was home to The Jazzhouse Club around 1962/63, where acts such as Ronnie Scott and Manfred Mann would play. Paul Simon was apparently a last-minute replacement for the no show Judy Collins. The building was demolished in the early 1970s and the residential development of Alison Close now occupies the site.

Greenwich Theatre Folk Club. Located on Crooms Hill, the club had John Martyn in 1968 and 1970.

Greenwich Town Hall. The Who (as The High Numbers) played four times in 1964 and all four gigs were apparently all far from being at capacity. The Town Hall was opened in 1906 and is on Wellington Street, Greenwich.

The Glenlyn

Address: 15 Perry Vale, Forest Hill, London, SE23 2NE
Train: Forest Hill (from London Bridge)

The Glenlyn was a 1960s venue situated just by the station, The Animals, The Moody Blues, Cilla Black, The Kinks, The Hollies (1964) and The Rolling Stones (1964) played here before it turned into a snooker room. The Who played over twenty times between 1963 and 1966 as The Detours, The High Numbers and as The Who. It was also known as the Glenlyn Ballroom and as of 2015 an Indian restaurant called Raj Tandoori.

Goldsmiths College
Address: Dixon Road, New Cross, London, SE14 5NW
Tube: New Cross (East London Line)
Capacity: 600

Goldsmiths College is a university venue which had Japan (1976) and The Electric Soft Parade (2004) play. Former student John Cale was made an Honorary Fellow of Goldsmiths in 1997. Other former Goldsmiths students include Alex James and Graham Coxon of Blur. The group, then called Seymour, played their second ever gig at the student union in 1989.

Granada (Dartford)

Address: 30 Spital Street, Dartford, Kent, DA1 2DL
Train: Dartford

Opened in 1935 as The State Cinema with a 1,500 capacity, it was designed by Beard & Bennett in the Art Deco/Neo-Classical style. The building has a brick façade with a central terracotta-tile surround to windows; the side elevations have little of interest.

It became The Granada in 1949. The Granada had Gene Vincent in both 1960 and 1961 and The Hollies in 1964. It closed as a cinema in 1978 and reopened as a bingo hall in 1991. The building was being used as a church in 2015.

Granada (Kingston-upon-Thames) (see Pl.11)
Address: 154–166 Clarence Street, Kingston-upon-Thames, KT1 1QP
Train: Kingston (from Waterloo)

The Granada (Kingston-upon-Thames) opened in 1939 and was designed by the architect George Cole (who designed many other cinemas including The State in Kilburn). While many cinemas offered some of the top names in the early days of rock 'n' roll, the Granada here at Kingston really did offer locals the best of the best. The list of the artists to have played this cinema is truly staggering and includes Little Richard (1962), Roy Orbison (1963 and 1964), Gene Vincent (1960, 1961 and 1964), The Rolling Stones (1964), The Kinks (1965), The Who (1967), Traffic (1967), The Tremeloes (1967), Marmalade (1967) and Johnny Cash (1968). The cinema closed in 1987 and became home to a nightclub called 'Oceana'. It was renamed in 2013 as 'Pryzm'. The building is Grade II listed.

Granada (Tooting) (see Pl.12)

Address: 50 Mitcham Road, Tooting, London, SW17 9NA
Tube: Tooting Broadway (Northern Line)
Capacity: 2,400

The Granada (Tooting) was opened in 1931. The exterior was designed by Cecil Massey and has four Corinthian pillars to the front above the entrance. The lavish interior was the work of set designer Theodore Komisarjevsky.

The Granada was the first cinema to be made a Grade I-listed building and as such the building is kept in beautiful condition, a venue from the early days of rock 'n' roll where The Beatles (1963), Jerry Lee Lewis, Gene Vincent (1959), Little Richard (1963), Roy Orbison (1963, 64 and 67), The Rolling Stones (1964 and 65) as well as Frank Sinatra (1953) and Pat Boone performed. The bill on 30 April 1967 featured The Walker Brothers, Cat Stevens, Englebert Humperdinck and Jimi Hendrix. The cinema later became a Gala bingo hall and is possibly the most lavish bingo hall in the whole of the UK.

Granada (Woolwich)

Address: 174 Powis Street, Woolwich, London, SE11 6NL
Tube: Woolwich Arsenal (DLR)
Capacity: 2,434

Opened in 1937 as a cinema, The Beatles played in June 1963. It became a bingo hall in 1966 and remained as such until Gala Bingo sold the building in 2011 for a reported £5 million to a church. The building is a Grade II*- listed building and is opposite the former Coronet venue – which is now also a church.

The Grand (see Pl.13)

Address: St Johns Hill, Clapham, London, SW11 1TT
Train: Clapham Junction (from Waterloo)
Capacity: 1,800

Opened in 1900 as a music hall and designed by Woodrow, the exterior has a red-brick, pink-Mansfield-stone dressing and is one of the most eye-catching buildings in the area.

No longer a music venue that regularly brings in the big names, The Grand once vied to be a contender in the early 1990s. Sebadoh, Hole, Pavement, The Manic Street Preachers, The Kinks and Suede are some of the groups that played here in its gigging heyday. A reformed Big Star played the Grand in August 1993.

The Grand is located out of the bright lights of Central London pretty close to Clapham Junction train station. Its distant South London location probably didn't do it any favours being a fifteen-minute train journey from Waterloo.

Situated opposite Clapham Junction train station, The Grand's magnificent red-brick frontage totally dominates and dwarfs the rest of the street. The Grand is now a nightclub that hosts gigs by mainly unsigned groups on the London circuit, although the odd noteworthy gig still slips in – such as The Wedding Present and Big Country, both in 2014.

Greyhound Hotel (Croydon)

Address: Park Lane, Croydon

The Greyhound had hosted ELO (making their live debut), David Bowie and AC/DC (1976) play. The venue was on Park Lane, opposite the Fairfield Halls, and was in the Nestle building. It later became a nightclub known as The Blue Orchid. The building, although empty for years, is still standing.

The Hanging Lamp. Based in the crypt of a church off from Richmond Hill, Richmond, folkie John Martyn appeared in 1968 and 1969.
Hayward Gallery. Paul Weller played on the roof of this gallery, which is part of the South Bank Centre, on 24 June 1997. Eight tracks were later released as a promotional CD, imaginatively titled 'Live From The Roof of The Hayward Gallery, 1997'. Location: Belvedere Road, SE1 8XX. Tube: Waterloo.
Hippodrome (Kingston). 1 St James Road, Kingston, KT1 2AH. The New Slang nights (run by Banquet Records) can have some special album release gigs such as Django Django, Palma Violets, Summer Camp, The Vaccines, Jaimie XX and Slaves in 2015. Others to have played include Frank Turner, Vampire Weekend and Example.

The Half Moon (Herne Hill)

Address: 1 Half Moon Lane, Herne Hill, London, SE24 9JU
Train: Herne Hill (from Farringdon)

This grand Victorian pub put on early gigs by U2 and Australian group The Triffids in its back room. Although the Half Moon in Putney claims to have had U2 play on its stage, the evidence shows that it was the Herne Hill venue that hosted the group. U2 played here three times: on 8 June 1980, 11 July 1980 and 5 October 1980. Indie band The Parkinson's played in 2003. It is currently closed.

The Half Moon (Putney) (see Pl.14)

Address: 93 Lower Richmond Road, Putney, London, SW15 1EU
Tube: Putney Bridge (District Line)
Capacity: 230

The Half Moon has been a regular music venue since 1963, although occasional music events have been staged since the 1920s. The Half Moon has a fine music pedigree, as its past performers reads like a whose who of modern music: Albert Lee, Dire Straits, Elvis Costello, Kate Bush, Nick Cave, Rod Stewart, various members of The Rolling Stones (the last to visit was Keith Richards in May 2000), Van Morrission and The Who have all graced the stage here. The Half Moon continues to host noteworthy gigs, either by up-and-coming groups or those who have had their fifteen minutes of fame. KD Lang made her UK debut on the Half Moon's stage.

Inside the bar of the pub are photographs of the many groups who have played the venue. The stage area has a low raised stage, a bar and is standing only. The Half Moon has always supported unsigned artists, but only accepts demos from serious groups who want to get signed (no hobby or covers bands). The venue stresses that the groups must also have a London following and should bring at least fifty paying punters when they perform.

The venue was threatened with closure in 2009 when tenant James Harris got into debt after takings fell by 20 per cent and the rent was doubled. Young's Brewery (the landlord) served notice on Mr Harris and had plans to turn the venue into a gastro pub, but fortunately the plans never came to fruitition and the pub remains as a live music venue.

House of Vans

Address: Archers 228–232, Station Approach Road, Waterloo, London, SE1 8SW
Tube: Waterloo (Bakerloo, Jubilee, Northern and Waterloo and City)
Capacity: 850

Located underneath Waterloo train station, this venue, run by the Vans shoe company, opened in 2014 and is dedicated to skate culture It is a multifunctional space housing an art gallery, café/bar, skate park and gig space. The Foo Fighters played under the alias The Holy Shits on 10 September 2014 as part of a series of three small gigs before their headline slot at the Invictious Games at the Olympic Park. Imagine Dragons and Bring Me The Horizon both played in 2015.

> **Kingston Polytechnic.** The Main Hall, Cambury Park Campus, Penrhyn Road, KT1 2EE, has hosted The Smiths (1983), U2, Barclay James Harvest and John Martyn (1970).
> **Kingston Tavern.** Elvis Costello's early group, Flip City, played this pub on Russell Garden's W14, in the early 1970s.
> **Lewisham Odeon.** Located at 1–5 Loampit Vale. The Who played a gig here in 1970. The cinema opened in 1932 with a 3,050 capacity, was closed in 1981 and demolished in 1991.
> **Locarno (Streatham).** Opened in 1929 by Billy Cotton and hosted Glen Miller, The Rolling Stones and The Small Faces. Later became The Studio, Ritzy and Caesars before being demolished in 2015. Location: Streatham Hill.

Indigo Club (also see O2)

Address: The O2, Millenuimn Dome, Greenwich, London, SE10 0DX
Tube: North Greenwich (DLR)
Capacity: 2,800 (standing)

The Indigo Club is the smaller, more intimate sibling of the O2 arena located inside the Millennium Dome. Indigo seems to be less busy with gigs than its older, bigger brother although The Who, La Roux, Blondie and the Black Eyed Peas have played here. Although a modern building, it does feel strangely like the Shepherds Bush Empire inside.

Lewisham Theatre/Broadway Theatre
Address: Catford Broadway, Catford, London, SE6 4RU
Train: Catford Bridge (from London Bridge)
Capacity: 800

Opened in 1932, this Art Deco theatre is a Grade II-listed building. It was also known as The Lewisham Concert Hall and is currently called the Broadway Theatre. Stevie Wonder, Eartha Kitt, Showaddywaddy (1983), Elkie Brookes (2003) and Suzi Quatro have all graced the stage here.

Mistral Club
Address: 2–4 High Street, Beckenham, Kent, BR3 1EW
Train: Beckenham Junction (from London Bridge)

The former Beckenham Ballroom was spread over two floors. Local boy Peter Frampton played many early gigs here before coming into recognition all over the world. Others who played the club include The Yardbirds (1964), Manfred Mann (1968), The Alan Price Set (1968), Black Sabbath (1968), Ike and Tina Turner (1968), Tyrannosaurs Rex (1968), King Crimson (1969), Fleetwood Mac (1971) and Mott The Hoople (1971). It became Tites Disco in 1974, Landtrys in the 1980s and then The Bridge Bar. Train: Beckenham Junction.

The Mick Jagger Centre
Address: Shepherds Lane, Dartford, Kent, DA1 2JZ
Train: Dartford (from Charring Cross)
Capacity: 350

Named after and opened by the famous local boy, of course, in 2000. The centre is an arts venue within Dartford Grammar School and is a fifteen-minute walk from Dartford train station. Unlikely to attract the most current or exciting names in the music scene, the centre offers the occasional artist of note, such as Sam Brown or Ian McNabb (February 2006).

The Miller
Address: 96 Snowfields Road, London Bridge, London, SE1 3SS
Tube: London Bridge (Northern and Jubilee Lines)
Capacity: 100

Run by the operators behind the Sebright Arms, this pub (formerly called The Miller of Mansfield) has had Grant Hart (of Husker Du), Winter Mountain (2014) and others in its upstairs room. There is a rehearsal studio in the basement.

Ministry of Sound
Address: 103 Gaunt Street, London, SE1 6DP
Tube: Elephant and Castle (Northern Line)
Capacity: 1,500

The Ministry of Sound is of course a clubbers' paradise, but a few bands have made it to the South London venue. The Cocteau Twins played in this former bus depot on 23 May 1996. In the underground station follow the exits to South Bank University.

> __Newlands Tavern/Stuart Arms/Ivy House.__ Address: 40 Stuart Road, Peckham Rye, SE15 3BE. Train: Croften Park (from London Bridge Station). A 1970s pub venue that had gigs by Dr Feelgood, Eddie and the Hotrods and Ian Dury, Graham Parker (1975) and Jeff Beck (1974). In 1974 Johnny Sox featuring a pre-Stranglers Hugh Cornwell played whilst the Elvis Costello led Flip City also gigged here. Gigs ceased in 1978. During the gigging years the landlords were Reg and Sue Fentiman. The pub was renamed The Stuart Arms in the 1980s and is currently called The Ivy House and is a community-owned pub. The pub dates from the 1930s and is a Grade II-listed building.
>
> __Old Royal Naval College.__ Home to the Greenwich Music Time festival started in 2014. In July 2015 the line-up included Ray Davies, George Benson, Tom Jones and The Gipsy Kings.
>
> __Old Vic.__ Rufus Wainwright played five nights on this theatrical stage in May 2007. Address: The Cut, SE1 8NB. Tube: Waterloo (Bakerloo, Jubilee and Northern Lines).
>
> __101 Club.__ Located at 101 St John's Hill, Clapham, SW11, the Television Personalities played in 1980. The building remains (as of 2014) but appears unoccupied and somewhat unloved.
>
> __Oval Cricket Ground.__ Address: The Oval, Kennington, SE11. Tube: Oval (Northern Line).The Who, America and The Faces played here in September 1971, as did Frank Zappa in 1972.

The O2/Indigo (see Pl.28)
__Address:__ Millennium Way, Greenwich, London, SE10 0DX

__Tube:__ North Greenwich (Jubilee Line)
__Capacity:__ 23,000 (seated)
__Live releases:__ Keane 'Live at The O2' DVD (2007) and Scissor Sisters 'Hurrah – A Year of Ta-Dah' DVD (2007)

Built as a celebration of the new millennium, the Millennium Dome was a controversial project hated by the media and seen as a very expensive folly with no long-term occupier signed up after the year 2000. The size of thirteen Royal Albert Halls, the O2 can easily claim to be the biggest new London venue in recent years, but given the Dome's difficult past and its location this question had to be asked: would the O2 follow London Arena's path and disappear after a whirlwind start? Seven years after opening in 2007 the venue was busier than Matterson Square Gardens and has firmly established itself in the music world, so the venue is a big success. The O2 is owned by AEG Europe.

The Millennium Dome opened as the O2 with a show by Bon Jovi on 24 June 2007. Gigs followed by Justin Timberlake on 4, 5, 7, and 8 of July, the Scissor Sisters on 26, 27 and 28 of July, Keane, Snow Patrol and The Rolling Stones. Prince played twenty-one nights in August and September 2007 as part of his 'Earth' tour.

Led Zeppelin reformed and played live for the first time since 1985 on 10 December 2007, as part of a charity gig for Ahmet Ertegun – the founder of Atlantic Records. When the gig was announced over one million fans applied for tickets, and a pair of tickets were auctioned on Terry Wogan's Radio 2 show for over £18,000 in aid of 'Children in Need'. The Eagles played a music industry gig here in 2007 to promote their album 'Long Road Out of Eden'. Take That, The Spice Girls, Linkin Park, Kylie, Alicia Keys, Celine Dion and Neil Diamond also appeared in the first twelve months of opening.

Those with floor/standing tickets will be directed to the dedicated entrance for the area. You will be lead past all of the bars and restaurants and will end up at the rear of the venue in a cold void which resembles a covered bus park, in what is possibly the worst customer environment a punter would want to find themselves in. If you have a seat in the very top row I hope you have a strong stomach and do not suffer from vertigo as they are very high up and appear to have a steep drop down.

The Entertainment District surrounding the O2 arena also includes the 2,200 capacity 'Indigo Club', which has featured Elvis Costello, Aimee Mann and Jools Holland, as well housing as cafés, bars and a cinema. The Indigo Club features a main area with an upper tier and the 'Kings Row' luxury seating area, and was the venue for Prince's aftershow parties. The O2 also contains The Brooklyn Bowl – a bowling alley/restaurant that also hosts gigs.

Orchid Ballroom

Address: 112A Brighton Road, Purley, Surrey, CR8 3AA
Train: Reedham (from London Bridge Station)

Paradise Bar/Six String Bar. Address: 460 New Cross Road, New Cross, SE14 6TJ. Tube: New Cross (East London Line). Bloc Party played in October 2003. Later became Six String Bar and currently a pub called The Royal Albert.
Paradise Club. This club at 3 Consort Road, Peckham had The Who in July 1962.
Park Tavern. This pub at 76 Elm Park, Streatham, SW2, put on gigs by second-division punk bands such as the UK Subs who played in September 1978.
The Peel. Address: 160 Cambridge Road, Kingston, London, KT1 3HH. Train: Norbiton. The Sir Robert Peel pub, otherwise known as The Peel. The venue catered for mainly unsigned or punk groups but still managed to attract the occasional 'known' act. Lords of the New Church, Ash, 'A', Napalm Death, Gary Moore, The Vaccines, Jamie T, Gallows, John Newman and The Quireboys were a few of the groups who have played here. Closed on 27 April 2014 when owners Punch Taverns went into financial difficulty, being demolished pretty soon afterwards. Banquet Records promoted many gigs here. The pub was well known for having strippers in the room behind the gig space.
Public Baths Hall. The building at 316 Malden Road, Cheam, SM3 8EP, was built in 1938. Those to have played include Cliff Richard in 1959 and The Who in 1966.

The Orchid Ballroom opened in 1950 and closed in 1973, and The Who (1966), The Troggs, Status Quo and The Hollies played in the intervening years. It later became a nightclub and currently has a private gym (Dynamics) in the basement of the long terraced building.

Plan B

Address: 418 Brixton Road, Brixton, London, SW9 7AY
Tube: Brixton (Victoria Line)
Capacity: 300

Plan B was a venue used by Plum Promotions (who have been involved with The Marquee, Betsy Trotwood and The Water Rats, to name just a few) that put on unsigned bands. Plan B started putting regular gigs on in 2005 and is a former Wimpy burger shop. It had a strong urban focus with Norman Jay and Basement Jaxx appearing. It is currently a nightclub called Phonox.

Pontiac Club

Address: Zeeta House, 200 Upper Richmond Road, Putney, London, SW15 2SH
Tube: East Putney (District Line)

The Pontiac Club was a 1960s R&B basement venue which was accessed on the far-right corner of the main building in the photograph. Belfast R&B group Them (featuring Van Morrison) played a few times in the early 1960s. As of 2014 it was called The Fez Club.

Purcell Room (Royal Festival Hall)

Address: Royal Festival Hall, Belvedere Road, South Bank, London, SE1 8XX
Tube: Waterloo (Bakerloo and Northern Lines)
Capacity: 367 (seated)

Opened in 1967, David Bowie showcased his album 'Space Oddity' here in 1969. Capercaillie, Clive Gregson and Christine Collister (1989) have also performed at the venue. As part of the Royal Festival Hall complex/South Bank Centre, the Purcell Room hosts a wide spectrum of artists.

The Purcell Room is located in the same building as the Queen Elizabeth Hall. This Brutalist concrete building was designed by Hubert Bennett

Queen Elizabeth Hall (Royal Festival Hall)

Address: Royal Festival Hall, Belvedere Road, South Bank, London, SE1 8XX
Tube: Waterloo (Bakerloo and Northern Lines)
Capacity: 1,100
Live release: Tim Buckley 'Dream Letter – Live in London' album, Jake Thackray 'Live Performance' CD (1970)

Pink Floyd were banned from the QEH when in 1967 they released bubbles into the crowd, subsequently ruining the seating (well the venue had only just opened!). It was also the venue for Tim Buckley's first London show in 1968. Patti Smith performed and recorded 'The Coral Sea' here in 2006 aided by My Bloody Valentine's Kevin Sheilds.

The building is also home to the Purcell Room and shares its Brutalist design with the rest of the South Bank Centre.

Red Barn. Location: 98–100 Barnehurst Road, Bexleyheath, DA7 6HG. A 1940s jazz venue where George Webb's Dixielanders played. The pub is still there.
Rose Of Lee The KT Bush Band featuring Kate Bush played this pub which later became 'Sports' and then 'Dirty South' which continued to put on bands – see Dirty South entry.
Rose Theatre. Located at 24–26 High Street, Kingston, KT1 1HL, Enter Shakiri played in January 2015.

Ram Jam/The Fridge

Address: 390 Brixton Road, Brixton, London, SW9
Tube: Brixton (Victoria Line)

This Brixton venue was run by brothers Rik and John Gunnell and was allegedly named in honour of Geno Washington and His Ram Jam Band. There is some debate as to the time it was in the basement of the first floor of the building. Those who played include The Moody Blues (1966), Otis Redding (1966), Cream (1966 and 1967), Jimi Hendrix (1966), Fleetwood Mac (1967), John Lee Hooker (1967), Nina Simone and Ike and Tina Turner. Renamed Clouds in the 1970s and became The Fridge in 1981 when run by Andy Czezowski. The Fridge relocated to The Ace Cinema in 1984 (see entry for The Fridge).

Rivoli Ballroom

Address: 350 Brockley Road, Croften Park, London, SE4 2BY
Train: Crofton Park (from Farringdon)
Capacity: 700

This South East London ballroom had The White Stripes playing to 600 fans on 12 June 2007, with the proceeds going to the Chelsea Pensioners Appeal. The Kings of Leon, Florence and The Machine (in 2009 and 2012) have also appeared. The building has also been used for several music videos including Tina Turners 'Private Dancer' and Elton John's 'I Guess That's Why They Call It The Blues'.

Built in 1913 as The Croften Park Picture Palace, the cinema was later converted into a ballroom.

Royal Festival Hall

Address: Belvedere Road, South Bank, London, SE11 8XX
Tube: Waterloo (Bakerloo, Jubilee and Northern Lines)
Capacity: 3,000 (seated)
Live release: Oasis 'Unplugged' MTV special (1996), Lou Reed 'Perfect Night Live in London'
CD (3.7.1997), Siouxsie 'Dreamshow' DVD (2005), New York Dolls 'Live at the Royal Festival
Hall' DVD (2004)

Originally constructed as part of the Festival of Britain (a feel-good festival after the Second
World War) in 1951, The Royal Festival includes in its complex The Queen Elizabeth Hall and
The Purcell Room (see previous entries) where mainly classical concerts are held. However, a few
contemporary musicians are occasionally let in: Bob Dylan (1964); Pink Floyd (1969); Fairport
Convention (1969); a benefit concert in 1972 featuring Mott the Hoople, David Bowie and Lou
Reed; New Order (1985); and Oasis (1996).

Since 1993 The Royal Festival Hall has hosted the annual Meltdown festival, where cultural
icons get to organise their own festival. Artists who have curated Meltdown include George
Benjamin (1993), Louis Andriesson (1994), Elvis Costello (1995), Magnus Lindberg (1996),
Laurie Anderson (1997), John Peel (1998), Nick Cave (1999), Scott Walker (2000), Robert
Wyatt (2001), David Bowie (2002), Lee 'Scratch' Perry (2003), Morrissey (2004), Patti Smith
(2005), Jarvis Cocker (2007), Massive Attack (2008), Ornette Coleman (2009), Richard
Thompson (2010), Ray Davies (2011), Anthony Hegarty (2012), Yoko Ono (2013), James
Lavelle (2014) David Byrne (2015) and Guy Garvey (2016). Meltdown guests have included
Lou Reed, Anthony and The Johnsons, The New York Dolls and Motorhead.

The Royal Festival Hall had a £115 million facelift starting in 2006, with the Hall reopening in
July 2008. Brian Wilson played a new set of songs over six nights in September 2008. Previously,
Wilson had performed 'Pet Sounds' in 2002 and 'Smile' in 2005.

Shakespeare Hotel. This Woolwich four-storey venue had Fleetwood Mac playing the late
1960s. Closed, although still standing at 12 Powis Street, SE18 6LF. Tube: Woolwich Arsenal.
Silver Blades Ice Rink. This ice rink opened in 1931 (as the Streatham Ice Rink) at 386
Streatham High Street, SW16. It became the Silver Blades in 1962 and The Pretty Things,
The Move (1967), The Kinks (1966) and Cream played here. Became home to the Streatham
Redskin's ice-hockey team. The site has been redeveloped and a Tesco store and an ice rink
now occupy the site.
St Mary's Hall. This Putney hall had The Who play live many times in 1963 and 1964.
Sundown. A small London-based chain of live music venues operated by Rank around 1972
(and closed soon after opening). There were three Sundowns all in Ranks cinemas. In Brixton
the Sundown was opened with a gig from Deep Purple, and the building is what later became
The Brixton Academy. In Mile End, the Odeon at 401 Mile End Road became a Sundown and
had Slade in September 1972, Fleetwood Mac in November 1972, and John Martyn and Sandy
Denny also played that year. Closed as a music venue in 1973 and reverted back to a cinema
although it was demolished in 1984. The Who played the Edmonton Sundown venue four
times in December 1973 and this was apparently the most successful of the Sundown venues.
Steppenwolf also played here. See Edmonton Regal entry.

The Star Hotel (Croydon)
Address: 296 London Road, Croydon, CR0 2TG
Train: Croydon (from London Bridge Station)

In the 1960s Jimi Hendrix played The Star – as did Fleetwood Mac – and Cream appeared in
1966. The rather fine building is now used as rented out rooms and its musical heritage appears
lost in the area.

Stockwell Swan

Address: 215 Clapham Road, Stockwell, London, SW9 9BE
Tube: Stockwell (Victoria and Northern Lines)
Capacity: 500

Opposite Stockwell tube station, the Swan puts on mostly tribute acts intimating groups like U2, Green Day, Red Hot Chilli Peppers and Queen in its 1930s-style building.

Tate Modern. This art gallery and former power station started a series of open-air free gigs called 'Late at Tate Britain' on the first Friday of each month starting in August 2006. Rough Trade started off the series with a showcase of its acts The Long Blondes and Scritti Politti. However, the first ever gig at Tate Modern was PJ Harvey on 1 September 2003 in the Turbine Hall, Bankside, SE1 9TG.

The Telegraph. Address: 228 Brixton Hill, Brixton, SW2. The 101-ers, featuring a pre-Clash Joe Strummer, played their first gig at this pub in 1974. The building later became a children's nursery and was being redeveloped in 2015.

Thames Rowing Club. This Putney-based club was a gig for Brian May in 1966 before he formed Queen.

Thomas A Beckett. Address: 302 Old Kent Road, Borough, SE1. This pub has been in live music use since the 1960s. An early pre-Clash Mick Jones played here in 1974. The pub remains but the gigs have gone. The pub was famous for being one of the places boxer Henry Cooper would train at.

Trocadero. Located at 1–17 New Kent Road, Elephant and Castle, this 3,500-capacity cinema was designed by George Coles for the Hyams and Gale Kinemas (which also ran The Troxy in Stepney) and was open between 1930 and 1963. Buddy Holly started his UK tour here with two shows in March 1958, and Teddy Boys (and Girls) threw coins at Cliff Richard while he was on stage here. Ella Fitzgerald appeared in 1962 when her show at the Lewisham Gaumont was transferred here due to a fire. Promoters pulled the show by Jerry Lee Lewis in 1958 when the scandal broke about his marriage to his teenage cousin. Rather shamefully this stunning building has been demolished and replaced by flats called 'Metro Central Heights'. However, a plaque has been erected on the building (by film critic Denis Norden, who used to work at the Trocadero) to mark where this fine building once stood.

Tooting Bec Common. Sting played two nights in a marquee here in December 1980.

Tooting Tramshed. Based at 46 Mitcham Road, Iron Maiden played here in July 1977. The building and name continue as a venue, but with under-the-radar acts.

Tunnel Club

Address: The Mitre Public House, 338 Tunnel Avenue, off Boord Street, Greenwich, London, SE10
Tube: Woolwich Arsenal (DLR)

The Tunnel Club was situated on the A102M Blackwall Tunnel southside approach. The club ran from The Mitre pub and had The Lover Speaks (famous for 'No More I Love You's') in August 1988. Billy Bragg (under the Spy Vs Spy pseudonym) had a residency here in the very early 1980s as opening for acts such as Blood & Roses, Doll By Doll and Doctor & The Medics. Bragg occasionally headlined and once had an unknown Housemartins as support. The club offered comedians as well as live music.

The Venue (New Cross) (see Pl.41)
Address: 2a Clifton Rise, New Cross, London, SE14 6JP
Tube: New Cross Gate (East London Line)
Capacity: 1,400

An imposing building, if only because of the starkness of the black frontage, The Venue has been here since March 1990. True, its glory years are in the past when acts such as Belly, Sebadoh, Julianna Hatfield, Ocean Colour Scene, Teenage Fanclub, Suede and Sheep on Drugs played here in the early 1990s.

The building has three floors with the stage area on the ground level. The days of originality have been left behind and the venue now puts on tribute acts exclusively. Come here for tributes to Blondie (Once More Into The Bleach), The Jam and Oasis.

The White Horse (Brixton)/Brixton Jamm
Address: 261 Brixton Road, Brixton, London, SW9 2LH.
Tube: Brixton (Victoria Line)
Capacity: 500

The Vaults. Basement Jaxx played this SE1 club in August 2006, previewing their new album 'Crazy Itch Radio'.

Wandsworth Prison. The 101-ers, featuring a pre-Clash Joe Strummer, played this prison three times in 1976. Elvis Costello's early band Flip City also played. Pete Doherty has spent time behind bars here. Located at Heathfield Road, SW18 3HS.

The Welcome Inn. Noteworthy for being the location of the first gig by Status Quo in 1967. A PRS (Performing Rights Society) plaque marks the approximate spot where the pub once stood, as it was destroyed by fire in 2006. Located on Well Hall Road, Eltham, a residential development now occupies the site ('The Edens', constructed by Weston Homes).

The White Lion. Address: 14–16 High Street, Putney, London. Tube: East Putney (District Line). Punk bands Crass and UK Subs played this pub fairly regular in the punk heydays of 1977/78. Continues to serve pints as a sports bar called Wahoo, and although live music may have left the building, comedy now takes to the stage. An impressive five-storey building with a white lion sitting majestically on the roof.

Wimbledon Palais Address: High Street, Merton, London. Originally an ice-skating rink, then an airship and balloon factory, it became a ballroom in 1922. The Beatles played a fan club gig here on 14 December 1963 to 3,000 fans with a steel cage separating the crowd from the group. It caused Lennon to remark that if the crowd pushed any harder they would come through as chips. The Rolling Stones played the venue several times in 1964. The Who (1965 and 1966), David Bowie and Pink Floyd all played before the Palais closed in 1967. It later became a furniture shop and then the HQ for the Shaftesbury Housing Association and later demolished.

Wimbledon Theatre/New Wimbledon Theatre. Address: 93 The Broadway, Wimbledon, SW19 1QG. Tube: Wimbledon (District Line). A Grade II-listed building designed by Cecil Massey and Roy Young. This 1,670-capacity Edwardian Theatre dates from 1910 and is perhaps the only theatre to have a Turkish bath in its basement. Spread over three floors, the theatre is the eighth largest in London. Artists such as Gracie Fields and Ivor Novello played in the 1950s. It attracts a strange mix of 1960's bands on the nostalgia circuit, and Bellowhead played here on their last tour in 2016.

Young Vic Theatre. The Who played this Waterloo theatre seven times in 1971.

The Clash played The White Horse in the 1970s. It reopened in February 2005 as The Brixton Jamm with a party thrown by Basement Jaxx. It focuses on club nights, although Alabama 3 have played the Jamm, and Pete Doherty played twice in one night in 2015.

The Witchdoctor/Savoy Rooms/Mr Smiths (see Pl.49)

Address: 75 Rushey Green, Bellingham/Catford, SE6 4HW
Train: Catford Bridge (from London Bridge Station)

The Rolling Stones played here in 1964, and others performers include The Who (1966), Georgie Fame and Marmalade. It was previously known as the Savoy Rooms (Savoy Ballroom) in the 1950s and in the 1970s became known as Mr Smiths. The building became notorious after a gangland killing between the Kray and Richardson gangs happened in the venue in 1966. It is currently houses a shop on the ground level and a church above.

The Windmill (see Pl.50)

Address: 22 Blenheim Gardens, Brixton, London, SW2 5BZ
Tube: Brixton (Victoria Line)
Capacity: 120

Looking like any other boozer that serves any council estate built in the UK since the 1960s, the Windmill is actually found down a Victorian backstreet. This little, obscure venue has started to earn itself a nice reputation, with *The Independent* newspaper naming it as one of the UK's top ten venues. Groups that have played the venue include Calexico, The Parkinson's, Eileen Rose, Do Me Bad, Things and Yourcodenameis:milo.

The Windmill puts on live music six nights a week and accepts demos from unsigned bands (demos to the above address) and rather admirably they book bands on the quality of the music, not on how many paying mates the group can bring along.

WEST LONDON

Acton Town Hall. Address: High Street, Acton, London, W3 6NE. Train: Acton Central. The building dates from 1910 and was extended in 1939. The Who played on 1 September 1962 (as The Detours Jazz Group at the gala ball to celebrate the reopening of the Hall). Moving forward some years, it was here that Mick Jones joined Joe Strummer and The Mescaleros on stage for a Fire Brigades Union benefit gig, shortly before Strummer died in December 2002.

All Saints Hall. Pink Floyd played their first 'underground' gig here in Powis Gardens, in a set that contained no r'n'b covers, which was a first for the group. Space rockers Hawkwind played three times in 1969. The church hall has now been demolished.

Bay 63 (see Subterania).

BBC Television Centre. In the glory days of *Top of The Pops*, this iconic White City complex had a few special performances outside the front of Television Centre. Green Day and Beyonce both played live sets in front of fans and were broadcast on TV.

Blue Moon Club. This club in Hayes had Cream (1966), Manfred Mann (1964), The Yardbirds (1964) and The Who (1965).

The Boathouse. Located near Kew Bridge, the venue offered Fleetwood Mac in 1968, Pink Floyd (1968), Slade (1972) and Status Quo (1972). Train: Kew Bridge.

Botwell House Club. The Rolling Stones played in 1963, The Zombies (1964), The Who (1965) and Them (1965) all played the club.

Brunel University. Address: Kingston Lane, Uxbridge, Middlesex, UB8 3PH. Tube: Uxbridge (Bakerloo and Metropolitan Lines). The Sex Pistols played the university's gym in December 1977, and U2 were the support act for The Photos on 12 December 1979. Hawkwind also played in 1979. Like so many of London's universities, Brunel's students union promotes club nights rather than gigs these days.

Burtons Ballroom. Located above the Burtons menswear shop in Uxbridge, The Yardbirds (1965), The Who (1965) and The Jeff Beck Group (1967) played.

Bush Hall/The Carlton Club (see Pl.7)

Address: 310 Uxbridge Road, Shepherds Bush, W12 7LJ
Tube: Shepherds Bush (Central Line)
Capacity: 200

Discovering Bush Hall is a pure joy; its chandeliers and plaster moulds could make you believe that you were really in a Prague concert room rather than the arse-end of the Central Line. Built in 1904 by an Irish publisher, who gave each of his three daughters a dance hall as a present, the Carlton Dance Hall (its original name) architecture was influenced by the French Renaissance.

The use of steel girders in its structure was almost unheard of in the early 1900s and has resulted in the original features (such as plaster-cast cherubs and harps on the walls) being preserved.

The venue hosted ballroom dancing, swing orchestras and even ceilidhs, before becoming a soup kitchen during the Second World War. During the 1950s and ʼ60s it became a bingo hall which had a secret life as a rehearsal room for Adam Faith, The Rolling Stones, The Who and even Cliff Richard.

The venue eventually became The Carlton Club offering late-night snooker and drinking. The venue was reborn as a music venue early in the new millennium and is now one of the most sophisticated venues in London. Those who have graced its stage include Nick Cave and The Bad Seeds, BMX Bandits, Erin McKeown, Alanis Morrisete, Chris Rea, REM, Kings of Leon and Granddaddy. On 14 August 2005 the Scissor Sisters played a secret gig here and previewed songs from their new, unreleased album (finally released in 2006). Former Suede frontman Brett Anderson played three solo shows at the hall in March 2007.

Chiswick Empire. Designed by Frank Matcham and opened in 1912 with a 1,948 capacity, Cliff Richard and The Drifters had a week's residency here in February 1958 and returned for another night in May 1959. Liberace was the last act to play the Empire in June 1959 before it was demolished – replaced by an office block (Empire House), shops and a supermarket. The Empire was at 414 Chiswick High Road, W4 5TF.

Chiswick Town Hall. Located at Heathfield Terrace, Turnham Green, W4 4JN, the hall had The Graham Bond Organisation play in 1966. The Pink Fairies held a Xmas party here in the early 1970s.

Chelsea Hospital. The White Stripes played an afternoon acoustic gig here for Chelsea Pensioners on 12 June 2007. The show was the group's first UK gig for two years. The Stripes played six songs as part of the promotion of their album 'Icky Thump'. Located at Royal Hospital Road, SW3 4SR.

Clarendon Hotel Ballroom. Address: The Broadway, Hammersmith, London. Tube: Hammersmith (District, Hammersmith & City and Piccadilly Lines). Capacity: 500. Live releases: 6 LP's called Stomping at The Klub Foot. Unfortunately this venue was demolished in the 1990s to make way for the present Hammersmith underground station (Electric Ballroom beware!). In its prime this art deco venue hosted gigs by U2 (July 1980), The Birthday Party (May 1982), Dr and The Medics (April 1984), Pop Will Eat Itself (Sept 1987) as well as Red Lorry Yellow Lorry, The Bolshoi and Ghostdance. On St Patrick's Day 1985 Elvis Costello and The Pogues played. Costello had played a special gig here in January 1980 to 300 *NME* competition winners. The Clarendon was home to Klub Foot shows which specialised in psychobilly groups such as Demented Are Go, The Meteors, Guana Batz etc. When the club closed some of the Klub Foot bands relocated to the LMS in Hendon (see LMS entry). A grand staircase lead to the large upstairs ballroom.

The Countdown Club. This club in the basement of 1A Palace Gate, Hammersmith, W6, saw the stage debut of Pink Floyd in January 1965. The Floyd played for an amazing five hours.
Douglas House. The Who played this Bayswater venue countless times in 1963. Located on Maida Avenue, Maida Vale, W2. Tube: Edgeware Road (Bakerloo Line).
Duke of Richmond. Located at 180 Earls Court Road, SW5 9QG, the KT Bush Band (Kate Bush) played this pub on 2 May 1977. Later renamed The Richmond and currently called Ping. Tube: Earls Court (District and Piccadilly Lines).

Ealing Rhythm and Blues Club

Address: 42A The Broadway, Ealing, London, W5 2NP
Tube: Ealing Broadway (Central and District Lines)

Ealing Rhythm and Blues Club, originally opened in 1959 as a jazz club below the ABC tearoom, was the location of the first gig by Blues Incorporated in March 1962. The March '62 line up of Blues Incorporated included a pre-Stones Mick Jagger singing (along with Art Wood), Charlie Watts on drums and Alexis Korner on guitar. The Ealing Club was the capital's first regular R&B venue and habitual visitors included Keith Richards, Brian Jones, Jack Bruce and Ginger Baker (the latter two would later form Cream). In May '62 The Marquee became Blues Incorporated's regular venue. The venue continued as a jazz club and Keith Richards believes the club had the worst condensation of any venue, with performers standing in the water dripping from the ceiling. Perhaps because of this problem the Ealing Club was originally known as the 'Moist Hoist', in honour of the tarpaulin that was hung above the stage to collect some of condensation.

The venue closed in 1965 and is now a club called the Red Room; the tearoom is an estate agents. The venue is directly opposite the underground station.

Earls Court (see Pl.9)
Address: Earls Court Exhibition Centre, Warwick Road, London, SW5 9TA
Tube: Earls Court (District Line)
Capacity: 22,000 (standing), 18,000 (seated)
Live release: Oasis 'There and Then' DVD, Pink Floyd 'Pulse' DVD

The land where the Earls Court Exhibition Centre stands was originally a showground where farmers and motor companies could display the efforts of their labours. The land was sold in

1935 to become a grand exhibition hall to rival the nearby Olympia. Earls Court Exhibition Centre was completed at a cost of £1.5 million and opened in 1937. An extension – Earls Court Two – was added in 1991 for £100 million and is linked to the original structure by folding shutters. The centre continued to host exhibitions, gigs and award ceremonies such as the Brits. Earls Court was the scene of the most memorable Brits show, when Pulp's Jarvis Cocker was so enraged by Michael Jackson's performance, which included children – at the time Jacko was having child abuse allegations made against him – that he got on stage and shook his money maker to the audience.

The foyer at the front of the building led into the massive second hall of building. This cathedral- like structure was vast and contained bars, merchandise and even a Pizza Express restaurant. Marked doors led to the standing areas and seats of the inner main venue. Once inside the main hall there was little to distinguish Earls Court from any other arena; it is vast with two video screens either side of the raised stage. The centre had a floor area in front of the stage that could be seated or standing, a raised lower tier, balcony, boxes and a gallery.

If you found yourself in the venue, you would be watching at the very least a major international act. Madonna brought her 2004 Reinvention tour to the venue, along with highly inflated ticket prices – the cheap seats being £100! At the height of their fame in 1995 Oasis sold out two shows here in record time. Morrissey played his biggest ever headline show at the time here, closing his 'You Are The Quarry' UK tour on 18 December 2004. The subsequent live CD 'Live at Earls Court', released the following year in 2005, was in fact recorded at various British venues in Morrissey's winter 2004 tour – not just Earls Court.

REM played two shows here on the 22 and 23 June 1999 supported by Stereolab (22) and Wilco (23). The Rolling Stones played six sold-out nights here in 1976 and Mick Jagger reportly called it 'the worst toilet he'd ever played in', but on the plus side it was here that Jerry Hall first saw him perform. However, a toilet or not, Pink Floyd played an amazing fourteen nights here in 1994 as part of their 'Division Bell' tour. U2 played on 31 May 1992 on their 'Zoo TV' tour and it was the first gig the group had played in the UK since June 1987. U2 returned on their 'Elevation' tour on 18, 19, 21 and 22 August 2001. Bono's father died on the morning of the 21st and Bono gave a moving speech about his dad during the set. Others who have played include Iron Maiden and Kasabian (December 2006).

The building was home to the 'Give it a Name Festival', which attracted groups like Him and Juliette and the Licks in 2007.

In 2013 planning permission was granted to demolish Earls Court and put 7,500 homes, a school and retail units on the site. Demolition was expected to take place in winter 2014, with the last event being a gig by Bombay Bicycle Club on 13 December 2014, who had, as a special guest, a veteran of Earls Court – Pink Floyds David Gilmore, which was a nice nod to the venue's heritage. That last gig was preceded by the first BBC Music Awards, which included Coldplay and Ed Sheeran playing live.

In May 2004 a 60 per cent stake in the centre and Olympia was sold for £245 million to a consortium. Earls Court One had 450,000 square feet of floor space, and the complex was owned by Capco, who also own the nearby Olympia.

Elgin Pub

Address: 96 Ladbroke Grove, London, W11 1PY
Tube: Ladbroke Grove (Hammersmith & City Line)
Live Releases: The 101ers 'Elgin Avenue Breakdown' (CD)

Joe Strummer's first band The 101ers had a residency in this pub in the 1970s, and Tom Jones played some early gigs here. The Elgin still remains as a pub, and live music still features on Fridays and Saturdays.

Ealing Town Hall. New Broadway, W5 2BY. Had several American blues artists such as Sunny Terry in the 1950s and 1960s.

Eel Pie Island Hotel/Colonel Barefoot's Rock Garden. Address: Water Lane at the Embankment, Eel Pie Island, Twickenham. Train: Twickenham. Capacity: 300–500. A hotel built in the 1830s on Eel Pie Island in the Thames that Charles Dickens referred to as a 'place to dance to the music of the locomotive band', in his novel *Nicholas Nickleby*. In the 1920s the hotel had tea dances and in 1956 a jazz club was started in the hotel. Jazz performers who graced the hotel's stage include Acker Bilk, Chris Barber, Ken Colyer, Buddy Guy, Howlin' Wolf and George Melly. The club was started by Arthur Chisnall as a social experiment to discover how the post-Second World War generation would develop and gain advice about further education. Maybe because of its isolated location and Chisnall's attitude, George Melly remembered it as a place where 'it was very difficult not to get laid'. Chisnall died in December 2006. In the 1960s, the hotel/dance hall hosted gigs by The Rolling Stones, The Who, Pink Floyd and The Yardbirds. Access to the island was via a small ferry until a narrow footbridge was constructed in 1957, which meant groups and their equipment had to be walked across to the venue as it was not vehicle friendly. The hotel closed in 1967 due to the owner not being able to afford the £200,000 bill for repairs, but reopened in 1969 as Colonel Barefoot's Rock Garden where Genesis and Black Sabbath played. The building burnt down in 1971 under mysterious circumstances and flats were later built on the site. The Eel Pie Club at the Cabbage Patch pub in Twickenham features musicians who played in the original venue. Websites that are devoted to the Eel Pie Hotel include www.eelpie.org

Elbow Room (Bayswater). Address: 103 Westbourne Grove, Bayswater, London, W2 4UW. Tube: Bayswater (Circle and District Lines). One of three Elbow Rooms in London (others include Islington – 89–91 Chapel Market, Islington, London, N1 9EX and Shoreditch – 97–113 Curtain Road, Shoreditch, London, EC2A 3BS.). There were also Elbow Rooms in Bristol and Leeds. This chain is co-owned by music producer Arthur Baker and mainly has DJs playing hip hop, garage and rock. The venues have had the occasional gigs by the likes of Ash, Boy George, Goldfrapp, The Pipettes and Mogwai, but are mainly bars and pool tables.

Fox and Goose Hotel. An Ealing hotel at Hanger Lane (A4005), W5 1DP, where The Who played in 1963. Remains as a hotel/pub. Tube: Hanger Lane (Central Line).

Farx Club/Northcote Arms Hotel

Address: 49–53 Northcote Avenue, Southall, London, UB1 2AY
Train: Southall (from Paddington Station)

The Farx Club was located inside the Northcote Arms Hotel and hosted Led Zeppelin (1969), Yes, Free, Mott The Hoople and Caravan. For many years the building was closed and was slowly falling into dereliction. However, by 2014 the building had been saved and had been converted into a care home. It seems somewhat fitting as by then the groups who played there could now also reside there too!

Feathers Hotel

Address: The Broadway, Ealing, W5 5JN
Tube: Ealing Broadway (Central Line)

The Who played at this Ealing hotel on The Broadway, W5 2PH (opposite the Ealing Club) on 15 November 1963, and Pink Floyd appeared in 1967. It later became the Townhouse pub and is currently a branch of Metro Bank.

Goldhawk Club

Address: 205 Goldhawk Road, Shepherds Bush, London, W12 8EP
Tube: Goldhawk Road (Circle and Hammersmith & City Lines)

This venue is forever associated with local boys The Who, being the location of their first gig and many more after that (as both The Detours and The Who) between 1963 and 1965. A plaque was erected in November 2014 to mark the association. Others who played include Adam Faith, Shane Fenton (Alvin Stardust), Screaming Lord Sutch and The Yardbirds (in 1964). It is now called The Shepherds Bush Club.

Granada (Greenford)

Address: 229 Greenford Road, Greenford, UB6 8QY
Tube: Greenford (Central Line)

Built in 1939 as a cinema and designed by Dixon, Braddock and Massey, The Rolling Stones (1965) and Gene Vincent (1962) appeared here. The cinema closed in 1966. Currently the building is a Tesco store, although there is planning permission to demolish and build a new store. Nothing remains inside to give any clues of its past, although its exterior is unmistakably cinematic.

The Greyhound
Address: 175 Fulham Palace Road, Fulham, W6 8QT
Tube: Hammersmith (District, Hammersmith & City and Piccadilly Lines)

The Greyhound started putting bands on in 1971, offering live music seven nights a week. Eddie and The Hot Rods played the venue in mid-1970s, and The Jam played in February 1977. Elvis Costello's first band Flip City played the venue frequently in the mid 1970's, often playing to an audience who had free admission. My Bloody Valentine (October 1988), The Pastels, Lush and Snuff (May 1989) were a few of the emerging indie bands who played the Greyhound in its final years.

Sadly, The Greyhound is no longer a music venue. For a while it was part of the pub chain The Puzzle, where there was more chance of finding a giant Connect 4 game rather than a guitar or amplifier, and is currently a bar called The Southern Belle.

The Gaumont (Shepherds Bush). Located at 58 Shepherds Bush Green, the cinema opened in 1923 and went on to be known as The Odeon, then becoming a bingo club called Top Rank and Mecca. Vince Taylor as well as Cliff Richard and The Drifters played in 1958. Although a listed building, the building has been redeveloped, and only the front façade remains. Now called The New Dorset Shepherds Bush Hotel.
The Golden Lion. The 101-ers, featuring Joe Strummer played this Fulham pub in May 1976. Located at 57 Fulham High Street, SW6 3JJ.
Hammersmith Working Men's Club. Located at 11 Rutland Grove, W6 9DH, the club opened in 1860 and has a 300 capacity. The Duke Special played the club in September 2006 and Supergrass played an acoustic set in support of their album 'Road to Rouen' in 2005. The Manic Street Preachers played in August 2010 to an invited audience to promote the album 'Postcards From A Young Man'. Others to have played include Oasis and Badly Drawn Boy.
The Hibernian Club. On the Fulham Road, SW6 1BY. The Manic Street Preachers (1991), Pulp (1992), Mudhoney and Blur (1992, on their 'Modern Life Is Rubbish' tour where they gave away a single of 'Wassailing Song') played this venue. Nearest tube: Fulham Broadway.

Hammersmith Odeon/Labatts Apollo/Carling Apollo/Hammersmith Gaumont/Eventim (see Pl.15)

Address: Queen Charlotte Street, Hammersmith, London, W6 9QH
Tube: Hammersmith (Hammersmith & City, Piccadilly and District Lines).
Capacity: 3,485 (seated)
Live release: Kylie Minogue 'Body Language Live' DVD, Michael Ball 'Live In London' DVD, Ian Dury 'Hold On To Your Structure' DVD (25/6/85), Gary Numan 'Beserker' DVD (11/12/84), Japan 'Oil on Canvas' DVD (1983), David Grey 'Life Live' DVD (2005).

Opened in 1932 as The Gaumont Palace, this Art Deco cinema was designed by Robert Cromie. The Gaumont became The Hammersmith Odeon in 1962. In 2002 the venue was sold to Clear Channel/Live Nation and in 2003 the seats were made removable to allow standing at gigs. In 2006 the venue became part of the MAMA Group and rebranded as The HMV Apollo from 2009 to 2012 when it was sold to AEG Live and Eventim.

Home of the big boys, The Odeon/Apollo attracts the cream of the music world and beer sponsors. As The Gaumont, Buddy Holly appeared in 1958. The Beatles played some Christmas shows at The Odeon from 24 December 1964 until 16 January 1965. Support Acts included Freddie & The Dreamers, Elkie Brookes and The Yardbirds. The Beatles returned for one show in December 1965. Kate Bush played three very rare shows here in May 1979 before returning thirty-five years later to play a series of twenty-two shows (called 'Before The Dawn') – her first since those gigs in 1979. At the end of 1979 four concerts for Kampuchea were held here and featured Queen, The Clash, The Specials, The Who, Wings and Elvis Costello. Blondie played their first London gigs here on 28 and 29 May 1977, supporting fellow New Yorkers, Television. Blondie returned for two more shows in September 1978 and eight more in January 1980, where the ticket price was £4.25. U2 played in March 1983. Elton John played a series of Christmas gigs here in 2004. REM played two nights here on the 29 and 30 May 1989 on their Green World Tour, after previously playing a show here on their 1987 tour on 12 September, supported by 10,000 Maniacs. Iggy Pop was here in June 1979 and returned in October 2005 with The Stooges to perform the 'Fun House' album in full.

Alan Tyler of The Rockingbirds namechecks the Odeon as the venue he shook Jonathan Richman's hand in the 1992 song 'Jonathan, Jonathan'.

Inside the venue the former cinema has some Art Deco features that have been restored with every recent refurbishment. The main floor area can either be seated or standing depending upon the arrangements for the performance.

Hammersmith Folk Club/Centre

Address: 73 Dalling Road, W6 0JD moving to The Kings Head pub at 474 Fulham Road
Tube: Ravenscourt Park (District Line), then Fulham Broadway

Originally at The Prince of Wales pub at 73 Dalling Road, W6 0JD, the club later moved to The Kings Head pub at 474 Fulham Road. Performers included Ralph McTell, The Furys, Liam Clancy and Shirley Collins. It was operational between the 1960s and 1980s.

Hammersmith Palais/Palais de Danse (see pl.16)

Address: 230 Shepherds Bush Road, Hammersmith, London, W6 7NL
Tube: Hammersmith (Hammersmith & City, Piccadilly and District Lines)
Capacity: 2,230.
Live releases: The Jam 'Precious' B side to 'Town Called Malice' (1982) and Toots & The Maytals 'Live at The Hammersmith Palais' album (1980).

Opened in 1919 as Palais de Danse promoting jazz music with an emphasis on Dixieland Jazz, the venue had the first maple sprung dance floor in Europe. Early visitors to the venue included

Hollywood stars Douglas Fairbanks Jr and Mary Pickford, as well as BBC radio broadcasts by Vera Lynn. The Palais was a popular dancing venue in the 1940s and remained open during the Second World War, when it became popular with American GIs. The venue was in the control of Mecca by the 1970s and started to feature rock tour schedules with gigs by David Bowie, The Police and Motorhead.

U2 appeared three times, in December 1980, December 1982 and March 1983. REM played two gigs at the Palais, on 28 and 29 October 1985. In the 1980s the venue was briefly renamed 'Le Palais' and was refitted to suit the disco crowds, becoming a regular venue hosting small-hours ITV show *The Hitman and Her*.

Other groups to have played the venue include Hard-Fi, My Chemical Romance, The Sex Pistols, The Kinks, Talking Heads, Massive Attack, PIL, The Cure and The Rolling Stones. Doves returned to the live circuit at the Palais in the winter of 2004. Graham Coxon and Gary Numan played in 2006. The venue was run by Barvest until the Palais closed to be demolished to make way for an office block in spring 2007. Some of the last groups to have played the venue include Kasabian (February), Idlewild, Jamie T, The Good The Bad and The Queen (March). The Fall were the last group to play the venue on 1 April 2007. The Palais was the venue for the Shockwaves NME awards for a few years before closing. The Palais was also the home to club 'School Disco' for many years, until the club moved to The Forum in February 2007 when the Palais's demolition was given the go-ahead by planners. However, the Palais lives on as it has been immortalised by The Clash in their 1978 single 'White Man In Hammersmith Palais' and has a musical timeline to the site's history on the entrance wall. The site is now occupied by 'Pure' – accommodation for students.

Kensington Park Hotel/KPH
Address: 139 Ladbroke Grove, London, W10 6HJ
Tube: Ladbroke Grove (Circle and Hammersmith & City Lines)

This pub/hotel/venue is spread over three floors. Tom Jones played some of his first London gigs here for the princely sum of £10. The building became the Chair Theatre in 1988 and later, in 1990, it became the Grove Theatre. Irish singer Mary Coughlan played in March 2014, and indie hipsters Superfood brought the ceiling down on 12 July 2014. Their gig had to be abandoned while it was repaired.

Lyric Hammersmith
Address: Lyric Square, King Street, Hammersmith, London, W6 0QL
Tube: Hammersmith (District, Hammersmith & City and Piccadilly Lines)
Capacity: 550 (seated)

Opened in 1979 by the Queen, the Lyric had originally been an opera house located further down King Street (designed by Frank Matcham), before being taken apart and relocated. Now a concreted exterior hides an internal seated nineteenth-century classical auditorium which has seen Richard Thompson take to its stage in 2005. The Magnetic Fields played three nights at the theatre in June 2004, promoting their album 'I'. Ryan Adams played two nights in May 2001 and former Larrikin Love frontman Edward Larrikin performed in December 2007 supported by Patrick Wolf.

Inn On The Green Address: 3–5 Thorpe Close (Westway), Portobello Green, London, W10 5XL. Tube: Ladbroke Grove (Hammersmith & City). The former Portobello Green Sports Club had TV Smith and Attila The Stockbroker play in late 2005. Former Clash man Mick Jones brought his new band Carbon/Silicon (also featuring Tony James of Generation X and Sigue Sigue Sputnik) to the venue for a six-night residency in January/February 2008. Closed in 2011.

Man in the Moon. This pub at 392 Kings Road, SW3 5OZ had Adam and The Ants play three times in May 1977. X-Ray Spexs also played in 1977.
Mead Hall. This Ealing hall had The Who in 1964.
Neighbourhood. See Subterania.
Northcote Arms Hotel. See entry for The Farx Club.

Maida Vale Studios

Address: Delaware Road, London, W9 2LG
Tube: Warwick Avenue (Bakerloo Line) or Maida Vale (Bakerloo Line)

Built in 1909 as The Maida Vale Roller Skating Palace and Club, the building was gutted in 1933 and turned into BBC radio studios. All the John Peel sessions between 1967 and 2004 were recorded here in Studio 4. Live gigs are also recorded in the studios where invited audiences (usually competition winners) can watch the action. Those to have played live sessions here include Blur.

Nashville Rooms (see Pl.25)
Address: 171 North End Road, London, W14 9NL.
Tube: West Kensington (District Line)
Capacity: 500
Live release: Elvis Costello B sides to 'Watching The Detectives' (1977)

Although now renamed 'The Famous Three Kings' and not putting on any live music any more, this building was The Nashville Rooms and as such it is steeped in the history of Punk and New Wave.

The Sex Pistols played in 1976 although it was over shadowed by designer Vivienne Westwood starting a fight in the audience. Wire made their live debut here in December 1976. Elvis Costello played the venue several times before making it big, and he even made a guest appearance here with The Rumour. The Nashville Rooms was also where Paul Simonon agreed to join The Clash. The Specials played, supported by Madness, in 1979. Adam and The Ants appeared in September 1977, and Joy Division played twice in August and September 1979. U2 performed their second London show on 2 December 1979, as a support act, to twenty-five people. The group returned to play a headline show and to a few more fans on 30 May 1980.

With all the punk gigs, and occasional violence happening at The Nashville Rooms, it's amazing to think that the beautiful glazed, curved inward entrance has actually survived intact – with no punk sticking their boot through it. Slightly more amazing is that this glazed entrance, which is highly individual, has not resulted in the building being listed for that feature alone.

Notting Hill Arts Club

Address: 21 Notting Hill Gate, London, W11 3JQ
Tube: Notting Hill Gate (Central Line)
Capacity: 218

Do Me Bad Things (2004), The Darkness (2001) and ex-Oasis Bonehead's The Seers played in April 2004. Wednesday night was Alan McGee's 'Death Disco' nights where live bands fitted between the spinning discs. Bobby Womack showcased his last album 'The Bravest Man Alive' here on 1 October 2012. Saturday afternoons are the Rough Trade 'Rota Sessions' where it's free entry to see some new bands perform.

Old Field Tavern. Located at 1089 Greenford Road, UB6 0AJ, this pub venue had gigs by The Who (when they were called The Detours, and was the venue for Keith Moons first gig) and Genesis. Demolished and replaced by a block of flats called 'William Perkin Court'.
Olympia. 'Extravaganza 70' was held here featuring Procol Harum on 29 May 1970 and Tyrannosaurus Rex on 30 May 1970. Primal Scream performed Screamadelica here in 2010. Others who have played include; Jimi Hendrix (1967), Rod Stewart (1977), The Cure (four times in 1992), Chemical Brothers (2008) and Bloc Party (2009). Address: Hammersmith Road, W14 8UX. Tube: Kensington (Olympia) (District Line) – note a limited service that only operates on some Olympia event days.
The Orange. See West One Four.

Porchester Hall

Address: Porchester Road, Bayswater, London, W2 5HS
Tube: Royal Oak (Circle and Hammersmith & City Lines)
Capacity: 600

Lily Allen played a special gig at this hall (which is next to the library and was built in 1929) on 4 October 2006 that was broadcast live by a mobile phone company. Arcade Fire played the hall twice on 1 and 2 January 2007 to promote their second album 'Neon Bible'. Others who have played include Amy Winehouse, Corrine Bailey Rae, Magic Numbers and Status Quo. The venue seemed to be popular with TV companies recording showcase gigs for television broadcast around 2006. The hall also featured in the film *Quadrophenia*.

Red Cow
Address: 157 Hammersmith Road, Hammersmith, London, W6 8BS
Tube: Barons Court (Piccadilly Line)

The Red Cow is no longer a music venue and no longer The Red Cow, it is now known as Latymers. As the Red Cow it had some very noteworthy gigs. The Jam played four gigs here in March 1977 and their 'In The City' album cover was shot here. In April 1976 an Australian group called AC/DC made their British debut at the Red Cow. A pre-Police Sting played here in January 1977, as a member of Geordie group Last Exit. Japan played to around 100 people here in 1977 and considered it their biggest gig at the time.

Riverside Studios

Address: Crisp Road, Hammersmith, London, W6 9LR
Tube: Hammersmith (District and Hammersmith & City Lines)
Capacity: 500
Live release: Paul Weller 'Studio 150' DVD

For two weeks in August 1988 Riverside Studios hosted gigs by In Tua Nua, Julia Fordham, Diesel Park West, Birdland, Spacemen 3, Tanita Tikaram and Love and Money. Paul Weller recorded the Studio 51 live DVD at these studios in 2004. The Counterfeit Stones and Suzi Quatro played in 2006.

Riverside Studios other function was as a theatre and art cinema, and was formally a BBC studio in the 1960s where The Beatles recorded many *Top Of The Pops* performances including 'Ticket To Ride', 'Yes It Is' (both on 10 April 1965) and 'I Feel Fine' and 'She's A Woman' (both on 16 November 1964). In 1974 future members of the Sex Pistols – Steve Jones, Glen Matlock and Paul Cook –secretly had keys cut to the building so they could rehearse here for free. The studio's were used to record Channel 4's *Pop World* (series ended in July 2007) where acts such as Girls Aloud, The Automatic and the Scissor Sisters have performed. In the 1990s the studios were also used for Chris Evans' *TFI Friday* where Blur, Oasis, Sleeper and a number of other

Britpop acts played live. Amy Winehouse performed two songs here ('Rehab' and 'You Know I'm No Good') in 2008 which were broadcast to America as her Grammy's performance.

The studios were demolished in 2015 (after one last hurrah, with *TFI Friday* returning for a final episode) and the site is to be redeveloped, a studio being part of the new build.

Ricky Tick. Located at 1A High Street, Hounslow (opposite the bus station), the venue had Jimi Hendrix and Geno Washington in the 1960s. Tube: Hounslow East (Piccadilly Line).
Rough Trade West. Address: 130 Talbot Road, London, W1 1JA. Tube: Ladbrook Grove (Circle and Hammersmith & City Lines). The original Rough Trade shop, but the poorer sibling to Rough Trade East, which attracts all the big names for in-store performances. Talbot Road left with the small fry.
St Marys College. This college in Twickenham (possibly at Strawberry Hill) had Cream in 1968. At Waldegrave Road, TW1 4SX the college had Genesis, Elton John, Status Quo and Uriah Heap all in 1970.
Stamford Bridge. The home to Chelsea Football Club had Bruce Springsteen play in 2008.
The Swan, Hammersmith. Another pub gig for Iron Maiden here in July 1977. Located at 46 Hammersmith Broadway, the building dates from 1901 and is a Grade II-listed building. Still open and functioning as a pub.

606 Club
Address: 90 Lots Road, London, SW10 0QD
Tube: Earls Court (Lines)
Capacity: 165 (standing), 130 (seated)

The 606 Club was a jazz club that was originally a thirty-seat basement venue at 606 Kings Road in the 1970s. The club moved to Lots Road in 1987 and has a strict 'UK musician's only' policy. Former Robbie Williams co-writer Guy Chambers played the club in February 2007.

Shepherds Bush Empire
Address: Shepherds Bush Green, Shepherds Bush, London, W12 8TT
Tube: Shepherds Bush (Central Line)
Capacity: 2,000 (standing), 1,278 (seated)
Live release: Paul Carrack 'In Concert' DVD, The Damned 'Tiki Nightmare' DVD (7/02), Sparks 'Live In London' DVD (1994), Status Quo 'Famous In The Last Century' DVD (27/3/00), Goldfrapp 'Wonderful Electric Live in London' DVD.

The Shepherds Bush Empire is the former TV studio where 1980s chat show *Wogan* was filmed. On this stage Terry Wogan introduced the top chart acts of the day and some young pretenders. Hall & Oates, Julian Cope, Kylie, Kate Bush and The Primitives all took to the stage here and mimed their hearts out. Prior to being a studio the building was a theatre, designed and built by Frank Matcham in 1903.

Since becoming a venue, The Empire has attracted almost every recording artist worth their salt on its stage. Performers such as Sheryl Crow, Blondie (on their 'Phasm 8' tour in November 2003), John Hiatt, Echo and The Bunnymen, The Feeling, Bob Dylan, Patti Smith, Bjork, Sex Pistols, Tom Petty, Radiohead, PJ Harvey, David Bowie (in 1997), The Rolling Stones (in 1999), Bon Jovi and KT Tunstall have all played here.

The Shepherds Bush Empire is one of the top venues in London, winning several awards. The ground floor is standing only, while upstairs is unreserved seating. The venue was closed in December 2015 when structural issues with the roof made the building unsafe for performances.

Southall Community Centre
Address: 20 Merrick Road, UB2 4AU.
Train: Southall (from Paddington)

Built in 1910 as a recreation centre for employees of a Danish margarine manufacturer (Maypole Dairy), the building became a hospital for First World War soldiers in 1915. In 1920 the injured solders had moved out and it became a community centre. The centre hosted gigs by Gene Vincent (1964), Jerry Lee Lewis, The Yardbirds (1965), The Animals (1965), The Who and The Small Faces. In 2008 the building was sold by Ealing Council and is now called The Centre Banqueting.

Starlite Ballroom

Address: Allendale Road, Greenford, London
Tube: Sudbury Town (Piccadilly Line)

This former Odeon cinema stopped showing movies in 1956. Reborn as the Starlite Ballroom, the venue had a pretty amazing roll call of bands that had played here; Cream (1966 & 1967), The Jeff Beck Group (1967), Pink Floyd (1966 & 1967), The Who (1966 and 1967), The Animals (1966), The Troggs (1966) and The Yardbirds (1966). The building still stands and was used as a snooker hall called Starlite Snooker – although in 2015 it was fairly derelict.

Subterania/Acklam Hall/Bay 63/Neighbourhood/Mode

Address: 12 Acklam Road, Ladbroke Grove, London, W10 5QZ
Tube: Ladbroke Grove (Hammersmith & City Line)
Capacity: 600
Live release: Gong 'The Subterania Gig' DVD (2000), The Fall 'Live at the Acklam Hall' cassette (also known as 'The Legendary Chaos Tape') (1980)

Starting in the 1970s as Acklam Hall, the venue hosted gigs by groups of the fledging new wave/independent scene including The Fall. Scritti Politti made their live debut here on 18 November 1978 on a bill that featured fellow Rough Trade band Cabaret Voltaire. U2 played as part of the 'Sense of Ireland Festival' in March 1980.

Renamed Bay 63 in the mid-1980s the Mighty Lemon Drops (supported by The Shamen) and Tallulah Gosh played in 1986. Changing name again in the 1990s, this time to Subternia, groups such as The Men They Couldn't Hang, Ruthless Rap Assassins, Paul Weller's Movement, Lunachicks and Swervedriver were all part of Subternia's attractions in 1991. Independent label Rough Trade curated the 'Acklam Hall Revisited' in 1996 with Tindersticks, Cocteau Twins, The Raincoats and Drugstore all performing. Other diverse artists who have played include Village People, Napalm Death, Psychic TV and Claudia Brucken (former singer of ZTT signings Propaganda).

The stage was on the ground level with a mezzanine floor overlooking the stage. No longer hosting gigs, the venue became a club called 'Neighbourhood' and was called 'Mode' in 2014, offering clubbers a home under the Westway. The internal layout has remained (albeit with a reduced stage area), although a church organ and pulpit now occupy the stage acting as the DJ booth, with a model spitfire suspended above. Mode had a brief return to live music in 2014 when Kasabian played a small show here and Blur played their comeback album 'The Magic Whip' in full in 2015.

> **Teddington Folk Club.** This club may have hosted folk legend Sandy Denny in 1966 but this fact did not save it from the wrecking ball in 2008 – a Travelodge now occupies the site.
> **Twickenham Technical College.** Here at Egerton Road, John Martyn performed twice in 1972.
> **Twickenham Stadium.** Address: Rugby Road, Twickenham, London, TW1 1DZ.
> Tube: Richmond (District Line). Capacity: 82,000 (seated). Live release: The Rolling Stones '40 Licks' DVD. The reformed Eagles played this rugby ground in June 2006. U2 played in 2005, and the Rolling Stones brought their '40 Licks' tour here. When the new Wembley Stadium opening was delayed in 2006 scheduled gigs by The Stones and Bon Jovi were moved to Twickenham Stadium instead. Rod Stewart played the stadium in June 2007, as did Genesis and the reformed Police played twice in September 2007. The stadium was built in 1909 with an original 20,000 capacity, which has steadily increased with various redevelopments and now covers a 35-acre site.
> The stadium is located on the northern side of A316 (heading towards London), or is a ten-minute walk from Twickenham rail station.

Tabernackle
Address: 34–35 Powis Square, London, W11 2AY
Tube: Westbourne Park (Circle and Hammersmith & City Lines)

The Tabernackle was built in 1889 as a church and was known as the Taj Mahal of North Kensington. The Powis Square area became a rock star hangout in the 1960s. The church closed in 1975 and there were plans to demolish this stunning building, but the building was saved when it was granted a Grade II-listed building status.

The Raincoats made their debut gig here in 1977. In the 1980s there were gigs by Misty In Roots and George Melly, and Joe Strummer played in 1988 – just as the venue was becoming known as a Rap venue. Lily Allen made her stage debut here in a 1990's panto, and The Rolling Stones launched their album Voodoo Lounge here in 1994. Others to have played include All Saints, Right Said Fred, Santana, Adele and James Blunt . The Good, The Bad and The Queen (featuring Damon Albarn and Paul Simonon) rehearsed here and played their first gig here.

The Target
Address: The Target roundabout at 256 Church Road, Northolt, UB5 5AW
Tube: Northolt (Central Line)

The KT Bush Band, featuring Kate Bush, played this pub to give her some live experience before being launched as a solo artist. The set consisted mostly of cover versions. It is now a McDonalds restaurant and there is nothing remaining inside to hint at its past, although it has retained its pub exterior.

The Toby Jug
Address: 1 Hook Rise South (A13), Tolworth, South-west London
Train: Tolworth (from Waterloo)

David Bowie and The Spiders From Mars brought their Ziggy Stardust tour here on 10 February 1972 and played to a reported audience of just sixty people. Strange to think that this obscure part of London hosted Bowie – after he had finally broken through to the mainstream – on a pub's stage. Even stranger is that Led Zeppelin, Traffic, Ten Years After, Status Quo, King Crimson, Jethro Tull and Fleetwood Mac also played the venue. The pub was demolished in 2000 and the site has remained empty since then – in limbo as various planning applications for a Tesco store failed.

The Troubadour (see Pl.38)
Address: 265 Old Brompton Road, Earls Court, London, SW5 9JA
Tube: West Brompton (District Line)
Capacity: 120

A folk coffee house in the 1960s, Bob Dylan and Bert Jansk performed here in 1963. Martin Carthy was a regular at the Troubadour in the early 1960s and Paul Simon, Joni Mitchell, Charlie Watts, Sammy Davies Jr and Jimi Hendrix have also played. The 1970s saw both Elvis Costello and Tom Robinson perform.

Today the premises have expanded either side of No. 265 and the basement performing area was refurbished in 1990. The Troubadour still attracts 'named' performers such as Boo Hewerdine (2005), Brendan Benson (2004), Albert Lee (2004), Deacon Blue's Ricky Ross (2005) and Amos Lee (2003/04/05).

The Troubadour hosts its 'Troubadour Sessions' for unsigned blues/R&B/indie/acoustic acts every Wednesday evening.

Three Tuns/Beckenham Arts Lab
Address: 157 High Street, Beckenham, BR3 1AE
Train: Beckenham Junction (from Victoria)

David Bowie started the Arts Lab in the Three Tuns Pub in 1969. Those who performed here include Peter Frampton, Steve Harley and Mick Ronson. The building remains but is now a Zizzi restaurant that has a Bowie themed interior and a plaque on the front façade celebrating the Bowie connection. When Bowie died the street outside the venue became a shrine to him. He lived in the town for a significant part of his career.

Under The Bridge
Address: Stamford Bridge, Fulham Road, London, SW6 1HS
Tube: Fulham Broadway (District Line)
Capacity: 550

Under the Bridge is aptly named, for the venue is located under the East Stand at Chelsea's Stamford Bridge football ground. Whilst Bruce Springsteen has performed above the ground this under the stadium venue has hosted gigs since 2011 from Adam Ant (2011), Jamie Cullum (2011), Jessie J (2012), Alicia Keys (2012), Texas (2013), Keane (2013), The Feeling (2013), Peter Andre (2014), The Fall (2014), Ian McNabb (2014) and The South (2014).

Wallington Town Hall
Location: Woodcote Road, Wallington, SM6 0NB
Train: Wallington (from Victoria)

David Bowie toured Ziggy Stardust at this town hall on 24 February 1972. Part of the London Borough of Sutton, the building is now the Old Town Hall and is home to the Orchid Hill Academy and College (previously Sutton College).

Uxbridge Womens Institute Hall. A pre-Faces Ronnie Wood played here when a member of The Thunderbirds in 1964. Located at 8 Kingston Lane, Uxbridge, UB8 3PN.

West Drayton Community Centre. A venue played by Ronnie Wood while a member of The Thunderbirds in 1964. Can be found at 90 Wise Lane, UB7 7EX.

Windsor Castle Pub. Joe Strummers 101'ers played three times in 1975 at the pub at 309–311 Harrow Road, W9 3RG. Others acts include Dr Feelgood (1974), The Cure, The Ruts and The Psychedelic Furs (1979). Tube: Westbourne Park (Circle and Hammersmith & City Lines).

The Winning Post. The Jam played this Twickenham pub in 1977 watched by members of Australian punk band The Saints. Located at Chertsey Road, TW2 6LS. Train: Whitton.

White Bear. A folk venue opened in 1966 by Dave Cousins and Tony Hooper of The Strawbs, at 198 Kingsley Road, Hounslow, TW3 4AR. Sandy Denny appeared in 1966. Hosted the Hounslow Arts Lab where in 1969 David Bowie performed. Became the Grail Folk Club in the 1970s. (Tube: Hounslow East).

White City Stadium. Teen idol David Cassidy played this stadium in Shepherds Bush in May 1974. Built in 1908 for the Olympics, White City was the first stadium constructed in the UK. So much for history – the stadium was demolished in 1985 to make way for the BBC White City complex.

White Hart (Acton). Located at 264 High Street, Acton, W3, the pub had David Bowie in 1970 on its Arts Lab night and Fleetwood Mac in 1967. However, the most interesting part of the gig history is that The Who (as The Detours) played twenty-eight times in 1963 (they had a short run of a Monday-night residency) and six times in 1964 (as The Detours, The Who and The High Numbers). Remains a pub but renamed The Red Back.

White Hart (Southall). Located at 49 High Street, Southall, this was home to Chris Barbers Jazz Club where Lonnie Donegan played. The Who played four times in 1964. The pub has since been demolished.

West One Four/The Orange
Address: 3 Northend Crescent, West Kensington, London, W14 8TG
Tube: West Kensington (District Line)
Capacity: 300 (standing)

A strange little venue, from 1988 and into the 1990s, The Orange hosted the occasional well-known singer-songwriters, as well as breaking some new acts. The stage was on the first floor. Both former Go-Betweens Robert Forster and Grant McLennan played solo gigs here in the early 1990s, and 10,000 Maniacs also played. The building has been since converted into a Sainsbury's Local store.

Zigzag Club
Address: 22–24 Great Western Road, Maida Vale, London, W9
Tube: Westbourne Grove (Hammersmith & City Line)

Malcolm McClaren protégées Bow Wow Wow opened the club in 1981, and The Birthday Party, The Sisters of Mercy and Gene Loves Jezebel played a joint gig here in July 1982. 1982 was a busy year at the Zig Zag as The Go Betweens, Lords of The New Church, Hanoii Rocks, Crass and Discharge all played the venue. The venue has now been demolished and replaced by flats.